Leisure in Post-War
BRITAIN

STUART HYLTON

First published 2012

Amberley Publishing
The Hill, Stroud
Gloucestershire, GL5 4EP

www.amberley-books.com

British Library Cataloguing in Publication Data.
A catalogue record for this book is available from the British Library.

ISBN 978 1 4456 0343 8

Typeset in 10pt on 12pt Sabon.
Typesetting and Origination by Amberley Publishing.
Printed in the UK.

Contents

Introduction

The principles of fun, from some of the world's great thinkers – and Norm Papernick:

> Fun I love, but too much fun is of all things the most loathsome.
>
> William Blake

> Those who can laugh without cause have either found the true meaning of happiness or have gone stark raving mad.
>
> Norm Papernick

> Sanity and happiness are an impossible combination.
>
> Mark Twain

> Happiness: an agreeable sensation arising from contemplating the misery of another.
>
> Ambrose Bierce

> I don't know why we are here, but I am pretty sure that it is not in order to enjoy ourselves.
>
> Ludwig Wittgenstein

The world has been searching for the true path to happiness since the time of Aristotle. In the mid-nineteenth century Utilitarians like John Stuart Mill came up with a philosophical theory which said that an action is morally right if it has consequences that lead to happiness, and wrong if it leads in the other direction. They tried to develop something called the 'felicific calculus' to measure the net amount of happiness produced by different courses of action. However, critics complained that it was impossible to reduce such complicated moral issues to a simple mathematical formula. After all, given recent events, a bus-load of bankers disappearing over a cliff may be the occasion for great national rejoicing, but does that make it morally right to saw through the brake-pipes? It's a tough one.

But the difficulty of measuring happiness does not stop the authorities from continuing to try. In 2009 the Office for National Statistics announced that it was one of their priorities to look for ways of measuring the emotional state of the nation since, as they put it, 'there is growing international recognition that to measure national well-being and progress there is a need to develop a more comprehensive view, rather than focussing solely on Gross Domestic Product'. To this end, they have even established a Societal Well-Being Division in their organisation (what next? Laughing Academies in our universities?). The new division has launched an online survey to take the nation's pulse on the matter. Naturally enough, this unscientific survey has courted controversy among pedants and xenophobes, who complain that (a) there is nothing to stop people voting more than once or, (b) worse still, to stop damned foreigners from muscling in on our survey. If the conclusion of the study turns out to be that true British happiness is to be found in losing to the Germans at football, we'll know who is to blame.

Nonetheless, politicians of all colours have backed this quest, which is strange, given that many people think politicians are as much to blame as any group for the nation's state of discontent. Perhaps they hope that a happiness index will bring better tidings than the conventional economic indicators, which are nearly always bad? Even as I was putting the finishing touches to this book in late 2010, Prime Minister David Cameron announced that his government would be backing the introduction of this new way of measuring well-being in the 2011 General Household Survey. He quoted Robert Kennedy on the limitations of Gross Domestic Product as an indicator, saying that 'it measures neither our wisdom nor our learning; neither our compassion nor our devotion to our country; it measures everything, in short, except that which makes life worthwhile'.

But it may be that fun has a more practical application for the politician, as an agent of social control. The fun theory was promoted in a competition by Volkswagen. Its central proposition was that you could alter the public's behaviour in certain socially desirable ways by making it more fun to do the right thing. They sponsored a number of experiments in Stockholm, and put the winning entries into practice to see whether they worked. In one, they modified traffic speed cameras so that they not only photographed and fined speeders, they also photographed those who kept to the speed limit and entered their names in a lottery. Winners got a share of the fines paid by speeders. This produced a 22 per cent reduction in traffic speeds, compared to the standard traffic camera. Another experiment tried to get more people to use the healthy option of the stairs, rather than the escalator. They converted the stairs to look like piano keys, and to play notes as people walked on them. They reported a 66 per cent increase in the use of the stairs. Who knows? Perhaps in future we will return home each night, our ribs aching from the constant round of mirth associated with simply being a law-abiding citizen?

This book has less scientific aspirations than measuring happiness and less political ones than changing behaviour. It simply sets out to document the changing face of fun in Britain. What have the British been doing over the past fifty years or so to have it, and are we any good at it? According to some commentators, the answer to the second question is 'not very'. Take this statement, made in the House of Commons in 1976:

> Although some material standards have been improved since 1946, it cannot be said that the majority of citizens of England are significantly happier. Far from it. There is a tension, a disquiet and a dismay in the nation that can be seen on the faces of the ordinary people.
>
> *Hansard*, Vol. 779, col. 909, 9 April 1976

The Member of Parliament who made this statement – John Stonehouse – made his own, rather radical, arrangements for leaving England. He left a pile of his clothes on the beach to fake his own suicide and fled to Australia with his mistress, before being arrested, repatriated and imprisoned.

But before we embark on this retrospective of fun, the bad news is that you've missed the high point. A study was published by the New Economics Foundation in 2004, looking at our nation's quality of life over the past fifty years. They looked not just at our material standard of living, measured by the aforementioned Gross Domestic Product, but also at social and environmental criteria like crime, family breakdown, economic inequality, state welfare spending, pollution, commuting costs, and so on. They concluded that 1976 was the best post-war year to have been alive in Britain. This, you may recall, was the year in which freak weather conditions caused massive destruction and twenty-two deaths, we were fighting with Irish terrorists and Icelandic fish-rustlers, we had the worst drought for 500 years and unemployment passed 1.5 million. It was also, you will recall, the same year that Mr Stonehouse gave us his assessment of the nation's state of mind. Happy days!

Just as we were about to enter this halcyon time in our national history, one Geraldine Norman introduced the 'hedonometer', described in *The Times* as 'a cheerfully unscientific way of gauging a nation's happiness' (*The Times*, 26 May 1975). Apparently, according to this instrument, Britain scored some way behind Botswana in terms of national well-being on almost every criterion. You may well ask, if we can't even beat Botswana when we are at the top of our game, what hope is there for us? Nor has the situation improved since; in 2010 the Gallup pollsters looked for signs of happiness in no less than fifty-three countries (*The Guardian*, 5 January 2011). They found that Nigeria came out top, scoring 70 on whatever scale of contentment they used in advance of the official UK government one. We miserable Brits came well down the table, with a depressing -44. And what do the Nigerians have to be so cheerful about? The list offered by the newspaper report included eye-watering corruption, growing sectarian violence, grinding poverty and – their second largest export after oil – the identity theft scam.

One commentator has even suggested that happiness might not be the right emotion for us to be measuring, and that we ought to look instead for an index of satisfaction. Perhaps our pampered existence artificially inflates our expectations of fun, and causes us to be more easily dissatisfied? Could it be that the sense of achievement in overcoming life's little adversities in (let's say) Botswana trumps any of the more expensive diversions we might have in a more affluent society like our own (I think I am right in saying that we are still just about more affluent than Botswana)? Maybe more of us need to have the opportunity to triumph over adversity in some small way. To that end, perhaps what we could really do with right now is a jolly good recession to increase the available supply of adversity – but what are the chances of that happening?

In the following pages I have looked at some of the ways in which post-war Britain has spent its leisure time trying to have fun, and also some of the ways in which the powers that be have sought to remove the last drops of mirth from it. These latter include those who seek to censor all sorts of fun, to protect us from ourselves; Lord Reith and his mission, which he passed on to his successors, to educate and improve us to within an inch of our lives through the medium of the BBC. Then there are the efforts of the press and other media to fill our heads with increasingly strident accounts of everything that's wrong with the world. (One suggestion is that our happiness could be greatly increased by censors banning the steady flow of bad news we get from the media. At present, much of the effort that goes into censorship by various bodies and individuals seems to be directed at things that might conceivably add in some small way to the national stock of fun – see the chapter on censorship.) But most of all, we will focus on some of our valiant, if often doomed, attempts to find ways of enjoying ourselves in our leisure time.

I suppose I should end this introduction by saying I hope you enjoy reading the book, but that's not really the British way, is it?

I would like to acknowledge my debt to the many books, articles and websites on which I have been able to draw, and which are listed in the body of, or at the end of, the book. Particular thanks go to my brother David for casting his expert eye over the motoring chapter and giving me much advice (which I hope I have followed correctly). I was helped with the illustrations by the photographic archives of Lincolnshire and West Sussex County Councils and my son Michael helped me prepare many of the other illustrations. If, despite all this support and good advice, any errors or omissions remain in the book, sole responsibility rests with me, and it is your solemn duty to spoil my day by reporting them to me.

1
Fun When We Were Young: Comics

Let's start with an easy one. We should be on safe ground with the comic, that innocent bit of childhood fun, with those cheery little cartoon characters that could make a rainy Sunday afternoon vanish in a trice! Surely even the British can enjoy these unreservedly, without becoming angst-ridden? Or can they?

Not always, it seems.

> It is not only American comics that should be banned, but also many of the other false practices that have been imported into this country. The sooner we return to a sane British way of life (built on traditional lines) the better for this great nation.
>
> *Picture Post*, 1952 – part of the Hulton Press
> group that published the *Eagle* comic

The hordes of Americans who were stationed in Britain during the war were blamed for all sorts of moral pollution – from the jitterbug (a form of unarmed combat disguised as dancing) to chewing gum. Among the most pernicious of these, in some eyes, was the imported horror comic. When the GIs returned home after the war (no doubt in some cases mentally scarred by some pretty blood-curdling experiences in the armed forces) they wanted rather stronger meat in their comic books than the bland tales of caped crusaders to which they had been accustomed.

The first of these to appear, in 1947, were *Eerie Comics*, quickly followed by a number of others, many of which quickly found their way across the Atlantic. An early edition featured on its cover a 'dagger-wielding, red-eyed ghoul threatening a rope-bound, scantily clad voluptuous young woman beneath a full moon'. Others featured more than threats; one teacher was horrified when she confiscated a comic depicting a drug addict beating a naked girl to death with a bicycle chain. These comics were populated by flesh-eating, grave-robbing, blood-drinking monsters of a kind that would definitely lower the tone of the neighbourhood. According to one British vicar, they were 'skilfully and vividly drawn, but often their content was deplorable, nastily over-violent and obscene, often with undue emphasis on the supernatural and magical as a way of solving problems'. Another genre was the fight stories magazine, which dispensed with the monsters and focussed on the violence. A short example of the latter is quoted in an article by George Orwell:

> He walked in stolidly and smashed a club-like right to my face. Blood spattered and I went back on my heels, but surged in and ripped my right under his heart. Another right smashed full on Sven's

already battered mouth and, spitting out the fragments of a tooth, he crashed a flailing left to my body...

The Penguin Essays of George Orwell, p. 93

Jane Austen it is not. Concern began to build up, both here and in America, about the content of these comics. America dealt with it rather more quickly and effectively. One of the leaders of the campaign over there was a psychiatrist named Fredric Wertham. He laid just about every youth problem of the age at the door of the comic, from juvenile delinquency, violent crime and social disaffection, to sexual deviancy, under which category he argued that Batman was gay and Wonder Woman promoted lesbianism (that last one I can understand; she certainly stimulated my interest in women). His criticisms nonetheless got the attention of a 1954 Senate Sub-Committee on juvenile delinquency and led the comics industry to take the pre-emptive measure of setting up a self-regulating body, the Comics Code Authority.

This vowed to regulate 'the portrayal of sex, violence and anti-social activity' in comic books, and introduced some quite strict measures, banning the use of words like 'terror' and 'horror' in titles, or the use of zombies, werewolves and the other traditional trappings of horror fiction. Even so, their actions did not prevent a moral panic breaking out, which caused police forces to set up anti-comic units, ritual burnings of such publications and oaths taken by Scouts and other youth groups not to read them and to boycott establishments that sold them. The combined result was a 50 per cent reduction in sales of these magazines between 1954 and 1956, and the disappearance of some of the best-known titles, like *Tales from the Crypt*. When the publication of this latter title ceased, its publishers focussed all their efforts on their other title, *Mad* magazine. Through the technicality of pitching it as a magazine rather than a comic, they were able to evade the tight restrictions of the Comic Code Authority. What the authorities missed was that this was the *really* subversive one. As Brian Siano (*The Humanist*) put it,

> It was the first to tell us the toys we were being sold were garbage, our teachers were phonies, our leaders were fools, our religious counsellors were hypocrites, and even our parents were lying to us about damn near everything.

No facet of American life, from Mickey Mouse to the President, was safe from the savaging inflicted by the idiot Alfred E. Newman and the other insane characters who inhabited its pages, and it was variously credited with or blamed for helping to create the 1960s counter-culture. It was also published in Britain from 1959 onwards.

But in early 1950s Britain, the focus was all on the horror comic. Concerned teachers, church-men, politicians and parents united under the title the Comics Campaign Council (CCC) to lobby against what one of them called 'the kind of depravity I never expected to find outside a madhouse'. This campaign was not entirely as disinterested as it seemed. Many of its leading lights were members of the Communist Party of Great Britain, who had a vested interest in attacking the United States and all it stood for in the way of cultural imperialism. As the Communist Party publication *Arena* said in 1951,

> the American threat to British culture, and to all that is good and vital in our national tradition ... comes from reactionary elements in United States society...

Similarly, one of the leading campaigners against horror comics in the media was the magazine *Picture Post*. But they again were not quite as disinterested as they might have appeared. As we saw at the top of the chapter, they were owned by the Hulton group, who published some of the more wholesome (or as some young readers might have seen it, tame), British competition. They are likely to have seen the threat to their sales from these imports for, although the sales of American horror comics in this country were quite small, we were told that the practice of children swapping them meant they reached a far wider audience (and influenced tastes more) than their sales would suggest.

Whatever their motives, the CCC proved to be a very effective lobbying body. Many people shared the views of this reader who wrote to the *Picture Post*:

> Who can look at these comics and escape the conclusion that there is a connection between them and the increasing volume of juvenile delinquency?

The CCC managed to get Dr Samuel Yudkin, an active member of the Communist Party and CCC campaigner, the opportunity to address the Conservative government's Education Committee on the subject. By 1954, even *The Times* was behind them:

> The problem which now faces society in the trade that has sprung up of presenting sadism, crime, lust, physical monstrosity and horror to the young is an urgent and a grave one ... There has been no more encouraging sign of the moral health of the country than the way in which public opinion has been roused in condemnation of the evil of 'horror comics' and in determination to combat them.
>
> *The Times*, 12 November 1954

Their campaign bore fruit in the form of the Children and Young Persons (Harmful Publications) Act 1955. The Act made it an offence to produce books, magazines or similar material likely to fall into the hands of children or young people that portrayed the commission of crimes, acts of violence or cruelty, or incidents of a repulsive or horrible nature, such that they would tend to corrupt the reader. This turned out to be something of a redundant piece of legislation, not least since the Americans were already turning off much of the supply of unsuitable material at its source. By 1962, only a dozen complaints had been made under this Act and no action had been taken in relation to five of them. It is thought that the first actual prosecution under the Act did not take place until 1970, when a British company was fined just £25 for re-publishing some of the early 1950s American horror magazines.

Not only was it rarely employed against imported material, it seemed the legislation – or the people applying it – were impotent when a home-grown version, apparently at least as deserving of prosecution, appeared in our newsagents. IPC Magazines produced something like 45 per cent of children's comics and magazines, including nursery favourites such as *Jack and Jill* and educational works like *Look and Learn*.

Although it cost only seven pence and attracted a readership aged seven and upwards, their publication *Action* was definitely not from the same mould as *Look and Learn*. At least, it was devoutly to be hoped that the tiny tots were not looking and learning. It first appeared in February 1976 and lasted (in its original blood-curdling form) only until October, when complaints about its violent content led to its withdrawal. A watered-down version, launched the following month, lasted until November 1977.

From the start, *Action* set out to shock. The cover carried strap-lines like 'Not for the nervous' or 'This comic is *not* suitable for adults', and offered such wholesome features as 'Death Game 1999' ('They call it a sport … its more like plain murder'); 'Shadowed by a Mad Axeman'; 'When Black Jack hits you … you stay hit' and 'Don't play Spinball!! You might end up looking like this!' (I leave it to your overwrought imagination to work out what 'this!' might have looked like). The press soon got onto it, and *The Sun* warned its readers about:

THE SEVENPENNY NIGHTMARE: DO YOU WORRY ABOUT WHAT YOUR KIDS READ?
– A giant shark snaps off a man's head in one crimson-splashed chomp. Then it tears apart another victim, limb from trunk;
– An international diplomat dissolves in agony as sulphuric acid gushes from his bathroom shower;
– The severed finger of a kidnapped boxing trainer delivered in a box – a warning to a black fighter to lose an important fight;
– Devil worshippers drinking human blood from chalices while their Satan-masked leader jabs a dagger into a human victim's chest;
– A sadistic warder dragging a boy prisoner along on his stomach from a rope attached to the back of his speeding car.

The Sun, 30 April 1976

The literary genius behind this publication was IPC Editorial Director John Sanders, and he was entirely unapologetic about it. He cited the fact that the youth of 1976 were already bombarded with violence by the rest of the media; he questioned whether items such as those listed above constituted violence, arguing improbably that 'violence is a highly emotive word. We prefer to say that *Action* gives rough, tough entertainment.' But then he fell back on the ultimate moral justification for his decision to publish – sales of his other titles were falling:

We would like to stick with traditional stories of Union Jacks fluttering over Boy Scout camps. But kids don't buy that any more.

Ibid.

Asked whether they had to be in this market at all, given IPC's host of other publishing interests, he replied:

Yes, we do. You might as well ask: Should Britain abdicate from the United Nations because we don't like what is going on in the world today. It's the same as saying, 'We don't like what the kids like, so we won't publish.' We can't turn our backs on this trend.

Ibid.

In the face of continued outrage from Conservative Members of Parliament and Mary Whitehouse, a child psychiatrist was produced by the publisher, to argue that children were much better than their parents at coping with horrifying material. He explained,

Children have such a short experience of life that they don't identify with pain and suffering in the same way as an adult. Youngsters are much better at separating fact from fantasy.

Ibid.

But the real clinching argument came from a spokesman for Joseph Holden and Sons, a leading comic distributor:

> The more violent comics are, the better they sell. *Action* is going like a rocket. More comics will have to follow suit and go in for blood and guts, or go out of business.
>
> Ibid.

Even with your market pitched at those of seven years old and upwards, it seemed, you could not go broke by underestimating the taste of the Great British public.

It's Wholesome! It's British! It's Biggles in Space!

One person who had no desire to go in for blood and guts was the vicar quoted earlier, the Revd Marcus Morris. He had a much better idea for saving young souls. Originally, this took the form of a character in a strip cartoon called Lex Christian, a fighting parson in the East End slums. Through successive promotions, a name change and a spot of time travel Lex became a flying priest, the parson of the fighting seventh, and eventually 'Dan Dare, Pilot of the Future … racing to the rescue of Rocket Ship no. 1, trapped by the silicon mass on the fringe of the Flame Lands'. As I write this, I do not have the first (14 April 1950) edition of the *Eagle* in front of me, in which these heroics were documented. So I can only assume, given the authorship, that the 'silicon mass' was some kind of devilish liturgy practised by the Catholic mutants of the planet Mekonta.

Dan's employer was the International Space Fleet, an organisation that specialised in compassion and reconciliation to a degree not normally associated with explorers who roam the universe in space ships armed with big guns. Frank Hampson, the creator of the strips, summed up the character of our hero:

> In the strip I tried to show a clear difference between good and evil. I preferred Dan Dare to prevail by intelligence, common sense and sheer determination.

There were other clues as to the comic's religious origins; moralising editorials, strip cartoons featuring unexpected action heroes – *The Great Adventurer* (the story of St Paul) and *The Road of Courage* (the story of Jesus himself). Even the promise of a 'pin-up for boys' would have come as something of a disappointment to many modern readers, consisting as it did of 'an accurate colour drawing of the new British Railways Turbine-Electric Locomotive'. Cutaway drawings to show the inner workings of some piece of machinery or other were a speciality of *Eagle*, though I do not recall that they ever did the Ark of the Covenant.

Eagle was nonetheless a runaway success. The first edition sold 900,000 copies and, at its peak in the mid-1950s, it had a circulation of around 2 million copies a week. The comic itself ran until 1969, but Dan Dare and some of the other leading characters were also featured at various times on computer games, radio serials (it ran on Radio Luxembourg five nights a week between 1951 and 1956, sponsored by Horlicks), CGI cartoons and other media. Its secret was that middle-class parents, who had hitherto looked down on comics as mind-rotting and, more particularly, proletarian, approved of *Eagle* and allowed their children to read it. A neat way of separating out the classes among the generation that grew up in the 1950s would be to get them to line them up according to who read *Eagle* and who subsisted on the likes of the *Beano* and *Dandy* (of which more later).

If Dan Dare had a fault, it was picking on people older than himself. His arch-enemy was the Mekon, born in about 1750 as the result of fiendish scientific experimentation by the Treens, residents of the northern hemisphere of Venus. He was super-intelligent, totally emotionless, evil and bent on world domination – but when you are over 200 years old and bright green, surely you are entitled to some little eccentricities? The Mekon's body was as weak as his mind was strong, and he travelled everywhere in a magnetically powered, mind-controlled personal transport resembling a Formula 1 bedpan (again, no doubt a necessity for a bi-centenarian). His great failing was in inventing ever more elaborate ways of killing off Dan Dare, from which he invariably escaped to appear in the next edition.

In a touching echo of the class system of the day, Dan was supported by his friend and 'batman', Spaceman First Class Albert Digby, a native of Wigan (a place that was not in the northern hemisphere of Venus, but just looked that way). Digby has been described as slightly gormless, idle and overweight but, once aroused by righteous indignation, unstoppable. Another fault, shared by all the characters, is the fatal tendency to alliteration – if startled, none of them could resist the temptation to cry 'suffering snakes!' or 'sizzling satellites!'

A striking feature of the Dan Dare strips was the quality of the graphics, which are still admired today. The main artist was Frank Hampson, who strived obsessively for scientific accuracy (insofar as scientific knowledge of life on Venus was available to a 1950s graphic artist). He even had science fiction author Arthur C. Clarke as science advisor to his initial strips. *Eagle* was reborn in 1982 with a new Dan Dare – the great-great-great-grandson of the original – at its centre and the Mekon as, well, an even more geriatric version of himself. By 1987 it had become more violent, with Dan on occasions even using a hi-tech gun. Naturally, this would never do, and the new *Eagle* folded in 1994.

Other Comic Contenders

We were a comic-reading generation, in the days before wall-to-wall television and games consoles monopolised youthful attentions. But there is only space to remember a few of these literary icons.

> We were given something called *The Children's Newspaper* which was extremely tedious. We wanted *Dandy* and *Beano* but we weren't allowed to have them.
>
> 1950s child, quoted in Pressley, p. 95

Before *Eagle*, parents looking for something wholesome for their children to read would turn to *The Children's Newspaper*. Launched in 1919, this was, as its name hints, a newspaper for children and was built around its founder's (Arthur Mee's) twin values of Christianity and the British Empire. The edition I looked at had as its front page story the Buchanan report on traffic in towns (see the transport chapter of this book); not immediately promising material for youngsters thirsting for heroes and villains (or possibly the dagger-wielding, red-eyed ghouls and rope-bound, scantily clad voluptuous young women of the American comics?) Despite its uncompromising approach to its young readers *The Children's Newspaper* sold 500,000 copies at its peak, but sales slipped to less than half that number after the war, as *Eagle, Look and*

Learn and other more appealing publications came on the market. Despite belated attempts to modernise itself *The Children's Newspaper* made its final appearance in May 1965.

Most of the characters in *Dandy* and *Beano* are one-dimensional, in that they possess one characteristic around which all their strips are based. Desperate Dan is preternaturally strong, if clumsy; the Smasher breaks things; Mitch possesses a Mummy (of the ancient Egyptian variety) and Harry a Hippo, both of which unsurprisingly manage to wreak havoc in a suburban environment. Others are incredibly hungry, incredibly nosey and there is a chap called Watson who is apparently a winker (note to editor: I have double-checked this).

But were they as harmless as they may superficially appear? During the war years they were irreproachably patriotic. They relayed all sorts of useful wartime messages to their young readers about recycling newspapers and 'if you find an unexploded mine on the beach, don't hit it with a rock'. More to the point, they lampooned Hitler and Mussolini ('Musso the Wop – he's a bit of a flop') unmercifully, to the point where it was (incorrectly) claimed that the names of the editors of *Dandy* and *Beano* were included on a Nazi death-list in the event of them invading.

Post-war, the picture is more ambivalent, because it emerges that a number of the characters have been forced to change their ways in response to concerns about the examples they were setting for their impressionable young readers. Although the authority figures in the stories generally prevailed over youthful rebellion, they relied on corporal punishment to a degree that would be unacceptable today. Children got whacked round the head or beaten by their parents or teachers, and bullies got beaten up by bigger bullies. The publishers became aware of growing unease about this, and a comic magazine character these days is apparently more likely to be punished by having his television remote control confiscated. Desperate Dan, who smoked tobacco in a pipe made from a bucket and went around tooled up with a six-shooter, was forced to go on a diet and had to hand in his gun in favour of a water pistol – not so desperate now, are you big fellow?

Worst of all, it appeared that Dennis the Menace was promoting homophobic violence. Dennis' arch-enemy, whom he constantly menaced, was Walter, known as the Prince of Softies. He was a gentle, bespectacled boy who liked sewing, picking flowers and holding tea parties for his teddy bears. It was decided somewhere that anyone who was that much in touch with their feminine side must be homosexual, and that Dennis was therefore guilty of gay-bashing. He (or rather, his illustrator) was ordered to desist forthwith and, moreover, Walter underwent his own transformation. He became someone who was 'completely happy about who he was and a confident, likeable character in his own right'. They even went so far as to give Walter his own girlfriend, so as to remove any doubts about his leanings (no doubt begging the question in some quarters of what was so shameful about him being gay?)

Opponents of political correctness were suitably appalled at this craven submission. What would it be next? Minnie the Minx giving girls hints on make-up? Lord Snooty lecturing the reader on the need for greater social equality? But there have been slight signs more recently of a return to the comic's anarchic roots. The *Beano* ran a controversial strip called *The Neds*, about a workshy ne'er-do-well Scottish family. They were also challenged over a schoolboy character called Simon Coe. A spokesman for the *Beano* described him as 'just a guy who overreacts dramatically to the annoyances in life that niggle us all'. This over-reaction took the form of such things as stuffing a child into a rubbish bin and kicking in a newsagent's door. But campaigners picked up on the fact that he appeared to suffer from some involuntary syndrome like Tourette's and was shunned by his schoolmates as a result. They feared that children with behavioural problems could end up being victimised in the playground (if those behavioural problems included stuffing their schoolmates into bins, they could well be right). But if the precedent of Dennis and Walter the Softy is anything to go by, Simon will no doubt in due course transform into someone resembling St Francis of Assisi.

Lord Snooty, though not to the best of my knowledge pilloried for any active wrongdoing, sent out some funny messages about class. This boy was the limitlessly rich Lord Marmaduke of Bunkerton, who lived in Bunkerton Castle, along with his pet stag Angus, his guardian, Aunt Matilda and a motley crew of youngsters who constituted his pals. These originally included Skinny Lizzie (a thin girl), Hairpin Huggins (a thin boy), Swanky Lanky Liz (a tall girl) and Gertie the Goat (a goat – you begin to appreciate the depth of characterisation that went into it). Again, after unimpeachable war service, in which he trounced Hitler on a regular basis, the peacetime nemesis of this Eton-uniformed anachronism became the Gasworks Gang, a bunch of dreadful working-class oiks. What were his largely working-class readership supposed to make of this? Anachronism or not, Lord Snooty's strip continued to be published until 1990.

Roy of the Rovers was a character aimed at the football-mad boy, in the days before football was considered a suitable activity for young ladies. He started life in *Tiger* in 1954 but got his own dedicated comic in 1976. At its height, this sold some 450,000 copies a week. Its principal character was Roy Race of Melchester Rovers, a player who could always be relied upon to snatch victory from the jaws of defeat (except that, in the issue I am looking at, he has been shot in the head and taken comatose to the intensive care unit – a position from which even he will find it difficult to score the winner from a last minute free-kick). His remarkable playing career (remarkable not least for its eventfulness – virtually every season he was embroiled in a championship or relegation battle, and he was kidnapped at least five times) lasted almost forty years. Then in 1993 he was involved in a helicopter crash in which he lost his left foot. Even the publishers recognised that, being one-legged and around sixty years old might suggest that his best playing days were nearly over. He was forced to hang up his one remaining boot and go into management. But if not every reader would find it easy to identify with a blond-haired lantern-jawed athlete like Roy, the comic contained plenty of other fantasy role-models with whom they could more readily associate.

One of the more extreme of these was *Mighty Mouse*, featuring Kevin Mouse. Do you remember the weedy boy at school who was always the last one to get picked for the football kickabouts in the playground? Kevin looked like someone who would have been picked after him. He was a medical student who was almost perfectly spherical, wore spectacles with lenses like the bottoms of milk bottles and had looks beside which Wayne Rooney would pass for a matinee idol. The reader was asked to believe that he was also a part-time player for First Division (think Premier League, younger readers) Tottenford Rovers, and was a player capable of mazy runs through defences beyond the specifications of George Best.

I found him in 1981, for reasons that were no more credible than the basic premise of the strip, faced with having to score a goal in an international match against Holland or lose his job as a trainee doctor at St Victor's Hospital. (Rather than leave you fretting about it, I will tell you now that he succeeded.) But, lest we are tempted to mock, there was no doubt an army of overweight, short-sighted schoolboys who drew great comfort from his exploits; and with childhood obesity now at epidemic proportions, who is to say that the time is not ripe for his return? Or would this simply result in a whole generation of youths stuffing themselves even more insensible in order to match his dimensions?

Turning to the girls, in *Jackie* it is not goals but a curiously chaste form of romance that the readers are looking for, preferably involving pop stars. The nearest it seems to come to intimacy in the material I saw is to be found in the form of a mathematics problem set in a February 1975 edition:

> A screaming fan pulled a 1-centimetre square patch of hair from Gary Glitter's chest. If there were 125 hairs in the patch, how many hairs are there on (a) his whole chest which measures 30 cm x 40 cm and (b) how much will she make if she sells each hair at £2.50 to other fans?

With the wisdom of hindsight, an editor might have had second thoughts about running an item involving young teenage girls and the more intimate parts of Garry Glitter's anatomy. We are not told the answer to the sum but, if the figure of 125 chest hairs per square centimetre is correct, it must qualify Glitter for residence in London Zoo.

The same edition offers hints on 'The Look of Love', or how to attract the adenoidal youth of your dreams (the secrets are apparently to avoid rough, scaly hands, a red nose and cheeks that are white and pinched, dry flaking lips, mascara scattered half-way down your cheeks, bad breath and smelling awful – unless of course you are going to a Halloween fancy dress party, in which case you might seduce a devotee of American horror comics). In the short story *When the World was New*, trainee God Heikon and trainee Goddess Senia meet at the foot of Mount Olympus and make the earth move (because they can, you know). In another feature, reassurance comes with the news that seventeen-year-old pop idol Donny Osmond 'has dated lots of girls back home in Utah. But don't worry – he says that he hasn't fallen in love with any of them, as yet!' Although you should know that his ideal wife would 'have to be a good housewife, and in particular good at cooking'. She 'should also know a little about his hobby, which as you know is electronics'. Renaissance woman indeed.

Tammy, by contrast, seems to encourage alarming masochistic tendencies in its young female readers. In a single edition, I found a young girl accused of witchcraft and about to be burned at the stake; a young female teacher who is sacked from her post at a famous public school by the wicked headmistress; a young wartime evacuee who is treated as a virtual slave by the wicked farmer's wife with whom she is billeted; a young girl who is imprisoned in a ghostly house; a young girl who is punished by her wicked Victorian mill-owner father for trying to help his downtrodden employees; a young girl sent to work as a servant in a country house in which she is victimised by the wicked other staff. Do you detect a pattern emerging? According to the editorial, this is 'the kind of picture story paper we think you want – crammed from beginning to end with thrilling and exciting stories and interesting features'.

Those seeking less troubled fantasy figures with which to identify could turn to *Judy for Girls*, in which they could read about *Jenny Johnson*, the schoolgirl zoo-keeper, *Kay Burrows*, the schoolgirl vet, or *Bobby Dazzler*, who was compensated for having to carry that name through life by being the only girl at the Westbury School for Boys. (Before anyone starts thinking that this was the result of some gigantic error on the part of the Medical Officer at her induction, she was there because her mother was the school matron.)

Bunty sets out to combine identity problems and agoraphobia for its readers. In one strip Carol Lawson runs Claremont College, an unorthodox educational establishment which specialises in teaching anybody anything. Her client in the week I read was a Mrs Ponsonby, a radical feminist and Secretary of the Feminine Freedom Fighters, who wants every last vestige of femininity removed from her daughter, Tommy (short for Thomasina, in itself a burden for any young woman to bear). Carol teaches her all the manly attributes – boxing, marching, stoking the school boiler and digging drainage ditches (probably spitting and swearing as well, but the editors of *Tammy* were too polite to say so) – and the training is well advanced when Tommy's mother rushes in with a change of plan. A relative has died and left them a fortune, but only on condition that Tommy has not been indoctrinated with any of her mother's funny feminist ideas. By now, it is implied, Tommy can belch and tell lies with the best of the lads – so far as we can tell, she may even have been on the verge of growing a beard and her voice breaking. But Carol comes up with an ingenious plan, with which she manages to hoodwink the solicitor who is sent to check on Tommy's female proclivities. She releases a mouse, and all of Thomasina's manly bonhomie evaporates into girlish screams. Reassured, the solicitor tells her 'I like an old-fashioned girl who needs masculine protection. There will be no difficulty about the will, I promise you!' There is probably a message for the readers about feminism in there somewhere, but it escapes me.

As for agoraphobia, *Bunty*'s feature 'A Walk with Danger' lists sixteen things for girls to be afraid of when walking in the countryside, including eagles, thunderclouds, ants, marram grass, swans and jellyfish (jellyfish – in the countryside?)

Are We Having Fun Yet?

While Dan Dare may have provided a positive role model, there was plenty of other stuff for the comic reader and their parents to worry about – violence and depravity in the horror comic, publications that incited violent behaviour, homophobia or class war among their readers, young girls having nightmares about an almost unlimited choice of incarceration, slavery, or other abuse up to and including being burnt at the stake, the fear on country walks of being savaged by ants, jellyfish … and Gary Glitter. I'm just surprised we all grew up as normal as we did.

2

Fun in the Sun: Holidays

This is the most miserable place on the south coast for the half-day tripper ... No whelk stalls in the street, no sixpenny dinners or ham and beef teas, no crowds of yelling bathers, no ventriloquists, phrenologists, cheap-jacks, fortune tellers ... anywhere in sight ... Its policy is to preserve itself from the jolly greeting of cloth-capped thousands – and until now it has succeeded very well.

David Cannadine describes early twentieth-century Eastbourne
in *Lords and Landlords*, quoted in Horn, p. 130

The older (seaside landladies) lament the difference today from pre-war times, when Newquay was filled up by professional people and middle-class families generally. Higher wages and holidays with pay and the poverty of the middle classes have changed all that. Now 'its just a different class of people we get. They're nice enough. But there's just no comparison with the people we used to have.'

Picture Post, 1952

What does the term 'holiday' mean to you? If anything conveys the meaning of fun, it should be a holiday. Yet, for much of the last century, for the average Briton, it meant leaning into a rain-bearing gale so strong you needed to be anchored by guy-ropes; being swaddled in the kinds of beachwear favoured by Antarctic explorers, on a beach made in equal parts of stones and broken glass; sandwiches containing real sand and seaside landladies who had been expelled from the Gestapo for unacceptable breaches of human rights. A nation's choice of leisure activities has much to tell us about their character. In this chapter, we look at some of the changes in British holidaying habits since the war.

In case you should think that the images of British holiday-making that I have just conjured up have been entirely replaced by the guaranteed sunshine of the Costa del Foreign, bear this in mind. Even at the height of the foreign package holiday boom in the 1990s, at least a half of all Britons took their holidays in the United Kingdom. This statistic comes from the British Resorts Association, who should know about these things (or at the very least devoutly wish them to be so – a press report (*The Guardian*, 31 July 1999) warned that estimated visitor numbers could be about as reliable as an off-form palmist's reading on Wigan pier). Even so, it may still be true – for when last I looked, Blackpool was still Europe's single largest holiday destination, attracting some 17 million visitors a year, and £4.5 billion was spent in United Kingdom seaside resorts in the year 2000.

But, within living memory, holiday habits were very different.

The Elusive Holiday

As the quotes at the top of the chapter suggest, holiday-making was to a large extent a middle-class preserve immediately before the Second World War. A proper holiday was an unimaginable luxury for a significant part of the population. Many lived in fear even of the statutory Bank Holidays, granted under nineteenth-century legislation, because for them holidays meant no wages and a painful choice between getting into arrears with the rent or seeing your family go hungry. By 1938, a campaign to secure a week's paid holiday for all workers had been running for twenty years, ever since Labour MP George Lansbury's first unsuccessful attempt to introduce it through a Private Member's Bill in Parliament. Clerical workers had for the most part had them since the previous century, and some of the more organised parts of manual labour had secured them; the print-workers were among the first to win them, in 1918. By 1938, just under 4.5 million people had paid holidays – but 15.5 million did not and, for them, the only possibility of getting away might be something like hop or fruit-picking in Kent. Many working-class people had never actually gone away for a holiday.

In the event, the Holidays with Pay Act 1938 did not radically change people's leisure habits – it recommended, but did not mandate, one week's paid holiday for all full-time workers. In any event, more pressing business with Mr Hitler interfered with whatever holiday plans people might have had. Even without such distractions, a holiday away from home – statutory or not – remained unaffordable for many of the 19.5 million workers who were trying to live on less than £250 a year. A *News Chronicle* survey of 1939 found quite a sharp divide between those earning over £4 a week, 90 per cent of whom felt they could afford a holiday, and those earning less than that figure, only a third of whom could. Only when post-war labour shortages forced wages up did holidays become a realistic prospect for many of this latter group. But even as late as the 1990s a European Union survey found that 35 per cent of British households could still not afford a week's holiday away from home (compared with just 12 per cent of Germans – no wonder those swine always managed to get their towels on the hotel poolside sun loungers first).

There was one group to whom the thought of recreation for the masses did not appeal. Many of the residents of the more genteel seaside resorts, used to receiving a nicer class of visitor during the holiday season, feared an influx of the great unwashed, who were well known to be frightfully vulgar. Their concerns are articulated in the quotes at the top of the chapter. The committee who had framed the legislation for paid holidays were for their part mindful of different problems – their concern was more with the financial pressures facing the low-paid holiday-maker. But there was a solution that met both their concerns – that meant that the proletariat could have their revels without frightening the horses in Eastbourne.

Holiday Camps

> If you didn't like team spirit, you were in the wrong place.
>
> Akhtar and Humphries, *Some Liked it Hot*, p. 43

> Roll out of bed in the morning
> With a big, big smile and a good, good morning.
> You'll find life is worthwhile
> If you roll out of bed with a smile
>
> Song, broadcast on the Butlins public address system at 7.30 each morning. Apparently the camp electricians were kept busy repairing loudspeakers suffering from cut wires.

The holiday camp was another Victorian invention, the first one opening on the Isle of Man in 1894. There were something like 200 – mostly small – holiday camps in Britain by 1938. By no means were they all commercial ventures – many were run by trade unions, political parties or benevolent organisations; some banned alcohol and profane language and the highlight of your week under canvas could be a lecture by Labour leader Keir Hardie or playwright George Bernard Shaw. Nonetheless, they had shown their ability to cater for a mass market. The two largest commercial ventures alone had enough capacity for 140,000 people in a season by that time.

Billy Butlin is generally acknowledged as the father of the holiday camp. Contrary to normal practice, the name of the mother is unknown. He was born in South Africa in 1899 but moved to Bristol as a small child, where his mother married a gasworker. Billy later emigrated to Canada, where he served in the Canadian army during the First World War. At the end of hostilities, he worked his passage back to England, collected his £5 pay and set out to walk the 160 miles from Liverpool to Bedminster, near Bristol. Bedminster was the winter quarters for the Marshall Hill Travelling Fair, and it was there that Butlin made his first investment in the leisure industry. For thirty shillings he bought a hoop-la stall. As the new season opened, Butlin revealed his first stroke of business genius – he made his hoop-la pedestals easier to hoop than those of his rivals! It meant he gave away more prizes, but he was soon netting profits that were ten times those of the competition. By 1929 he had made enough to open an amusement park on the south side of Skegness Pier and was the entrepreneur who introduced the British motoring public to fairground Dodgem cars.

At some stage in his life, Butlin had been traumatised by a holiday at Barry Island which had been ruined by a seaside landlady trained at the concentration camp School of Hospitality. Following the common practice of many landladies of the period, she threw her 'guests' out of the house during the day, whatever the weather, rather than have them clutter up the place. Butlin decided he could do much better. In 1935, he bought 200 acres of turnip field just north of Skegness and set out to turn it into a holiday camp that would eventually cater for up to 8,000 campers. The development was done on a shoestring; the money almost ran out and the water supply was not turned on until days before the opening, in April 1936. (His camp at Bognor was even less finished when he opened it in 1960. Some of the first campers had to be offered alternative accommodation at Clacton, though some turned down the offer and spent part of their holiday installing doors and window frames in the chalets.)

But the package he offered was an attractive one – a roof over your head (all day, if the holiday-maker so wished!), three square meals a day and free entertainment, all for 35 shillings per person per week.

During the war years, the camp was requisitioned by the Royal Navy, who renamed it the HMS *Royal Arthur*. Under this name it became one of the very few holiday camps to be sunk by naval gunfire (and almost certainly the only one to be sunk twice). In fact these 'sinkings' took place only in the fevered imaginations of the German propaganda machine, who had clearly got it into their heads that the title HMS meant that it was a proper ship that they could claim to have sunk. In fact, the camp was handed back to Butlin relatively unscathed in 1946.

Meanwhile, other camps had followed Skegness. Clacton was built on the site of some boating lakes and miniature golf courses, which Butlin bought in 1936. He opened another funfair there the following year, with the holiday camp opening in 1938. By 1937, Butlins had gone public, with a share capital of £220,000. The following year, he paid £12,000 for 120 acres of land at Filey. Construction was under way when Herr Hitler put something of a dampener on seaside holidays. Never one to miss an opportunity, Butlin struck a deal with Hore-Belisha, the Minister of War, for the government to buy the camp and finance its completion, in return for Butlin being able to buy it back for an agreed sum at the end of hostilities. This he did, managing to reopen it for holidays towards the end of the 1945 season. At its peak, this camp could take 11,000 visitors and it even had its own railway station from 1947, at a time when most holiday-makers did not have the option of the private car.

Until Butlin and Captain Harry Warner, another big operator of the time, revolutionised the cost of holidays, a camp would typically charge around £2 10s per person per week. This is roughly in line with the cost of a week's accommodation at one of the less than salubrious bed and breakfast establishments at the time. Given that the average industrial wage was then only around £3 10s, it meant that even holiday camps were restricted to the better-paid skilled manual and clerical workers. But Butlin managed to reduce his costs radically, enabling him eventually to offer a couple a week's holiday, with full board and free entertainment, for that same £3 10s. It gave Butlin a new slogan, (though the original idea was Captain Harry Warner's, when he opened his first camp, in 1931):

Holidays with pay. Holidays with play! A week's holiday for a week's pay.

In fact, Butlins were very keen on their slogans – to judge from the evidence, the clunkier the better (the first one on the list below admittedly comes from Shakespeare's *A Midsummer Night's Dream*, but the standard goes rapidly downhill from that point). Here are a few examples from across the years:

- Our true intent is all for your delight (1930s)
- You make new friends at Butlins – where you will meet the kind of people you'd like to meet (late 1950s)
- You'll have a really wonderful time at Butlins by the sea (1960s)
- Butlinland is freedomland and Holidays are Jollydays (1970s)
- A little bit of this and quite a lot of that (early 1980s)
- Let's Butlin it and Butlin it, and you'll do it again (mid-1980s)
- Play happy families (late 1980s)

Although for the first few years Butlin's clientèle was as much middle-class as working-class, the camps later came to be regarded in some quarters as a type of ghetto for the proletariat. But they were undoubtedly big business; at their height, one in twenty of all British holiday-makers went to Butlins. By the late 1950s and early 1960s Britain had over a hundred holiday camps and Butlins alone exceeded a million campers in 1963. The other big players were Warners and Pontins. Butlin's promotional material spoke highly of the amenities in his chalets, calling them 'AN EDEN-ON-SEA and almost an earthly paradise'. They incorporated 'electric light, running water, comfortable beds with interior sprung mattresses … a luxurious home of your own'.

Other features of the early Butlins camps included

- no choice of meals, nor of who you could sit with to eat them, though you had the consolation of compulsory cheering whenever a waitress dropped a plate;

– early morning reveille over the tannoy, with Radio Butlin welcoming you back to the world of the living with 'There's a new day a tumblin' in';

– Redcoats marching through the camp in the evening, beating a drum and singing 'Come and join us, come and join our merry throng' in order to round up any campers who were not felt to be enjoying themselves enough and shepherd them back to the ballroom;

– a house system, with the camp divided up into Gloucester, Kent, Windsor and York houses, competing with each other throughout the week;

– a sports field, scenes of such epic contests as the three-legged race, the egg-and-spoon race and the donkey derby;

– For the youngsters, the opportunity to become Butlins Beavers (or Warners Wagtails) and subject to the tender mercies of their new 'aunties'. Slightly more creepily, Warners also had an Uncle Arthur who drew the children, pied piper style, from their chalets in the morning by playing his recorder, and led them down into Warner's private woods for nature studies while their parents slept in.

Even in those entertainment-starved days, there was evidently a good deal of scepticism about this formula for enforced mateyness, but there was sufficient suspension of disbelief on the part of most campers to enable it to work to some degree. This apparently lasted until Friday nights, which were notorious for their sexual liaisons and the (often alcohol-fuelled) brawls which followed them. Butlins was at one stage the nation's largest beer retailer and had a well-practised routine for dealing with difficult drunks. They would drive them out into the countryside in a van and leave them to sober up as they found their way back, on foot.

But for those who were not on passion (or inebriation) bent, there were a wide range of trophies to be won. Holiday Princess, Lovely Legs, Knobbly Knees, Best Ankles, Glamorous Grandmother, Ugliest Face, Shiniest Bald Head, Shaver of the Week (sponsored by Philishave) and Best Cigarette Roller (sponsored by Rizla). You had to be very average indeed to come away from your week at Butlins without winning something.

For some unimaginable reason there were those who accused holiday camps of being regimented, and the proprietors were at pains (sometimes painfully so) to point out that this was not the case. The following appeared in an advertisement feature sponsored by Butlins in the local papers in 1960 (the emphases are theirs):

Some people say 'Oh, Butlins – its like the army – do this, do that, like a lot of sheep'.

Obviously people who say this have never been near a Butlins camp, because nothing could be further from the truth.

Butlins is everybody's holiday and it is planned to let you do what you like. Of course there are organised entertainments. Of course you have meals within stated times. Of course there are bright lights, fun and gaiety. But is there any sizeable holiday resort where there isn't?

The point about Butlins is that it provides for ALL TASTES and ALL AGES but no one, repeat no one, seeks to force you to do anything. Butlins provide all amusements for all people. But its your holiday. You do what you like. There is POSITIVELY NO REGIMENTATION.

No regimentation – and that's an order. Methinks they do protest too much.

As well as being holiday camps, Butlins became known as finishing schools for the entertainment stars of the future. Many famous names cut their teeth as Redcoats. Clacton

Butlins alone brought on the likes of Dave Allen, Roy Hudd, Des O'Connor and, in 1958, an early professional performance by a young Cliff Richard. Butlins were very protective of the Redcoat name. When another holiday company bought the former Butlin camp at Barry Island, they tried continuing to employ redcoats, until the threat of legal action from Butlins forced their coats to turn blue.

During the 1960s, the camps were hit badly by the boom in foreign holidays. Butlins made its first ever loss in 1965 and Fred Pontin tried to get in on the trend by launching Pontinental Holidays. But the glory days of the holiday camp were over. Attempts to repackage them as holiday centres, villages or parks were not spectacularly successful, and all three of the market leaders were sold on between 1972 and 1983. Billy Butlin got a good return on his initial £1.50 investment. In 1972, the business was sold to the Rank Organisation for £43 million.

Package Holidays

It may come as a surprise to learn that the package holiday is not a twentieth-century invention. According to P. J. O'Rourke, the first package tour (or, more accurately, the first American one) left New York on board the steamship *Quaker City* in June 1867. Among the passengers was one Samuel L. Clemens (better known to us as Mark Twain) and its progress was recorded in the most popular travel book of its generation, *The Innocents Abroad*.

But there are many British claims to be the first well before that; Thomas Cook started in the package holiday business as early as July 1841, ferrying temperance workers from Leicester by rail to a rally in Loughborough. It was indeed a package; for the one-shilling fare, they got the return 12-mile rail trip, ham sandwiches, tea, cricket and other sports. Even more emphatically a package was the twenty-day excursion to Paris being offered by Joseph Crisp of Liverpool by 1845, and Cook himself was offering package tours to Europe by 1855. An even earlier claim, more dubious but striking in its own way, was a cut-price rail excursion to an event in June 1836, organised by the Bodmin and Wadebridge Railway in Cornwall. The 'attraction' was a public hanging in Bodmin, but records do not tell us whether lunch was included.

The first modern Continental package tour was organised by a Russian émigré called Vladimir Raitz. He settled in London and in 1949 took a holiday in Calvi, Corsica. There he met a socialite with local connections called Nicholas Steinheid, who offered to use his influence to help him set up a holiday company serving the area. Raitz, a London School of Economics graduate, did the sums and calculated that he could offer holiday-makers a two-week package holiday for less than £35. This was still a considerable sum for anyone to find, but was still less than half the cost of just the return air fare to Corsica by British European Airways. At this time, BEA had pretty well sewn up a monopoly in flying Britons abroad for their holidays, and one of the major challenges Raitz faced was getting the civil aviation authorities to licence him. But undeterred, and financed by £3,000 left him by his grandmother, Raitz founded Horizon holidays in October 1949. At this stage, the company was just a part-time sideline to his day job as a journalist.

As anticipated, the civil aviation licence proved a major stumbling block. It did not come through until March 1950, and then only on condition that the customers were limited to 'students and teachers only'. The final cost of the first package, which took off in May 1950, came to £32 10s. To call it 'basic' conveys an unwarranted air of luxury. The first tour party consisted of eleven 'teachers' and twenty-one 'friends' (that is, people who went just for the return flight, a quick look around the site and a dip in the Mediterranean. Unlike most other package holidays since, this one had no holiday-makers from the previous week to fill the plane on the return journey). The party was met at King's Cross station and ferried to Gatwick, where the transport took the form of a Second World War Douglas Dakota (a civilian conversion of a military transport plane). This carried thirty-two passengers and flew at a leisurely cruising speed of 150 mph. Nervous passengers afraid of heights would have taken comfort from the fact that, being unpressurised, it operated at no more than 3,000 feet. The journey to Calvi took six hours and required a refuelling stop at Lyon. On the credit side, the planes were cheap. Raitz could hire one for the return journey for just £305, or less than £10 a passenger.

The airport at Calvi did not have even so much as a shack for a terminal. It was an airstrip that had been built by the US Navy in 1943 to support the invasion of Italy. But the locals, unused to a sudden influx of tourism, made up for the lack of facilities with the warmth of their greeting, turning out the town band and garlanding the visitors with flowers. The grandly named Club Franco-Britannique, their holiday home, was also unpretentious in the extreme. For many of the guests, the accommodation was the same tents that had been used by the military personnel who had built the airport seven years before. The remaining facilities consisted of what was fetchingly described as 'a sanitary block', an open-air dining area, a dance-floor and a bar made out of bamboo. But, on the plus side, the holiday-makers could enjoy a package which included as much of the local plonk as they could drink, and at least two meals a day containing meat (no small consideration when Britain was still on rations).

In year one, Raitz's target was a modest 350 customers, but he missed even that by fifty. For the first few years, the company led a hand-to-mouth existence. But, on the positive side, for a number of years Horizon had a monopoly in the market, and were able to offer a growing range of destinations, including Majorca, Sardinia, Minorca and a sleepy little Spanish resort with only one hotel called Benidorm. One of his other early and possibly less cheery venues was Lourdes (1953). But other operators eventually got into the market, no doubt encouraged by June 1954 amendments to the Convention on International Civil Aviation that helped stimulate a mass market in tourist charter flights.

By the 1960 holiday season, operators were offering two weeks in Majorca for thirty-nine guineas. A fortnight in St Remo would cost you forty-four guineas, a ten-day tour of the Swiss Alps fifty-one guineas and the Grand Tour (a fifteen-day tour of Rome, Florence, Venice and Capri) sixty-five guineas. With rising numbers of tourists came tumbling prices; an overseas holiday that would have cost the family £80 in 1951 would have cost them about the same (despite inflation) in 1970; and between 1969 and the early 1990s the cost of a fortnight in Torremolinos halved in real terms.

But in the early days, abroad was still exotic territory indeed. Car-borne British tourists would honk and wave if they saw another British car. According to one intrepid adventurer:

> It was like going to the moon. Nobody had ever been to France for a holiday where we lived. They all went to Blackpool. They'd never heard of anyone going abroad except in a war. They made us so worried that we made a will the day before we left.
>
> Akhtar and Humphries, *Some Liked it Hot*, p. 84

But the die was cast and these upstart rivals had not escaped the gimlet eye of the domestic tourist industry. The president of the Scarborough Hotels Association, Harry Lund, chose the safe setting of his association's annual dinner to launch his gastronomic attack on 'the garlic and olive oil gang of the press and radio':

> Those writers, usually women, who belittled bacon and eggs and the incomparable meats and vegetables of England, while praising starch-laden Continental breakfasts and main meals consisting of dollops of spaghetti with a little tomato sauce.
>
> *The Manchester Guardian*, 11 December 1956

But his antipathy was not shared by a party of eighty Derbyshire miners, who (for reasons which are not immediately clear) decided to spend their holiday in Riccioni, on the Adriatic Coast. Fearful of the cuisine, they took with them their own cook (note, not a chef) and beer supplies, but were as surprised as anyone to become converts to the local wine and pasta.

Package trips were aggressively marketed; hundreds of potential holiday-makers packed into public halls to see films promoting this new and exotic form of leisure. One of the complaints of seaside local authorities at home was that they could not match the promotional budgets of the package holiday companies. By 1960, some 3,500,000 Britons were holidaying abroad each year. Regional airports began to develop their own markets; Manchester hosted charter carrier Euravia from 1961. Numbers continued to boom; by 1979, it was claimed (no doubt by that palmist on Wigan Pier again) that 10 million Britons took overseas holidays, and this figure was said to have doubled by 1987.

But despite the growth of the industry, it suffered a reverse in the 1970s. On 15 August 1974 the second-largest tour operator, Court Line (Horizon was by now just one of the brands under which it traded) went under. Almost 50,000 tourists were left stranded overseas and a further 100,000 were threatened with the loss of their deposits.

The package tour has had a number of distinct impacts on the British way of life. It has increased the appreciation (or at least the consumption) of wine, a beverage seen by many pre-war Britons as something foreign and suspect. It has helped drive up the standard and variety of the food we eat at home and it has done much to introduce the British and their Continental neighbours to each other (though whether the familiarity is always appreciated – on either side – may be a matter on which the jury is still out).

Effects on the Domestic Competition

Notwithstanding the claims of the British Resorts Association, British resorts suffered from the post-war boom in foreign travel; their (often Victorian) infrastructure was outdated and neglected. Seaside piers suffered particularly badly in the war years. They were originally built to enable tourists arriving by boat to get ashore without getting their feet wet. Come the Second World War and it was decided that visitors – especially German ones – should not be given such kid glove treatment, and many piers were at least partly dismantled. (Perhaps instead they could have lined the beach with seaside landladies, surely a sight to dishearten even the most fanatical storm-trooper?) Nor was the incentive for seaside local authorities to invest in upgrading the infrastructure particularly strong – money spent on leisure gardens and promenades hardly generated a commercial return.

Even so, some resorts were entrepreneurial and able to re-invent themselves; in the 1980s, the attractions of the heritage industry began to be fully appreciated and were seized upon by many of those resorts that had one. Some, as part of their strategy, went in for niche marketing. By 1999 the British Tourist Authority began a drive to attract the pink pound – gay tourists from America – to resorts like Blackpool, Bournemouth and Brighton, offering dedicated gay venues and gay events. Blackpool characteristically even provided the amenity of gay bingo (and no, I don't know how its rules differ from the standard variety).

Other areas also went into decline. Blackpool was the nation's thirtieth most deprived borough, according to 1991 census figures (which were recorded before the economic boom that undoubtedly followed when gay bingo was introduced). In some resorts, struggling hoteliers gave up on the tourist trade entirely and took instead to earning a less seasonal income from benefit claimants, giving the tabloid newspapers the gift of headlines about the 'Costa del Dole'. Some resorts became controversially associated with the housing of asylum seekers. According to some reports, you were more likely to be surrounded by foreigners in places like Margate than you ever were in Benidorm.

Few can have suffered a decline more terminal than that of New Brighton. In its heyday it was a thriving resort, with a tower over a hundred feet higher than Blackpool's (but demolished in 1919). By the 1970s, changes in the tidal flows of the Mersey had ripped out its beach and the pollution from that river left bathing to those with a taste for dangerous sports; its main entertainments complex had been destroyed by fire and not replaced. The pier was closed in 1972 and demolished five years later. A survey of visitors showed that over half the sample would not return to New Brighton even for a day trip and over 70 per cent automatically rejected it as a future holiday destination. Its approval ratings for things like beach quality, scenery, cleanliness and 'a good place for a holiday' had slumped to between 0 and 15 per cent. 'It is rare to find … so black and unrelieved an image,' concluded a despairing market researcher.

One of the criticisms of the Almighty as a designer of the human anatomy is that He put the area devoted to recreation too close to the sewage outfall. The same can be said of Britain's seaside municipal authorities. For years they solved their sewage problems by dumping it into the sea, uncomfortably close to where their visitors bathed. Government scientists colluded with the authorities in ignoring this, insisting upon extraordinarily high levels of proof before accepting that this constituted a health hazard. In Blackpool by 1950, a debate had been raging for over a decade about the dangers of such a policy, but the authorities still felt able to say in that year's promotional booklet:

> Blackpool sea water is specially beneficial to health. Sufferers of all kinds of ailments acknowledge this … Sea bathing improves the complexion. Be sure to have a salt water bath or swim each day you are on holiday.
>
> Walton, p. 125

Complaints nonetheless proliferated and, in 1957, the Coastal Anti-Pollution League (later becoming part of the Marine Conservation Society) was formed by a couple who had lost their child to polio, brought on by bathing in polluted waters. While the League (probably for legal reasons) praised the good beaches more than they condemned the bad, it hardly did much for the reputation of domestic holiday-making. Despite the best efforts of pressure groups, in 1994 seventy-four out of about 500 British beaches failed to meet the Marine Conservation Society's water standards and about a hundred failed European Union water bathing requirements.

The Stately Home

> The [National] Trust is a noble thing, and humanly speaking immortal. There are some silly mortals connected with it, but they will pass.
>
> Beatrix Potter, a not always uncritical friend of the National Trust

The growth of the newly mobile motoring classes after the war coincided with an extended period of financial difficulty for the owners of many historic homes, as their running costs ran way ahead of the income generated by their estates. Higher taxes for the better-off and death duties provided another inconvenient burden for many hard-pressed aristocratic owners.

One solution was to open your stately pile to the great British fee-paying classes. One of the first to go down this road was the Duke of Bedford. He inherited his title in 1953, along with a £4.5 million bill for death duties and a house – Woburn Abbey – that was crumbling about his ears. He decided to open it to the public for six months as an experiment and, somewhat to his surprise, attracted 181,000 visitors. Within seven years, he was getting over 430,000 visitors a year and generating an income of £53,875. One of the first visitors stole the Duke's dog, and this may have been instrumental in his decision to diversify into the safari park business (anyone trying to slip a lion under their coat deserved all they got). He even let the estate out as a film set. Admirers among you of that seminal piece of cinema *Nudist Paradise* (1958) may have been too engrossed by the dialogue and characterisation to notice that it was set in Woburn. What worked for the Duke of Bedford worked for others and, by 1965, over 500 houses across Britain were open to the public. 'Doing a stately home' became part of the weekend's leisure for a large part of the population.

About a fifth of the properties open to the public were owned or managed by the National Trust. Among those forced by the 40 per cent tax band and other financial pressures to sell off large parts of the estate they inherited in 1930 had been the Marquis of Lothian. He had been Private Secretary to Lloyd George, the architect of the 40 per cent tax band for the wealthy. Lothian was later one of the driving forces behind the National Trust Act 1937, which allowed the Trust to accept gifts of houses, along with endowments of land or capital, on a free-from-tax basis.

The explosion in the Trust's membership since the Second World War is eloquent testimony, among other things, to increasing car ownership and the public's improved ability to get to what are often very rural idylls. The Trust was formed in 1895 and in the first half century of their existence their membership only rose from 100 in 1895 to 7,850 in 1945. By the end of their second half-century numbers had increased to almost 2.2 million and by 2007 were up to 3.5 million.

Saucy Seaside Fun

> The marvellous thing about a joke with a double meaning is that it can only mean one thing.
>
> Ronny Barker

'Do you like Kipling?'
'I don't know, you naughty boy, I've never kippled!'

> Caption to a McGill postcard that sold over 6 million copies – a world record

'I like seeing experienced girls home.'

'But I'm not experienced!'

'You're not home yet!'

George Orwell, The Art of Donald McGill

Ever since the 1860s, comic seaside postcards have been an intrinsic part of the British holiday experience. They have sold in their millions (16 million a year at their peak), predominantly to working-class holiday-makers, and were part of a tradition of bawdy humour that extended back into vaudeville and music hall (and before that to Chaucer's *The Miller's Tale* in the fourteenth century) and forward into the *Carry On* films and comedians from Max Miller to Benny Hill. They were a marvellously democratic medium, providing a vehicle for communication whose limited writing space was a relief to those of equally limited literary abilities.

However, they raised quaintly paternalistic questions about the moral policing of the lower orders among those who considered themselves their betters. In seaside resorts the length of the land, Watch Committees gathered to pontificate on whether this postcard or that was suitable for the masses. This produced a delightfully confused picture across the country, with cards deemed to be fit for consumption in Blackpool being ruled indecent and banned in Bournemouth. The police in Skegness were given powers to prosecute if a particular card was thought to give rise to 'unnatural and lustful desires', but the constabulary felt unable to advise on whether particular cards aroused such feelings with them, when a representative of the card manufacturers called in on them for advice in 1958.

The undoubted doyen of the seaside postcard was Donald McGill. In a career that stretched from 1904 to 1962, he is estimated to have produced around 12,000 cards, populated by an entire cast of weedy victimised husbands, loud domineering wives, voluptuous barmaids and their lascivious customers. Around 200 million copies of his designs were sold over this period. But the Conservative government that took power in 1951 was on a mission to reverse what they saw as a decline in moral standards that had begun in the war years. Committees were set up to sit in judgement on taste and decency of all sorts of artwork and literature. Inevitably McGill's postcards came under their scrutiny. There were several small cases, then a more major one heard at Lincoln Assizes in July 1954, where McGill – by now eighty-one years old and with failing eyesight – was charged under the 1857 Obscene Publications Act. A number of cards were produced in evidence, but one of the key ones showed a man holding a giant stick of rock in such a manner as to suggest that he was tossing a caber. Those who were so inclined might also have interpreted it as showing someone who was both massively over-endowed and suffering from those unnatural and lustful desires they worried about in Skegness (though I have never seen unnatural and lustful desires with letters running through the middle of them). The caption was 'A stick of rock, cock?'

McGill submitted a written defence, in the course of which he stated,

> I have carefully considered the cards complained of ... and I set forth my observations in respect of each card with explanations to show my mental approach ... I would desire to point out that in quite a number of cards in question I had no intention of 'double meaning' and, in fact, a 'double meaning' was in some cases later pointed out to me.

That sounded too naïve to be true from the king of seaside postcards, a man who classified his output by its score on the vulgarity scale, from soft, through average to strong (strong were by far the best sellers). The court evidently thought so, too. He was fined £50 plus costs, but far worse was the fact that thousands of postcards were confiscated and destroyed, and nervous retailers up and down the country cancelled repeat orders. Several of the manufacturers, who lived a precarious existence at the best of times, went bankrupt.

Later, the government's line softened a little, and then a lot. McGill was one of those who gave evidence to the parliamentary Select Committee whose deliberations led to the 1959 reform of the Obscene Publications Act (which is discussed in more detail in the chapter on censorship). McGill also later quit the industry, complaining of its degeneracy. By the time he died, in 1962, the postcards were starting to be recognised as works of art, and serious collectors (or deltiologists) went on to pay serious money for them. Film director Michael Winner collected them and a collection assembled by comedian Ronnie Barker sold for £60,000. The ultimate establishment accolade came in 1994, when Queen Elizabeth II posed for a series of McGill illustrations. Well, not exactly. The Royal Mail issued a series of commemorative stamps on which the Queen's head appeared alongside a series of McGill cartoon characters. Unfortunately for the purists (or should that be impurists?), the characters were removed from their saucy comic context and were lacking any double entendre captions, but it is nonetheless a striking illustration of how far public taste had moved since that 1954 prosecution.

Quite how anyone could argue that McGill's naughty but innocent products could have corrupted and depraved their readers, as the 1857 Act requires, remains a mystery. George Orwell wrote an article on the art of Donald McGill in 1941 and suggested one possible line of argument:

> Codes of law and morals, or religious systems, never have much room in them for a humorous view of life. Whatever is funny is subversive, every joke is ultimately a custard pie, and the reason why so large a proportion of jokes centre round obscenity is simply that all societies, as the price of survival, have to insist on a fairly high standard of sexual morality. A dirty joke is not, of course, a serious attack on morality, but it is a sort of mental rebellion, a momentary wish that things were otherwise.
>
> *Horizon*, September 1941

The downside is that the sending of seaside postcards has fallen by 75 per cent in recent years, as the mobile phone has replaced the post office as the communications medium of choice for many holidaymakers. The world that the cartoon characters inhabit is similarly outdated. The attitudes and preoccupations that they reflect have not changed much since the 1970s (possibly because many of them are simply reprints of old ranges). I ask you – mobile phone messages from the seaside? Where's the fun in that?

Caravans

One form of holiday-making that it seems natural to associate with the post-war rise in mass car ownership is the touring caravan. There certainly are masses of them; at the last count, some 500,000 touring caravans and 120,000 motor homes. Apparently, if all the touring caravans in Britain were placed end to end (and, at peak holiday times on the road, you could be forgiven for thinking that they already have been) they would stretch from Lands End to John O' Groats three times. The Caravan Club alone has almost a million members and, in 2004, nearly one in five adults who holidayed in the UK did so in a caravan.

In fact, caravanning has a much longer pedigree than mass car ownership. Mrs Jarley, a character in Charles Dickens' *Old Curiosity Shop* (1841) lived and travelled in a caravan, and they were widely used in the nineteenth century to house agricultural workers and travelling showmen. In the mid-nineteenth century, Romanies began abandoning their tents in favour of horse-drawn caravans. But they were by no means purely for the working classes. Both Harrods and Fortnum & Mason used to hire them out to their wealthy customers. But modern caravanning really dates from 1885, when an eccentric Scot named William Stables placed an order for a horse-drawn 'land yacht' that he called *The Wanderer*.

Caravanning quickly became a popular pursuit of the wealthy, who dubbed themselves Gentlemen Gypsies. Their luxuriously appointed 'vans sometimes had running water, libraries and pianos, and some would travel with staff to do the domestic chores and look after the horses. This was their idea of communing with nature, and in some respects it was, compared with modern caravanning. Their 'caravan site' was any convenient roadside verge and their supermarket the nearest farm, and by 1907 there were enough of them to justify the formation of the Caravan Club of Great Britain and Northern Ireland.

In 1915, someone had the bright idea of hitching a caravan to one of those newfangled motor cars. The horse-drawn traditionalists considered this development utterly vulgar, a betrayal of the leisurely spirit of the caravan. It would be tempting to say that the association between car and caravan has never subsequently been broken but, during the Second World War, a number of motoring caravanners got round the petrol ration by converting their 'vans back to horse-power. Others, fearful of the bombing of their town or city, used their caravans for an impromptu evacuation to the safety of the countryside. Some even became temporary shelter for those who had been bombed out of their homes.

To many non-caravan owners they are notable for adding to the misery of a British holiday by performing the function of a mobile traffic jam. Things used to be even worse: the Road Traffic Act of 1930 abolished the 20 mph speed limit for motor cars but retained it for towed caravans; even until 1958 the towing speed was limited to 30 mph and then it was only raised to 40 mph. Small wonder that, in the days before motorways made overtaking easier (at least for that part of your journey), caravanners used to attract the opprobrium of the motoring classes like no other road users.

British caravanning had its own equivalent of Henry Ford, a man who brought the activity within the financial reach of a mass market. Sam Alper served in the Second World War as an electrical engineer on aircraft. After leaving the forces, he went to work in his brother's caravan business, which he soon found himself running. It did not take him long to work out that, at prices from £500 upwards, caravans were too expensive for many potential customers. Before the war, this was partly addressed by companies who used to hire them out. Another – not always successful – approach was to build your own caravan. The results all too often resembled garden sheds on wheels. Alper applied his engineering skills to come up with a more affordable version. His 1948 prototype for the Sprite was eventually marketed at just £199, and made ingenious use of the scarce raw materials available at the time. The sides were made of tempered hardboard, the roof of war surplus barrage balloon material and the wheels, suspension and brakes were also war surplus – from a Spitfire fighter.

Being so much cheaper than the competition, Alper had an uphill task to persuade the public that his product would not just fall to pieces. He did so by means of a series of highly successful publicity stunts. In one, a Sprite caravan was towed 10,000 miles around the coast of the Mediterranean Sea; another was towed over the highest mountain pass in Europe and yet another taken as far north as the Arctic Circle. The stunts worked; Alper sold 500 'vans in his first year and, by 1965, launched the Sprite Alpine, which was to become the biggest-selling British caravan of all time.

In addition to producing the cheapest caravans, Alper also set out to make some of the smallest. His Sprite Cadet of 1970 was just 8 feet and 6 inches long. Fitting all the essentials for living into such a small space would tax anyone's ingenuity, and users of some models recall that, in order to shut the toilet door, you first had to clutch your knees to your chest.

But the very success of the caravanning movement lead to one of its major freedoms being curtailed. By the early 1960s, the caravan population had become so numerous that it was deemed necessary to remove the age-old right of caravanners to pull up and make camp for the night wherever on the roadside they wanted to, and to restrict them to using properly organised camp sites, where they could spend their time with others who shared the common interest... of owning a caravan. Quite right too – why should they have all the fun?

Are We Having Fun Yet?

> There's sand in the porridge and sand in the bed,
> And if this is pleasure, we'd rather be dead.
>
> Noel Coward, *The English Lido* (1928)

You don't seriously expect holidays to be fun, do you? They rank alongside bereavement, divorce and redundancy as major creators of stress. Just think of all the things that they give you to worry about: have you packed the passports and the right clothes? Did you lock all the doors, turn the heating off and cancel the milk and papers? There's traffic congestion on the roads ('are we nearly there yet?') and flight delays at the airport, not to mention you flying off to Spain and your luggage to Los Angeles. And that's before you have arrived at the not-quite-completed hotel where, naturally, they have never heard of you. Then there's the biggest stress factor of all – prolonged and intimate exposure to your nearest and dearest, the family who, for fifty weeks of the year, you only manage to avoid murdering thanks to your ability to leave for work in the morning, five days a week.

No, holidays are not there for fun. The useful purpose they serve is to reconcile you to the fact that the rest of your life is not really as bad as you sometimes imagine it to be. The best a Briton can hope for from a holiday is to achieve a tranquil acceptance of the hand that fate has dealt him. Paul Theroux does a pretty good job of capturing British holiday-making skills in his 1984 book *The Kingdom by the Sea*:

> Wherever a road came near the seaside cars parked and piled up, and people in them, always very old people ... They sat in their cars and stared out at the sea. They were on every beach road ... I saw them everywhere, eating sandwiches, drinking tea out of plastic cups, reading the paper, looking fuddled. They always faced the water. They were old couples mostly, but they never seemed to be holding conversations ... they did not seem to be looking at anything in particular. Their expressions were a little sad, as if they were expecting to see something beyond the horizon or under the surface of the waves ... It looked sombre enough to be an English recreation.

This is a real British holiday. And if this is not you now, dear reader, this is where you are headed. This is how we do things.

3
Fun on a Plate: Food

We went to France for our holidays and took six large sliced loaves of bread with us. We still had one left after thirteen days. It was still good to eat. This is a tribute to a Leicester bakery.

Letter to the *Leicester Mercury*, quoted in Cooper

On the Continent people have good food; in England they have good table manners.

George Mikes, 1949

Food – one of our most basic needs and surely one with great potential for bringing us pleasure? Trouble is, we as a nation have a reputation for not being very good at it. Jackie Mason said that England was the only country in the world where the food is more dangerous than the sex. In some eyes, the two are not unconnected; it has been suggested that many Britons shy away from too intense a passion for food because, as a sensual pleasure, it is a bit like sex and therefore embarrassing. The term 'gastro-porn' has been coined to describe lavishly illustrated cookery books (I think they must have been looking at the ones featuring Nigella Lawson). Nonetheless, the British public has continued since the war to spend more and more on eating out; our dietary horizons have broadened to the extent that, in many towns and cities, you have access to the cuisine of a positive United Nations, in supermarket and restaurant; cookery books sell like best-selling novels and our televisions bring us wall-to-wall coverage of celebrity chefs. There's even a dedicated food channel, which must be like watching your microwave go round. We seem to have gone from a situation where we were all reluctant diners, seeking no more from food than to keep body and soul together, to at least some of us being obsessive foodies whose lives revolve around their next culinary experience. But are we having fun with food?

As with motoring, we like to imagine there was a golden age of culinary excellence – we may for example cast our minds back to Charles Dickens' time and his accounts of sumptuous banquets. The reality is that, if you were sent back to those times, the odds would be that most of you would be going to bed hungry most nights. Even if you had food, it was an age of widespread adulteration, and you could be consuming pickles coloured with copper or verdigris, beer enlivened with sulphuric acid and mustard containing lead chromate. But the worst public alarm was caused by that most staple of diets, bread. There were claims that London's bread contained alum dissolved in human urine, that purgatives sometimes had to be added to offset the constipating effect of the alum, and that one part in six of the loaf could be made up of ground-up lime, chalk or even human bones. Yum!

Out of Austerity

Coming forward in time, we still start from a very low baseline. British cuisine was in a particularly sorry state in the immediate post-war years. Rationing had served the nation well during the war years, insofar as it ensured that nobody starved (indeed, parts of the population were possibly better nourished during the war than they had been during the preceding peace). But it tended to provide a diet that was far more nutritious than appetising. Also, rationing dragged on far into peacetime; it would not be removed entirely until 1954, and in some cases where items were taken off the ration, it was only because there were no supplies of them left to ration. Monotony of the diet and the total absence of many of the foodstuffs that make eating interesting were having a corrosive impact on morale. Morale was not helped by the fact that the watery wartime ales were not restored to their pre-war strength until 1950.

The prospects for eating out were no better. Despite the fact that tourism was, by the late 1940s, our biggest net dollar earner, the British Tourist and Holidays Board carried out a review which found that Britain's awful service and even worse cooking was driving potential overseas visitors to the Continent, in search of something decent to eat. Government regulation was in part to blame; the Catering Wages Board Orders meant that hoteliers could not afford enough staff to run their establishments properly, and another regulation hanging over from the war years restricted the price you could charge for a hotel or restaurant meal to five shillings, which hardly encouraged caterers to explore the frontiers of excellence. Others blamed the class system. They claimed that the people who influenced the quality of our food at this time had all been to public school, where the standard of catering was so horrific as to render them incapable of knowing what proper food was supposed to taste like. As far as the quality of the service was concerned, often appalling working conditions and starvation wages did much to kill off any pride the serving staff might have taken in their jobs. One Morecombe waitress summed the attitude up, when asked what the soup of the day was: 'I don't know – I don't work in the kitchen. It could be anything.'

Gradually, champions of good cooking began to emerge. Elizabeth David published her *Book of Mediterranean Food* in 1950, followed the next year by *French Country Cooking*. Both were enthusiastically received, and huge influence was later claimed for them, though it seems unlikely that they had much impact on the eating habits of the majority of Britons. In the popular press, most early forays into foreign cuisine were tentative in the extreme. This from a 1953 edition of *Good Housekeeping*:

> Anyone who has kept house in Europe or has had a holiday on the Continent is likely to be familiar with Italian pasta … Italy is the land of its birth and the country where it forms the staple diet of the people, especially the peasants. It is eaten plain as a preliminary course, or combined with meat and fish in an almost endless variety of main dishes.

The 'meat sauce' they recommended to go with it pushed out the boat with a whole quarter-teaspoon of mixed herbs and no less than a tablespoon of chopped onion to spice it up. In this and other early 'Italian' recipes, macaroni was recommended as a more easily obtainable form of pasta and cottage cheese provided a very inadequate substitute for mozzarella. Their 1956 recipe for pizza involved frying it.

But not every Briton was a potential willing convert to even these modest forays into Continental cuisine; when television chef Philip Harben tried to introduce his viewers to 'pasta from Italy' he received over sixty complaints from the BBC Viewing Panel, calling for 'more everyday dishes' and his French onion soup was equally (forgive the pun) panned. Some even gloried in the ineptitude of British cooking, as this letter to the *Daily Mail* shows:

The reason the French mess everything about in casseroles and such-like dishes, is that they cannot procure the quality of meat obtainable in Britain; and they wouldn't know how to cook it anyway.

Quoted in Cooper, p. 9

It will come as no surprise that the British Travel Association also backed the British cooking of the day against the world's best:

Most of the people who do the complaining (about British food) are, in fact, British themselves – most of whom are quite content to eat some of the abominable muck served up in other countries just because it is foreign and has a foreign name and, therefore, must be good.

Ibid., p. 165

The diets of most people were probably influenced less by these dubious Continental practices, and more by the introduction, in 1950, of Bird's Eye 'frosted' foods, which gave them 'fresh' fruit and vegetables all year round. However, by the late 1950s, the choice of foodstuffs available to British kitchens was expanding enormously. What appeared not to be expanding was the imagination of the British housewife, if this extract from *The Times* is to be believed:

Every day seems to produce new kinds of frozen foods and within the last year or so frozen food cabinets have begun to appear in village shops all over the country. Greengrocers too are becoming adventurous. Green and red peppers, sweet corn, aubergines and avocado pears are commonplace today, not just in London but in small country towns and every greengrocer now seems to have little bags of garlic as a matter of course ... Yet in the face of all this abundance, this really stupendous variety, huge numbers of English women still plod on in a rut, buying 'the usual'.

The Times, 21 January 1957

Along with the proliferation of vegetables, a new set of role models was also starting to emerge.

Celebrity Chefs

Right from the post-war reopening of broadcasting in 1946, radio and television had their own celebrity chefs, in the form of people like Marguerite Patten and the aforementioned Philip Harben. In that age of austerity, their main purpose was to show the struggling housewife how to make the most of her meagre rations. Indeed, so hard were the times that the rations Harben cooked on camera were apparently his own. But the word 'austerity' is one that you would never associate with the most famous of the immediate post-war television chefs.

We tend to think today of someone like Gordon Ramsay being one the more edgy examples of the celebrity chef, but the mid-1950s onwards saw the heyday of Fanny Cradock, the queen of celebrity chefs and someone who would have sent the likes of Ramsay whimpering back into the pantry with his tail between his legs. Such was her well-deserved reputation that she was known within the BBC as Lady Macbeth, and the *Independent* felt quite relaxed about breaking the convention of not speaking ill of the dead in their 2009 centenary retrospective of her. It began:

She had mad glittering eyes, the face of a supercilious horse, the maquillage of a French clown and
the demeanour of a woman in constant search of an argument. She was rude to everyone.

The Independent, 19 February 2009

It all got a bit personal and unpleasant after that. She was a bully, an appalling snob and – so
some people thought – a pretty rotten cook to boot. *The Guardian* journalist Simon Smith
tried living solely off her recipes for a week; by the end of it, the heart attack that could not
have been far off would have been a blessed release from a diet of green cheese ice cream and
swans made of meringue (among her real classic pieces of pretentiousness were peach melba,
served on a carved ice swan, and a meringue Taj Mahal). Smith also tried her steamed chocolate
pudding that the recipe described as 'incredibly light'. Smith's verdict:

Yes it was – but in the sense that a breeze-block is light. It also has gut-expanding capabilities like
thermal insulation foam.

The Guardian, 14 October 2006

She also seemed to serve cream with just about everything – including pig's kidneys. While
recipes of baroque complexity and life-threatening richness may have impressed a Britain just
coming out of the austerity years, nouvelle cuisine it was definitely not. Nonetheless she was
the queen of British cooking for twenty years from the mid-1950s, and is claimed by Delia
Smith and Jamie Oliver, among others, as their inspiration. Among her less exotic creations,
she is credited with the invention of that 1970s dinner party staple, the prawn cocktail.

Her life was just as extraordinary as her television persona. As a year-old infant, she was
abandoned by her mother into the care of her grandmother. She married an RAF pilot at the
age of seventeen, who died in a crash four months later, leaving her widowed and pregnant. She
followed her mother's tradition by abandoning her daughter to her parents and, later, walking
out on two sons. She eventually married four times (two of them bigamously), abandoning
her second husband, and then her third after just eight weeks of marriage, to move in with a
Major John Cradock of the Royal Artillery. He himself had a wife and four children (whom he
apparently never saw again). Although she stayed with him for forty years and took his name,
they were not actually married until 1977, by when their main television career was over.

How they stayed together remains a mystery, for she humiliated and bullied him unmercifully
in front of the cameras, as she did everyone with whom she worked. Their television appearances
gradually became more and more bizarre, with Fanny cooking dressed up to the nines in a ball-
gown and tiara, and Johnny in full evening dress and monocle. Although they were almost
beyond parody, the Two Ronnies, Benny Hill and other comedians loved to play them, with
'Johnny' in the role of drunken silly ass, causing kitchen mayhem. But the comedians could
scarcely outdo the real thing, and popular mythology has Johnny telling the audience at the
end of one programme, 'Great cooking is making doughnuts like Fanny's.' (In this particular
case, the words actually came from the show's host, but the attribution naturally stuck with
Johnny.)

Unsurprisingly, Fanny's rudeness was eventually her downfall. In 1976, she was called upon
to advise an amateur chef in a television competition. So poor was her advice and so rude and
condescending her treatment of the unfortunate woman that an outraged public complained in
droves. She was never given another television cooking appearance, and her public appearances

in retirement were limited to being a faded celebrity on quiz and chat shows. Characteristically, when she discovered that the other guest on one of the chat shows on which she had been booked was actually a female impersonator (Danny La Rue) she stormed off the set.

In addition to her 'skills' as a chef, she enjoyed careers in journalism and as a novelist. Johnny died in 1987 and she survived him by seven years. Small surprise that two biopic dramas of her life have since been made. In this and other ways (many of them unintended), Fanny and Johnny added immeasurably to the gaiety of the nation, if not necessarily to their appreciation of what constitutes good food.

Lyons Corner Houses and Their Offspring

Lyons Corner Houses were one of the great British dining institutions of the immediate post-war period. Their evolution can in some respects be used as a barometer of a decline in certain aspects of the nation's dining standards since the war – moving from silver service by efficient uniformed waitresses to self-service, eating with your fingers from a paper bag. Where will we go from here – face down in one huge communal trough of swill? First opened in 1909, the Corner Houses were huge establishments on four or five floors, each one employing some four hundred staff at their peak. They were part of the massive Lyons catering industry that also included some 250 teashops, found in many towns and cities. So large and complex was their business that, by the 1930s, they were employing so many musicians to entertain their customers that the company had to establish a separate orchestral department. They also developed the world's first business computer, the Lyons Electronic Office 1 (or LEO 1). One of the features of Lyons establishments before the war were their black-uniformed waitresses, known as 'nippies', but post-war the tea shops went over to cafeteria service.

A square meal in a round bun.

An early advertising slogan for Wimpy

Lyons Corner Houses, and the even more genteel Fullers Tea Rooms, were not the most welcoming environment for the growing youth market. Lyons tested various new formats in an effort to widen their appeal, and in 1954 tried out an experimental fast food section within their Corner House in Coventry Street, London. This was named after a hamburger-guzzling character in the *Popeye* cartoons, one J. Wellington Wimpy. The Wimpy Bar proved so popular that they were soon opening free-standing Wimpy Bars at a rate of knots. By 1970 there were over 1,000, trading in twenty-three countries. Their arrival chimed with a fashion for all things American and the opening of a branch could be the occasion for much excitement in a town. Sometimes a word of explanation was also needed (no doubt for the benefit of older readers) as to what a Wimpy Bar was. This from the press coverage of the opening of a town's first Wimpy Bar in 1957:

What is a Wimpy?
A pure beef hamburger that has the reputation of being a meal in itself. It has found favour in London's West End – and in Buckingham Palace. The Queen offered Wimpys to her guests at an important reception recently.

Hylton 1997, p. 89

We can fondly imagine Her Majesty inquiring of Prince Philip, 'Does one want fries with that?' In addition to hamburgers (then 1s 3d each), Wimpy also offered a variety of frankfurter sausage known rather dubiously as the Bender, milk shakes, quaintly English delicacies like toasted teacakes and fish and chips, and a dessert of doughnut, ice cream and chocolate sauce called the Brown Derby. Further excitement came in the form of tomato ketchup, dispensed from genuine squeezable plastic tomatoes.

Given that they were one of the few establishments to remain open after the pubs had closed, some Wimpy Bars began to attract the unwelcome attentions of teddy boys, mods and rockers, and others who had reached that point where a good fight would mark the end of a perfect evening. The Northampton Wimpy Bar became the first establishment in town to have bouncers on the door, and its proprietor had to have his own personal bodyguard because of the threats made to him.

A rival, in the form of McDonald's, began to eat into their trade from 1974, prompting Wimpy to start a rather slow process of converting from their traditional table service to the over-the-counter service of their rival. In 1989 they were taken over by Grand Metropolitan, who had also just acquired the Burger King chain. The counter-service Wimpy (the 'Bar' part of their name was soon dropped, though few of us seem to have noticed) then started to be converted into Burger Kings.

Other catering brands, soon to become familiar parts of the dining landscape, also made their appearance around this time. A tiny American-style diner opened its doors in Reading in 1958 – the nation's first Little Chef – while Bristol in 1953 saw an old coaching inn reopened as a Berni Inn. For less than eight shillings these latter offered a menu that more or less defined eating out for the masses at this time – prawn cocktail, steak and chips and a choice between black forest gateau or cheese, accompanied by a medium sherry. One of the reasons they could do it so cheaply was that they dispensed with the need for a trained chef, requiring only someone capable of operating a grill and a deep fat fryer. By the late 1960s over a hundred Berni Inns were open up and down the country.

We see here the start of the American takeover of our eating habits but, before we get onto that, what is English food, and do we have fun with it?

Going out for an English

> Chicken tikka masala is now Britain's true national dish, not only because it is popular, but because it is a perfect illustration of the way Britain absorbs and adapts external influences.
>
> Robin Cook, when Labour Foreign Secretary

According to Fanny Cradock there is no such thing as English cuisine – even good old Yorkshire pudding comes from Burgundy. Another strong candidate for our national dish also has foreign antecedents. Fish and chips have their roots in not one but two Continental culinary traditions. In the sixteenth century, exiled Portugese Jews brought to Britain the practice of frying fish encased in batter. This was at that time of limited application, unless you were very rich, lived close to the sea, or had access to river fishing rights that were not controlled by the local gentry. In eighteenth-century France, the wives of fishermen who returned without a catch developed the practice of cutting fish shapes out of potato and frying them as a substitute meal. This, too, was imported to Britain. When the *Daily Star* broke news of this to the nation in 2004, under the characteristically understated headline 'Le Great Breetish Feesh and Cheeps: it's Frog Nosh Claims Prof', it provoked a hostile reaction from far-right political parties.

The one bit of credit Britain can claim is for putting the two together in the nineteenth century, and this is fought over by Joseph Mallin of London and John Lees, the claimant from the north-west. But the real credit needs to go to the railways that made it possible for people living in inland towns and cities to have an affordable supply of fresh fish. The fish and chip business has remained cosmopolitan ever since. In the 1950s it was dominated by groups such as the Italians and Cypriots, whereas in recent years its proprietorship has taken on a decidedly more Oriental nature. Going back further, even its raw ingredient, the humble potato, was of course an American import.

In fact, Robin Cook (quoted above) was perhaps more right than he thought; some of the food we might instinctively class as 'foreign' has more of a claim to a domestic origin than foreign interlopers like Yorkshire pudding. Much of the 'Indian' food we eat in this country bears little resemblance to anything consumed by the residents of the SubContinent, but has been developed over here to suit western palates. Chicken tikka masala and balti both have claims to be Anglo-Indian dishes. The former was, according to some accounts, a response by an Indian chef somewhere in Britain to a discerning English (or possibly Scottish) customer who demanded 'gravy' with his curry, while Baltis originated in the West Midlands in the 1980s (the word comes from the Hindi for 'bucket').

In fact, for as long as there has been international trade, nations have been borrowing each other's cuisine. We may have borrowed from the French, but they in turn borrowed from the Italians who, before them, had taken recipes from the Greeks, who got their inspiration from the Egyptians and Persians. So, in thinking about what constitutes a national cuisine, we can go one of two ways. One is to see what we can learn by going back into history, to see what the natives were subsisting on before all this foreign exchange got under way; the other is to see what is characteristic about the food the nation eats today, whatever its origins.

Taking the historical route first, in my tireless quest to bring you the facts I delved back as far as the fourteenth century to see what Britain was eating. For the wealthy, it seems there was already a steady international trade in foodstuffs. A wide variety of herbs and spices were available (just as well for disguising meat dishes, in the days before refrigeration) and a wide range of Continental wines were imported. Most of the country was within two days' ride of the coast, making all kinds of fish and seafood available – at a price – and virtually anything that walked or flew could find its way onto the meat course. Imported exotic fruits such as lemons, dates and pomegranates might also form part of the rich man's diet.

The choice for the poor peasant was much more restricted. Bread was the staple in the days before potatoes, and could be made of combinations of wheat, barley, oats or rye. There was a wholegrain brown bread called 'tourt' which, when it got old, was cut into slices and used as plates. When it ceased to function even as a plate, it was fed to the pigs (presumably that saved the family from having to find a dishwasher that could take bread). There was even a form of bread made of ground peas, bran and beans, though this was known as 'horse-bread' and was normally reserved for animal feed.

The other great staple was pottage, a form of porridge made of oats and whatever scraps of meat or vegetable that came to hand. I rapidly came to the conclusion that the diet of our ancestors was not going to tell us much about our modern culinary traditions (except for one thing: there was a widespread medieval belief that green vegetables were harmful to you, unless they had first been boiled to destruction, which may help to explain British cooks' treatment of them in more modern times).

So, let us turn to the food we all eat today. Based on sheer volume, baked beans must come high on our list of national foods. Apparently no other nation on earth has our appetite for them. The UK market in baked beans is worth some £300 million a year, and our leading supplier, Heinz, produces 1.5 million cans of the things per day. What does it say about the culinary refinement of a nation whose favourite food is notable mainly for its dramatic after-effects? If you want to find the cause of global warming, look no further. (I know you are going to ask, so let me tell you that their windy effect is caused by oligosaccharides in the beans reacting with the gut flora *methanobrevibacter smithii* in the lower intestine. I'm glad we cleared that up.)

Another foodstuff with gaseous qualities is Britain's supposed least favourite vegetable, the Brussels sprout, which has been part of the nation's diet since 1796. Despite being almost universally hated, we Brits still eat them in large quantities (we grow one of Europe's largest crops – over 80,000 tonnes, and little of it exported – compared with the whole of America, which produces just 32,000 tonnes). Why? Are we the only nation in the world too polite to tell the cook that they are inedible? Foreigners tell us that it is our cooking practices that make them that way. After six or seven minutes' boiling (by when the cooking has barely got going by British standards) they start to release sinigrin, which gives off the sulphurous smell that makes strong men retch. There is only one British way to cook Brussels sprouts, which is to boil them until they are reduced to a grey slime, then throw them away.

The same cooking principle is applied to the British treatment of peas – or mushy peas, as the characteristically British version is known – except that the person who wrote down the original recipe forgot to add the bit about throwing them away. They generally include a food colouring which appears to be radioactive. Another name for mushy peas is 'Yorkshire caviar' so, if you are looking for an evening of unashamed luxury, you know where to head for. In the trendier parts of London, they call them avocado dip.

Cucumber sandwiches, by contrast, are barely a foodstuff at all – more a statement of social ambition. Served on tiny crust-less sandwiches of bread cut so thin that you can see through it, and with the cucumber (which is in any case 89 per cent water) peeled, they have no calorific value and taste of nothing.

Haggis is the dish for which Scotland is most famous. It is made by stuffing a sheep's innards with ingredients slightly less palatable to humans than their original contents. Like every other foodstuff (except possibly soup), it is also available in Scotland in a deep-fried version. The bad news for the Scots is that it may not be a Scottish dish at all. The first British reference to it appears in a Lancashire cookbook of around 1430. Before that, there is evidence that haggis (or something very like it) was served at the Coronation of French King Louis III in AD 878, and there are references to it in ancient Rome and even in Homer's *Odyssey*. A little national pride may be salvaged from the fact that Scotland still holds the world record for haggis hurling (which may well be the best thing to do with a haggis) and, if you can better 180 feet 10 inches, you could earn yourself immortality in the *Guinness Book of Utterly Useless World Records*. Another more than useless record is the £2,500 charged for a haggis flavoured with Balvenie Cask 191, one of the world's rarest single malt whiskeys. Some small comfort can at least be taken from its contribution to the tourist industry; apparently 33 per cent of American visitors to our shores believe the haggis to be some kind of exotic Scottish creature. (No doubt the Loch Ness monster is one of their main predators.)

On the same principle as haggis, of finding a use for even those parts of the animal that are self-evidently inedible, we have pork scratchings. These are deep-fried, salted and carefully unspecified pieces of a pig's anatomy, cunningly manufactured to give you the experience of eating someone else's toe-nails. They are apparently high in nutrition and low in weight (albeit even lower in palatability) which may explain why they get taken on Arctic and Antarctic expeditions, for use when people get desperate.

Marmite was discovered by accident in 1902, while trying to develop a material for road-mending from spent brewer's yeast. It must be one of the few foodstuffs to be marketed on the premise that half of those who try it will hate it. The lovers and the haters of Marmite are passionate rivals on the subject, and even lobbied Parliament and the Speaker about it during the 2010 general election campaign (I suppose their carers thought it would do them good to get out for the afternoon).

In a similar vein was the advertising campaign dreamed up for that modern British classic, the Pot Noodle. Recognising that most people regarded them as an unhealthy and slatternly way of eating, the advertisers played upon the idea of them as a guilty pleasure, akin to visiting a prostitute or a sex shop. Strangely enough, you tend not to see sex shops or prostitutes trading on their similarities to a Pot Noodle. It is another example of Britain's love-hate relationship with its food. In 2004, Pot Noodle was voted Britain's most hated brand, yet it still manages to command some 77 per cent of the (admittedly rather specialised) pot snack market, with 155 million of them emerging from their Caerphilly factory each year.

The Cornish pasty is notable mainly for its engineering qualities. It was designed to be robust enough to be dropped down a mineshaft to a hungry tin miner. He would then eat it, holding the crimped part of the shell in his dangerously dirty miner's hands (the lead seams contained quantities of arsenic), prior to throwing the crimp away. Again, it seems they may not be of Cornish origin. The earliest reference to pasties is thought to be in a thirteenth-century charter granted by Henry III to the town of Great Yarmouth (which is about as far east as you can get from Cornwall without your hat floating).

Finally, passing mention must be made of the impact of the class system on English eating habits, adding a further degree of torment to the socially aspirational diner. It does not stop at what you eat (prawn cocktail? Rice salad? Tinned fish? All frightfully proletarian, my dears, according to Kate Fox). You may also be condemned by your chosen brand of marmalade (thick-cut Dundee marmalade is socially superior to Golden Shred) or even what you call your evening meal and when you eat it (there are separate social pigeon holes for the 'dinner', 'supper' and, heaven preserve us, 'tea' brigades).

Such is the deeply depressing cavalcade of British cuisine. The French can, without a hint of irony, use the words '*amuse-bouche*' to describe food, but in English the words 'fun food' become the biggest oxymoron since 'fun run'. 'Fun size' has in fact become advertiser-speak for the smallest (and therefore least pleasurable) version of chocolate bars one can buy. Small wonder we have in recent years embraced foreign gastronomy with such enthusiasm.

Going out for a Foreign

The history of Indian food in Britain goes back far longer than one might imagine, starting with the first attempts of the East India Company to colonise the SubContinent from 1608. Before long, lascars – seamen, mainly from Bengal – began arriving in London. There were an estimated 1,400 of them living in the city by 1810, though many were living in such dire poverty that they hardly constituted a sound basis for a restaurant trade. Nonetheless, curry powder was available to the British consumer from 1780 and the first dedicated Indian restaurant appeared in 1809. The Hindostanee Coffee House in London's Portman Square promised a house 'for the Nobility and Gentry where they might enjoy the hookah with real Chilm tobacco and Indian dishes of the highest perfection', all served in a pseudo-colonial setting. The one thing the coffee house did not serve was coffee. Colonial expatriates returning home brought back many of the recipes with them, and soon versions of them got included in the English domestic repertoire. Mrs Beeton's 1861 *Book of Household Management* contained no less than fourteen curry recipes, as many from India as it did from Scotland, Ireland and Wales put together.

Various other Indian restaurants followed during the reign of Victoria, but the first really influential one of modern times was the Shafi, opened in Gerard Street, London in 1920 by two north Indians, Mohammed Wayseem and Mohammed Rahim. It became a kind of community centre for London's growing expatriate Indian population, as well as a training ground for others who would go on to set up their own establishments. While these catered mainly for the expatriate Indian population, Veeraswamy's Indian Restaurant, which opened in Regent Street in 1927, became popular with the fashionable set. It too set out to create a colonial atmosphere, and became known as 'the ex-Indian higher serviceman's curry club'. It was taken over in 1935 by a Member of Parliament, Sir William Steward, who owned it for forty years and spent much time scouring the world for genuine ingredients. Its great claim to fame is that it was there that lager was first introduced as an accompaniment to Indian food, during a visit by the Prince of Denmark.

Indian restaurants gradually spread, first through London and in those seaports which became the base for a settled Asian population, and then in the major cities. Although we call them Indian, about three quarters of them were actually Pakistani-owned in the days before Bangladeshi independence in 1971. Thereafter, geographical variations became more evident. Over half the restaurants were now actually Bangladeshi, most of them coming from a single area – Sylhet. But from Birmingham north the number of Bangladeshis decreases and the number of Pakistani proprietors increases. In areas like Manchester and Bradford almost all the restaurateurs are Pakistani, Kashmiri or north Indian, whereas in Glasgow and areas of London like Southall they are mostly Punjabi.

Chinese restaurants began to appear in Britain around the start of the twentieth century, usually associated with areas of Chinese settlement around ports like London and Liverpool. Maxims in Soho was founded in 1908 by Chung Koon, a Chinese ship's cook who settled here. Another establishment, Wong's in Limehouse, was also open before the Great War. It was not as quick as Indian food to form part of the domestic repertoire – the first Chinese cookery book did not appear in England until 1932, while many specialist Indian ones were published in Victorian and Edwardian times. As late as April 1914, no less a journal than the *Hotel Review*, publishing a review of a new Chinese restaurant, still laboured under the misapprehension that a noodle was a 'bird of prey'. By 1939 there were at least nine Chinese restaurants in London, mostly in Soho. During the war years the Ministry of Food, desperate to diversify the nation's boringly rationed diet, brought in 'a Chinese Housewife' to give a recipe for chop suey on their radio programme *The Kitchen Front* (which was aimed at 'working-class housewives').

But it was the aforementioned Chung Koon's son John who helped to establish Chinese food as a mass-market interest. He it was who came up with the idea of the Chinese takeaway (he opened the first one in Queensway in 1958). But his real stroke of genius was to get Billy

Butlin to install a Chinese kitchen in each of his holiday camps. The menu was limited, to say the least, consisting of chicken chop suey and chips and, well, that was it. But it had the effect of encouraging a whole generation to experiment further with what passed for Chinese food. By the end of the 1960s most towns had their own Chinese takeaway, many of which also mastered the exotic secrets of that other foreign cuisine, fish and chips. Much of the decline in the numbers of fish and chip shops (they fell from a peak of 35,000 in 1927 to 8,600 by the turn of the century) was down to them diversifying into Chinese and other forms of takeaway. By 1984, the nation could boast some 7,000 Chinese restaurants and takeaways.

The Decline of the English Diet

> In the highly mechanised countries, thanks to tinned food, cold storage, synthetic flavouring matters, etc. the palate is a dead organ …
>
> George Orwell, *The Road to Wigan Pier*

As we saw, the diet in the austerity years of post-war Britain was relatively nutritious but dull. Today, we have greater choice of food than we have ever had but, nutritionally, the way we have chosen to exercise that choice leaves much to be desired. One of the reasons why we can now produce so much more food is that food production has been industrialised. The origin of much of our food is now the factory, rather than the farm. By as early as 1973, food manufacture had become Britain's largest industry, employing some 8 per cent of the manufacturing labour force. Over 2,000 food additives were in use by the 1970s – extending its shelf-life, reducing its price, improving its appearance, increasing its palatability and otherwise playing about with its properties. In their defence, many of these additives explain how we have been able to move from a situation a century ago, where many of the population were on the brink of starvation, to one of relative abundance. But the British seem to have developed a particular fondness for highly processed food. According to Blythmann, in 2003 we ate more ready meals than the rest of Europe put together and more than half the crisps and savoury snacks consumed in Europe. Partly as a result of this, according to present trends, a third of British adults will be obese by 2020.

Eating out

As we also saw at the start of the chapter, the British restaurant experience was also at a pretty low ebb in the immediate post-war years. In 1951 journalist Raymond Postgate founded the Society for the Prevention of Cruelty to Food and launched the first *Good Food Guide*, as an act of rebellion against what he saw as 'a lifetime of suffering' on the part of the British public. His criteria for inclusion in the *Guide* were at first modest in the extreme:

> Any place where food could be eaten without nausea, where the helpings were not derisively tiny and the staff not directly rude.

In the first edition, only 11 of the 484 restaurants listed outside London were serving foreign food, and only one of these was offering non-European food. The system for producing the book was designed to make it incorruptible. No inducements for inclusion or advertisements were accepted, reviewers were volunteers who paid for their own meals and submitted their reviews anonymously. The review team nonetheless attracted a number of the great and the good, including future Cabinet minister Roy Jenkins, cricket commentator John Arlott and novelist Kingsley Amis.

Fellow food critic Egon Ronay was equally outspoken about the catering industry of the day:

> What they do in Wales could be called gastronomic rape, except that they don't seem to derive any pleasure from it.
>
> Quoted in Sandbrook, p. 129

What can be established beyond a doubt is that the Great British public now spend a lot more of their time and money eating out. In 1964, the public spent £480 million on dining, and less than 3 per cent of the working population were employed in catering. By 1997 this had risen to £13.6 billion, and something like 10 per cent of the working population were in the catering industry. We will come on to whether we are having more fun as a result shortly. But hardly less dramatic than the growth in the market is the way it has changed. This is where we spent our money in 1964:

Restaurants, cafés, snack bars: 45 per cent
Canteens: 13.1 per cent
Hotels and holiday camps: 12.9 per cent
Fish and chips: 12.5 per cent
Pubs: 9.1 per cent
Catering contractors: 4.6 per cent
Other caterers: 2.8 per cent

By 1997, the much bigger pie was sliced as follows:

Pub catering: 37.5 per cent
Restaurants: 19.2 per cent
Burgers: 8.5 per cent
In-store catering: 6.8 per cent
Pizza/pasta: 6.2 per cent
Fish and chips: 5.5 per cent
Ethnic (eat-in): 4.5 per cent
Ethnic takeaway: 3.9 per cent
Fried chicken: 3.8 per cent
Roadside catering: 3 per cent
Other fast food: 1.3 per cent

A number of trends can be seen from these tables. One is the dramatic move of the pub industry into food, as it struggled to cope with competition from cheap supermarket drink, the breathalyser, the smoking ban and other reverses to the industry. Another is the American takeover of the café/snack bar trade. Almost a fifth of our spending on eating out now goes to American-style fast food chains of pizza, burger and fried chicken stores. A third is the growth of the ethnic food trade, which by the end of the last century had cornered something approaching 10 per cent of the market. In the following sections, we will look at some of the post-war developments in our dining habits.

Coffee Bars and Milk Bars

One of the factors that led Lyons to diversify their offer in the first place was the rapid growth in the fashion for coffee bars in the 1950s. Coffee bars (or originally, coffee houses) have again been part of the British way of life for almost as long as the existence of coffee was known to us. The 'first coffee house in Christendom' began trading in Oxford in 1650, two years before London's first establishment opened in St Michael's Alley, Cornhill. Around a thousand of them had opened by 1675. In addition to providing refreshment, they became vital centres for communicating news and gossip. In the nineteenth century, temperance campaigners tried using coffee houses as an alternative attraction to tempt the working man away from the demon drink (though without conspicuous success).

In 1945 Gaggia developed a new type of espresso machine and cappuccino (named after the colour of the robes worn by Capuchin monks) was born. The scene was set for the growth of an edgy alternative culture based in the coffee bar. The first of these, the Moka, was opened in Frith Street, Soho, in 1953, and spread rapidly throughout the land, as this newspaper report from 1954 shows:

> 'Expresso', the latest coffee craze from Italy, was greeted enthusiastically by guests at the opening party of 'Palomino' in Duke Street, the first restaurant in town to install one of the glittering machines which produce this kind of coffee.
>
> In a setting which is an attractive blend of South American and contemporary styles Mr J. W. Clough, the proprietor of 'Palomino', introduced his guests to 'cappuccino', the frothing creamy drink so different from the average English white coffee … The editor of the *Berkshire Chronicle* was … initiated into the habit which has swept London in the last year and is now steadily spreading into the provinces.
>
> Hylton 1997, p. 57

If coffee drinking has survived and flourished over the years that followed, the coffee bar's counterpart, the milk bar, was certainly more of a transitory phenomenon. Their real glory days were the immediately pre-war years, with more than a thousand British outlets trading by 1936. Richard Hoggart, no fan of American fads, savaged them in the 1950s:

> Compared even with the pub around the corner, this is a peculiarly thin and pallid form of dissipation, a sort of spiritual dry rot amid the odour of boiled milk. Many of the customers – their clothes, their hairstyles, their facial expressions all indicate – are living to a large extent in a myth world compounded of a few simple elements which they take to be the American dream. They are a depressing group….they have no aim, no ambition, no protection, no belief.
>
> *The Uses of Literacy*, pp. 248–9

The milk bars' main function, of providing somewhere for youth to hang about, was gradually taken over by fast food outlets, shopping malls and the waiting rooms at the Magistrates' Courts.

Fast Food

Fast food has always been with us. It is said that the ancient Romans ate more of it than modern westerners do, and that when historians delved into Bristol High Street's past they found evidence of no less than five cookshops (the medieval equivalent of a takeaway) existing there in 1470. Its early name – Cook's Row – might have given them some sort of clue. Every age and every nation seems to come up with its own variety of fast food – the pizza, the sandwich, the burger – and it can variously be as good or as bad for you as any other comestible. That is, until science took over.

That modern icon of fast food, the burger, first made its appearance in various parts of the United States in the 1880s and led a blameless existence for half a century. In 1940 it came to form part of the menu of a barbecue shack in San Bernardino, California. This establishment was the first McDonald's. In 1948 they opened their first proper restaurant, in which they applied Henry Ford's production line methods to food manufacture and the 'catch 'em young' marketing techniques of the Disney Corporation. By 1953, they had got into franchising the McDonald's business model. Today they are the world's largest food retailer, with 1,500,000 staff working in 31,000 outlets in 119 countries, and the model for all their rivals.

Successful fast food has to be tasty and cheap, and this is where the science comes in. One essential ingredient of tasty savoury food is fats. Mediterranean countries got their fats from healthier sources, like olives, but those of us living further north tended to rely more on animal fats. About a century ago, a process – called hydrogenation – was found for turning liquid fat into solid blocks. It also meant that solid blocks of fat could now be made from vegetable oils that were cheaper and had a longer shelf-life. They were called trans fats, and exist in small quantities in natural sources like meat. Up until the 1960s most people consumed very little in the way of trans fats, but some modern processed foods can contain up to 40 or 45 per cent of them. The United States National Academy of Science says that trans fats are 'not essential and provide no known benefits to human health'. Worse than that, they break down in the body in a different way to natural fats, with the dire consequences for obesity that we will come to shortly.

Second in this scientific rogues' gallery are sweeteners. Traditionally, things like honey or refined beet or cane sugar have been used to sweeten food, but in the 1960s scientists discovered how to increase the fructose content of corn syrup, to create High Fructose Corn Syrup (HFCS). It was cheap (not least because it evaded the import tariffs to which many natural sugars were subject), easy to transport and to blend. However, the body once again absorbs it in a different way to natural sugars (that is, much more quickly), making the consumer more prone to obesity, insulin resistance and diabetes.

The third bit of science came in the form of food additives. As we saw, an estimated 2,000 of these were in use by the 1970s, to improve the taste, texture, smell or appearance of cheap ingredients, increase their shelf-lives or achieve other ends. Food has long been adulterated by some pretty nasty additives – as we have also seen, time was when arsenic was used as a food colouring, and ground bone and chalk were both used to whiten bread. Today the search is ongoing for evidence that additives are toxic or carcinogenic – a constant tug of war between regulators and ingenious food scientists. Not all of the potentially harmful additives are the complex products of the scientists' laboratory. About 80 per cent of the salt in our diets comes from processed foods, and an excess of this can lead to high blood pressure, heart disease and strokes. A 2007 survey found that a single Pizza Hut meal could contain up to twice the recommended daily salt intake for an adult.

But don't the British just love their fast food! A worldwide survey in 2008 found that the United Kingdom had the highest number of fast food outlets per head of population of any nation in the world. Our per capita expenditure in them is the highest of any European country.

All the Trouble in the World

For the past decade or more there has been a constant battle between the fast food industry and the promoters of healthy eating. In the course of this, various scientific experiments have established (to varying degrees of satisfaction by rival parties) that fast food is to blame for just about every ailment known to man, bar dandruff (though I may have missed that particular study). We only have space to list a small sample:

Food poisoning: The problems start before the food even enters the restaurant. According to some accounts, the American meat-packing industry appears to be poorly regulated and this leads to the contamination of the meat with salmonella and *E. coli*. This can be spread to humans via under-cooked burgers, with potentially fatal consequences. *E. coli* has apparently become the leading cause of kidney failure among American children.

Obesity: Experiments with animals found that those fed with fast foods put on large amounts of weight. The film director Morgan Spurlock decided to extend the experiment to a human being – himself. He ate nothing but three McDonald's meals a day and took the government recommended minimum daily exercise. The results are documented in his 2004 book *Super Size Me*. After thirty days he had put on 24.5 pounds, increased his body mass index by 13 per cent and was suffering from a range of ailments, from liver malfunction (doctors likened the state of his liver to pate) to failures in the marital bliss department. Obesity is now ranked as America's number one health threat, resulting in some 400,000 preventable deaths per year, through heart attacks, diabetes and other weight-related problems.

According to the British Heart Foundation, Britain has the fastest-growing rate of obesity in the developed world. Between 1995 and 2002, the incidence of obesity in English children aged two to fifteen doubled in boys – from 3 per cent to 6 per cent – and almost doubled in girls – from 5 per cent to 9 per cent. Imperial College London even went so far as to propose that fast food restaurants offset the threat they pose to human health by distributing statins – the medication that reduces cholesterol in the blood – along with their food.

Addiction: Some American research has suggested that fast food is highly addictive, possibly to the same degree as heroin or tobacco. They believe that high-fat foods stimulate opioids or 'pleasure chemicals' in the brain, and that their removal throws the subject into the state of anxiety generally known as cold turkey (or perhaps that should be cold turkey twizzlers?) This particular conclusion is questioned by others in the scientific community. However, a separate 2008 survey found that 45 per cent of Britons felt they were so fond of fast food that they could not give it up (slightly higher even than the proportion of Americans feeling that way).

Stupidity: Another American study concluded that an excess of fast foods caused students to score significantly lower than their classmates on a range of academic tests. Again, this report (in the *Times Educational Supplement*, 22 May 2009) proved controversial.

Global warming: Researchers at the University of Manchester have calculated that lamb curry ready-meals eaten in the UK amount to an annual carbon footprint equivalent to 140 million car miles, or 5,500 times around the world. Before you conclude that fast food diners are all farting their way to global oblivion, this calculation also took into account the carbon cost of the rearing of the animals and the energy involved in slaughtering them, cooking the meals and things like transport and refrigeration.

Rats: Our streets are now nightly left ankle-deep in the detritus of discarded takeaway food. This has been a major contributor to the dramatic rise in the rat population, so you can add Weil's disease to the catalogue of illnesses for which fast food can at least be indirectly blamed.

Nouvelle Cuisine

> Its so beautifully arranged on the plate – you know someone's fingers have been all over it.
>
> Julia Child on *www.foodreference.com*

While one large sector of our population was busy stuffing their arteries with lard and their brains with toxic additives, another one was engaged in starving itself into poverty. *Harper's & Queen* magazine coined the term 'nouvelle cuisine' in 1975 to describe a marriage of the culinary traditions of France with those of health-conscious California. As such, it can be seen as a reaction against the cream- and rich sauce-laden traditional cuisine of France, favoured by the likes of Fanny Cradock.

This was not the first time the term had been used in French culinary circles. In both the 1740s and the 1880s/90s it was used to describe new waves of invention in the kitchen. One writer even tried to claim that the Siege of Paris in 1870, during the Franco-Prussian war, led to the introduction of 'nouvelle cuisine' as starving Parisians were reduced to eating cats, dogs, rats and the entire contents of the Paris Zoo (apparently elephant's trunk proved to be a particular delicacy). But '*gigot de chien flanque de ratons*' – dog's leg served with small rats – was not so much 'nouvelle' as 'desperate' cuisine.

The traditional description of 'nouvelle cuisine' is in terms of healthy, high-quality ingredients, lightly cooked and artistically presented in more manageable portions. But there are others – far more cynical than myself, naturally – who have an entirely different view of it. According to no less an authority than *uncyclopedia.wikia.com*, 'nouvelle cuisine' was invented by overworked chefs, who used it to drive the excess customers away from their establishments without resorting to anything as unsubtle as food poisoning.

Their version tells us that the key characteristics of a 'nouvelle cuisine' meal are that you start with a plate several times larger than is required to hold the quantity of food involved (in France, they call them 'American plates', presumably in recognition of transatlantic portion sizes). Said plate is first dusted with some kind of powdery food-type substance, so as to suggest a possible health hazard. It is then covered with random stripes and swirls of ketchup or other edible liquids in the manner of a Jackson Pollock painting, to show how artistic the chef is. You are not supposed to eat these swirls. If the diner so much as smudges them, chef will throw a tantrum.

The food is then served in microscopically small portions, so as not to interfere with the artwork on the plate. So as further to minimise the distraction caused by the food, the different items forming the meal are not spread around the plate, but are piled on top of each other. This apparently has the further advantage that items that did not turn out too well can be hidden below the others. At this stage, a magnifying glass may prove a handy addition to standard items of cutlery. On the subject of cutlery, *Uncyclopedia* also recommends the provision of an angle grinder, since – in pursuit of the maximum freshness – no item of 'nouvelle cuisine' is allowed to be cooked for more than twenty seconds. Some chefs go even further, and use food preparations such as a liquid helium marinade, though this can make the food stick to your lips and cause frostbite.

Side dishes of vegetables or potatoes, to sustain you at least until the next course, are out of the question. What you can just about see on the main plate is what you get. Anyone going out to a restaurant suspected of nouvelle cuisine tendencies is strongly advised to get a tin of spaghetti hoops in at home for their main meal.

The bill will, of course, be in inverse proportion to the amount of food provided. The logical conclusion will be when the diner is charged a sum adjacent to the National Debt for being shown a photograph of a meal. Dieticians have apparently raised concerns with *Uncyclopedia* about the impact on diners of regularly trying to subsist on 'nouvelle cuisine'. Symptoms are said to include gnawing on things (like table legs, or other diners) and, in extreme cases, bits of the diner falling off from malnutrition and requiring surgical re-attachment.

So there we have 'nouvelle cuisine' – not so much a way of eating as a form of conceptual art. Some commentators believe that it may no longer be the culinary force it once was, but that its evil influence has managed to permeate into the mainstream of catering. While it may have left your tummy rumbling, it should have pleased the eye and (perhaps more important to some) was for a time seen as

the most rarefied of all forms of *haute cuisine*, epitomising gastronomic excellence and good taste.
Roy C. Wood, *The Shock of the New: a Sociology of Nouvelle Cuisine*

All of which brings us on to the subject of ostentation in food.

Expensive Food

If 'nouvelle cuisine' can be defined as child's portions at adult prices, there is an end of the food market whose prices go far beyond the grasp of all but the most grasping of adults. Just as personalised car number plates are God's way of telling someone that they have too much money, so the top end of the food market is more to do with lavish (and often tasteless, whatever they may say about the food itself) ostentation. Think of the excesses of the City fat-cats and what image comes to mind (after the Porsches, that is)? It is, of course, the excesses of champagne-fuelled, expenses-paid lunches in ultra-expensive restaurants.

What they call the tasting menu at one of our best-known Michelin-starred restaurants comes in at a modest £160 per head (plus an optional 12.5 per cent service charge – and these are 2010 prices, so they probably will have gone up by the time you read this). Add to this a wine list the size of a telephone directory, from which you can pay anything up to £6,950 for a single bottle of red wine, and even up to £35 for a pot of tea, and it is clear how one typical party of six found no difficulty in racking up a bill for £2,750. I am perfectly prepared to accept the word of its many admirers that the service at this establishment is exemplary and the food memorable. I would certainly remember spending this sort of money on a meal – possibly to the point of being traumatised by it. And what food! One of the items on the tasting menu has been described as follows:

> A mousse is sprayed into a golf-ball-sized sphere and 'cooked' in liquid nitrogen. The 'ball' is then placed inside your mouth all in one. It evaporates almost instantly and you experience all the flavours one by one as smoke (actually some kind of vapour) pours from your nostrils.

That's not cooking – that's a chemistry lesson; that's showing off! If I were spending that kind of money on a meal, I would want something a little more enduring than some kind of oral explosion. And I would want a doggy-bag. There is a lingering suspicion that at least some of the business customers would not mind if they were eating soap, provided the bill was outrageously large enough to impress their clients.

But there are examples of ostentatious consumption beside which even this establishment pales into insignificance. In the following section, I have not hesitated to quote examples from throughout the world, since the market for pointless stupidity by the excessively rich is truly global and British idiots have to compete on a world stage. So how do they justify the prices charged for premium foodstuffs?

Some may be expensive because they are genuinely difficult and costly to produce. Saffron is probably the world's priciest spice, at anything up to £4,200 per pound. It comes from the flowers of the saffron crocus and to make a pound of it requires anything between 50,000 to 75,000 flowers. This would require you to grow, harvest and process an entire football field's worth of the little blighters.

Others are expensive because they are rare and irreplaceable. If you fancy splicing the main-brace with a tot of Wray and Nephew's original rum, a bottle of their 1915 brew (re-bottled in 1940) would set you back £26,000. This is because only four bottles survive from the days before the company changed its distilling process (and there are presumably thought to be three other people, beside yourself, who would be silly enough to pay that sort of money for one). However, this is cheap compared with wine prices. A bottle of 1945 Château Mouton-Rothschild sold at Christie's in 1997 for £86,925, the price of a house at the time. Mind you, it was a big bottle (a jeroboam) and I suspect it must have been a good year.

If you cannot manage rare and irreplaceable, then rare alone will often suffice. White truffles are proving increasingly difficult to track down and the largest find of 2008 (at a fraction over a kilogram) sold at Christie's for a modest £129,000. At this price, a £111 cheese sandwich, manufactured in Somerset and containing £92 worth of white truffle, starts to sound like good value.

Sometimes rarity can be manufactured by setting impossibly specific standards of provenance. The world's most expensive potato is La Bonnotte, which is cultivated only on the island of Noirmoutier off the Atlantic coast of France, on fields fertilised by the local seaweed and regularly covered by the sea. Apparently (and unsurprisingly) they taste salty, so you do at least save money on the condiments. Just 100 tons of these potatoes are grown each year and they are only sold between 1 and 10 May. More to the point, they can cost anything up to €500 per kilo. Meanwhile, over in Japan, Yubari melons, grown in just one town on the island of Hokkaido, can fetch up to £19,000 a pair.

Sometimes the price of food is justified by the charitable motivation behind it. Apparently it is all right to produce obscenely lavish and expensive foodstuffs if it is being done to support, say, starving children in India. In 2008 Burger King produced what they called the world's most expensive burger. At £95 the list of ingredients included wagyu beef, *pata negra* ham, onion straws fried in Cristal champagne, Modena balsamic vinegar and pink Himalayan rock salt. What it could really have done with was some La Bonnotte fries. A rival for the title of most expensive burger made its appearance at Nino's Bellissima in New York. At $175, it included Japanese Kobe beef, Parisian foie gras, Matsutake mushrooms and a white truffle mayonnaise. This one at least came with its own small side order of fries, though the dusting of gold leaf may be felt by some to have tipped it over slightly into the realms of vulgar ostentation.

All of which goes to show that even humble fast food may be prey to excess. The twelve-inch 'Pizza Royale 007' offers lobster marinated in cognac, caviar soaked in champagne, sun-blushed tomato sauce, Scottish smoked salmon, venison medallions, prosciutto and vintage balsamic vinegar. The sprinkling of twenty-four-carat gold flakes also helps to bump the price up to $4,200. Yet more white truffles (and I thought they were supposed to be rare) featured in the world's most expensive cheese on toast, selling at £345 a slice back in 2006 (for charity, naturally).

Still hungry? Ready for dessert? I can offer you an ice cream sundae at $1,100, which has three Belgian truffles (at $100 each) just for the sundae to stand on, a side order of Beluga caviar (with ice cream?) and an infusion of gold leaf. But even this is bargain basement compared with the Frrrozen Haute Chocolate which, at £16,120, is not unreasonably regarded as the world's most expensive pud. It contains no less than fourteen different exotic cocoas, 0.2 ounces of edible gold and a side of *La Madeline au Truffe* (itself the world's most decadent chocolate, at £1,675 a pound). But what really racks the price up are the gold, diamond-encrusted spoon with which you eat it, and the gold bracelet set with one carat of white diamonds wrapped round the serving dish, both of which the eater gets to keep. For some reason, it is available only to special order.

A cup of tea to finish the meal? It will not taste right unless it is made with a teabag like the one the PG company commissioned to mark their seventy-fifth anniversary. Manually encrusted with 280 diamonds, it is valued at £7,500. Or perhaps coffee? The Kopi Luwak develops its unique qualities by being passed through the digestive system of a civet cat in Sumatra, before being sold on to you at upwards of $300 a pound. If the thought of all this rich food (or of the process for producing Kopi Luwak coffee beans) has upset your digestion, a glass of water may be better. Kona Nigari is desalinated water, high in minerals, from the deep seas off Hawaii. It is also high in price, at $16.75 an ounce.

If we are not already firmly in it, we now enter the realms of total insanity. Make way for the £100,000 cupcake. This was specially manufactured for an event in Glasgow called Glam in the City. In an attempt to produce a Scottish foodstuff even less digestible than a deep-fried Mars bar, the designers substituted chocolate sprinkles on the cupcake with scatterings of small diamonds. It is to be hoped that they are not moreish. But the ultimate prize has to go to the fruit cake produced by a Tokyo pastry chef for Christmas 2005. It came in at $1.65 million for one small cake, on account of the 223 small diamonds with which its icing is exquisitely set. Its creator swears that the cake is edible, and if that is not conspicuous consumption, I don't know what is.

A Postscript on Pretension

Derek Cooper's admirable 1967 volume *The Bad Food Guide*, to which I refer at several points in this chapter, paints a horrific picture of the worst of English cuisine and catering at that time. It should be sufficient to persuade even the most jaded twenty-first-century restaurant-goer that standards have risen by leaps and bounds in the intervening forty-odd years. He reminds us of one characteristic of at least part of the industry at that time, one that may still send shudders through diners of a certain age.

This was the gratuitous use of French – often pidgin French – in the menu, to disguise (and no doubt bump up the price of) some very ordinary cooking. Peterborough in the *Daily Telegraph* quotes the example of a diner who asked the waitress why the pâté, supposedly a speciality of the house, appeared to have come out of a round tin. The waitress went off to consult the chef, and came back with the news that 'he's never seen *pâté maison* come in tins any other shape'. Elsewhere he reported finding *potage* of the day, *gâteau* cake and *fromage* stilton; stew becomes an upmarket *ragoût* (and fish fingers, no doubt, *doigts de poisson*).

Where the food is not translated into incomprehensible French, it may be burdened down with English verbiage which is not only unnecessary but stretches the boundaries of the Trades Descriptions Act to its very limits. The Frankenstein products of some giant food factory are brought to our plates as 'garden' peas, 'farmhouse' bread or 'home-made' preserves. How refreshing it would be, suggests Cooper, if menus continued to do this, but honestly. We might look forward to a dessert of 'powder-fresh milk, chemically dyed haddock, turnip jam and lard-rich ice-cream'.

Also popular in the 1960s was the themed restaurant, where the proprietors poured all of their effort and money into the décor, rather than the food. Cooper cites as models the nautical theme (staff dressed in sailor-style T-shirts, with various pieces of flotsam, jetsam and other quayside rubbish artistically arranged about the place, toilets labelled 'mermaids' and 'mermen'); the Continental (names like the 'Capri' or the 'Casa' something, with bull-fighting posters and Chianti bottles with candles stuck in them); or the homespun twee ('The Crinoline Lady' or 'The Copper Kettle', all mob caps and hand-knitted sponge cakes). But they would all have to go some way to match for sheer awfulness this 1966 local newspaper report of a new restaurant opening:

> Visitors to the newly reopened restaurant were particularly impressed with the gay decorations. The South Sea Island motif, with palm trees, tropical fish in tanks, native basketwork and 'thatched' roof bar, is a truly delightful setting. The waitresses in their hula skirts lend an authentic touch to this gay new nightspot. Hawaiian music is discreet and the diner is transported thousands of miles away by the ingenuity of it all. Well done, says *The Herald*.
>
> Quoted in Cooper, p. 54

Are We Having Fun Yet?

But are we having fun with the abundance and rich variety of food now available to us? We have one sector of the population stuffing itself with fast food which – if all the studies by its detractors are to be believed – is the culinary equivalent of Russian roulette; another searching their highly decorated plates, vainly looking for something of substance to get their teeth into; and yet a third using food as a means of showing off (and showing off does not count as fun – my book, my rules). Somebody's having fun, but I suspect it is only the restaurateurs and food manufacturers, laughing all the way to the bank.

4

Fun in a Box: Television

The attraction of television is insidious ... Will there be a readjustment of social habits? Shall we become incapable of creating our own diversions? ... Shall we become lazy-minded, taking our entertainment and ideas automatically from the screen?

John Swift, *Adventure in Vision* (1950)

For better or worse, one of the defining features of our post-war leisure activity (if the word 'activity' is not hopelessly misused in this context) is our addiction to the idiot's lantern in the corner of the room. It has been blamed for most of the ills of society but we love it, devoting much of our leisure time to the passive consumption of this chewing gum for the eyes.

This chapter will not be one of those sentimental strolls down the memory lane of 1950s and 1960s viewing. There will be none of that 'do you remember when we had proper programmes, like *Emergency Ward 10* and *Crossroads*?' unless reference to them is needed to make a wider point. What we are most interested in here are the dramatic wider changes that took place in the institution of television in the post-war years – the monopolistic edifice of the Reithian BBC into which the fledgling television service was reborn after the wartime interval; the types of programme to which traditional BBC values gave birth; the dramatic growth in television owning and watching (some may say despite the content of those early programmes); the battle over the maintenance of the BBC monopoly and the emergence of its brash new commercial rival; the ratings battle of the two stations and the BBC's response to competition; the growth of concerns about the influence television was having on our lives and those of our children, and attempts to regulate it in 'the public interest' (not to mention the lively debate over who determined that).

The Growth in Viewers and Influence

Television will be of no importance in your lifetime or mine.

Bertrand Russell speaking in 1948, quoted in Miall, p. 137

When television broadcasts were interrupted by the outbreak of war, they were in the middle of showing a Mickey Mouse cartoon, and 'Mickey Mouse' was a pretty good description of the service when it reopened (with the same cartoon) after the war in 1946. At this time, there were only around 20,000 households with sets, most of them located within thirty miles of Alexandra Palace, from where the early broadcasts were transmitted. Like Bertrand Russell (quoted above), few took the medium seriously at this stage. As late as 1949, a survey showed that two out of three households had never even seen a set in action, far less owned one.

Despite the limited coverage and scope of the service at this time, the BBC found (possibly to their surprise) that the number of licence fee-payers was growing rapidly, from 50,000 in June 1948 to 100,000 in March 1949. A BBC survey of that year found

> unmistakeable signs of TV becoming less and less a 'rich man's toy' – indeed by the start of the year although TV was still relatively common in wealthy than in less comfortable homes … more than a half the TV sets in use were in lower middle class and working-class homes.
>
> Quoted in Kynaston 2007, p. 305

A major leap forward came in 1950, when the BBC opened its first high-powered transmitter outside London, at Sutton Coldfield. Described as 'the world's biggest and most advanced television station', it brought the wonders of television within the reach of most of the West Midlands. Its introduction coincided with a further significant growth in set ownership. By March 1950, there were 343,882 sets licensed – still only about one home in twenty nationwide, but a major increase on the previous year's figure. Coronation year saw a further doubling of set ownership. A television audience of over twenty million watched the Coronation service in Westminster Abbey in 1953 (although there were only around two million sets licensed). Some 10.4 million went round to friends and neighbours to watch it and another 1.5 million saw it in pubs, halls and other public venues.

The numbers of licensed sets had grown further, to 4 million, by 1955. It would be on 22 September of that year that the arrival of commercial television provided the next big stimulus to set ownership. But on day 1, the commercial operation would be on scarcely less of a Mickey Mouse footing than its BBC counterpart had been, when it re-opened after the war. Only four of the planned commercial stations were operating and it was estimated that only 190,000 homes were able to tune into the opening night. It would be a few years before commercial television became the notorious 'licence to print money' that it was later described as being.

But the die was certainly cast for the growth of television. The numbers of combined radio and television licences exceeded the numbers of radio-only licences for the first time after 1957; licensed viewers reached 10.5 million by 1960 (by when 72 per cent of the population had the combined licences) and 13 million by the end of 1964. By this time, non-ownership of a television was becoming something of a conscious lifestyle choice, bordering on the mildly eccentric. In 1970, when only 2.3 million people bought a separate radio licence, compared with the 15.6 million combined licence holders, the authorities finally threw in the towel and scrapped separate radio licences altogether. By 1994/5 99 per cent of the population had a set and the debate was more about how many sets people had. In 1965, only 3 per cent of households enjoyed the luxury of a second set. This rose to almost a quarter by 1979 and by 1991, there were more people with three or more sets in their homes than there were suffering the privation of having just one.

BBC Values, BBC Programmes

Until 1955, British broadcasting was the subject of a monopoly (unless you count the ratings war they fought with German wartime propagandist Lord Haw Haw). The British Broadcasting Company (as it was called when set up in 1922 – it became a corporation with a Royal Charter in 1927) was given the remit 'to inform, educate and entertain'. Its first Director General was a dour Scottish product of those madcap funsters, the Scottish Free Church, who certainly gave the impression that he regarded the 'entertainment' part of his job as by some margin the least important of the three. John Reith is described in Miall's book as 'at his worst, morose and consumed with self-pity'. He could give the impression that his idea of fun was watching it drizzle. He ceased being Director General in 1938, but his baleful influence continued to stalk the corridors of Broadcasting House for many years after the war.

As well as its desire to give the public something better than they thought they wanted, another aspect of the Corporation's painful consciousness of its monopoly position was its desperate anxiety not to exploit it by showing anything remotely controversial. This applied particularly to anything of a political nature, but also covered other pillars of the establishment, such as the church and the monarchy. As A. J. P. Taylor observed, it was ironic that the only way the BBC could maintain its independence was by never exercising it.

In the war years and for a decade afterwards, one of the main manifestations of this was the so-called 'fourteen-day rule', whereby the Corporation was not allowed to broadcast on any subject that was due to be debated in Parliament within the next two weeks. It was said to protect the BBC from attempts to interfere by the government, but it killed current affairs broadcasting stone dead. This came to a head in February 1955, when one of the BBC's few attempts to be courageous over current affairs broadcasting, the television programme *In the News*, was barred from discussing the atomic bomb under this 'rule'. The programme's panel agreed this was a ridiculous restriction and, later that year, the BBC decided that it would no longer be bound by a 'rule' which was in fact just a convention. The Postmaster General, the minister responsible for television, tried to impose it on them, but was forced by a united media campaign to back down.

A third element of the BBC perspective was the widespread belief within the Corporation that television was some kind of novelty that would never amount to anything much, and should not be allowed to distract the Corporation from its core business of radio. Reith was actively hostile to it when it was first introduced and the BBC establishment distrusted visual media, associating it with movies and the music hall. They feared that

> the high purposes of the Corporation would be trivialised by the influence of those concerned with what could be transmitted in visual terms.

In their view, television could be

> brushed aside; it was not a medium to be taken seriously: pantomime horses and chorus girls were its natural ingredients; it was not suitable for news or current affairs.
>
> G. W. Goldie, pp. 18–19

Trivial or not, the BBC took its usual high-minded approach to the new service and, as early as 1950, set up a Television Panel of 2,500 members of the public who, they hoped, would help them to deliver 'a keener, more sensitive and more intelligent appreciation on the part of all who see it of the world about us'.

At about the same time, they set out guidelines for children's television:

> Television Children's Hour aims to enrich children's lives and to foster their development by the stimulus and enjoyment of what they see and hear. The aim seems to have several elements:
> – to entertain and be liked by the children;

– to satisfy the parents that the programme is fostering children's development in ways of which they approve;

– to satisfy instructed professional opinion that programmes are soundly constructed and well executed. This refers to both the entertainment value and aesthetic competence, and to the educational and psychological judgement which the programmes will reflect. So far, television has to some extent not come under the vigilant gaze of psychologists and educationalists.

They got 300 households with children to respond to questionnaires about the early pre-school children's programme *Andy Pandy*, from which they learned:

– that Andy was generally liked, though the children were concerned that he couldn't talk;

– that the children regarded the television as entertainment and were not prepared to get down from their chairs even when invited;

– that they regarded Andy as a younger child, to be played with and tolerated, but not as an equal.

Their dismissal of television, coupled with the higher costs of production (the scenery and costumes for a radio play come cheap by comparison), not to mention the initially low viewing figures, made it difficult to secure the share of the Corporation's budget needed to develop the service. In 1947 the Corporation spent just £716,666 on its television programming, compared with the £6,556,293 it put into radio. Even by 1951 the service's entire budget for television programmes was just £3 million.

Well into the 1950s, even as commercial television was coming up to challenge them, there were still those in the BBC who saw television as no more than a distraction from its main mission. A new recruit to the Corporation in 1956 was told by one of its executives that television could not last, because its cost was eating up too much of the licence fee. In that same year, the BBC appointed Gerald Beadle as its Director of Television. He was a man who did not even own a set and who saw the appointment as a gentle winding down towards retirement.

Before 1950, television was not even represented on the board of the BBC and thereafter it was represented, not by the Director of Television but by George Barnes, the Director of the Spoken Word (was there a director of the unspoken word?). The prejudice even carried over to the *Radio Times*, where television listings were still published as a four-page supplement, very much the junior partner to the radio pages. All this so frustrated BBC executive Norman Collins that he was forced into an alternative and ultimately very lucrative career, first lobbying for and then running a commercial television service. Collins had been a high-flyer at the BBC, responsible for such hits as *Womans' Hour*, *Dick Barton Special Agent* and the successful television coverage of the 1948 Olympics. He was tipped as a future Director General of the BBC, until their lack of support for television and being bypassed for promotion drove him out. He would not have helped his cause with the BBC by writing, after a study tour of American television in 1949:

Once television is truly national it will become the most important medium that exists. Everything that it does or does not do will become important. The very fact that it is in the home is vital. Its only rival will be the wireless, and the rivalry will not be strong ... the first casualty of television, possibly the only casualty, is not the local cinema or the country theatre, it is sound radio.

A fourth constraint was the amount of talent available to the Corporation. Even despite limited broadcasting and relatively limited audience figures, many variety agents were resolutely opposed to exposing their artistes on the early television, which they saw as consuming a lifetime's material in a single broadcast. As a result, the BBC's live shows consisted in large part of dull (and cheap) Continental cabaret acts.

The final limitations on the output were the technical shortcomings of the medium in its early years. The primitive technology meant the pictures were small (a magnifier to place in front of the screen was a commonly available accessory), dim and indistinct, and of course in black and white (or green and white in the case of my father-in-law, one of many who built the family's first television from war surplus radar parts. Also, one of the more bizarre early accessories was a multi-coloured Perspex screen you could fix in front of your television screen. It gave some sort of an illusion of colour by having a band of blue (for sky?) in front of the top of the screen, a band of red in the middle and a band of green – to represent grass – at the bottom – whatever was showing on the screen). The Corporation also had very little equipment for making programmes. Coverage of the Coronation pressed into service virtually every camera the Corporation possessed. Last but not least, the new medium had much to learn about how to present itself. Most television dramas were simply photographed stage dramas; they failed to learn from, or were unable to deliver, the lessons of Hollywood.

It does not sound like a recipe for fun and, sure enough, it produced a schedule of programmes that varied from the stultifyingly boring to the infuriatingly patronising. According to Lewis,

> there was about them a strong flavour of evening classes run by a well-endowed Workers' Educational Institute: cookery lessons from the TV chef, the goatee-bearded Philip Harben; gardening hints from the TV gardener, the venerable Fred Streeter; *Music for You* – nothing too demandingly classical – conducted in a black tie and introduced with a few ingratiating words by Eric Robinson; and, for nursery tea, the dancing, or rather jerking, puppets, Muffin the Mule, Andy Pandy and the Flower Pot Men.
>
> Lewis, pp. 208–9

As for the early sports programmes, this was an account of their coverage of the 1952 Boat Race:

> This was a ludicrous performance, television-wise. The cameras died in an explosive series of blinding flashes; for sound we were transferred to the Light Programme commentary; their launch ran out of petrol. TV did produce a blurred and bad picture of the finish, but that was about all.
>
> Clarke, quoted in Sandford, p. 360

All of these shortcomings were evident to television's critics. In February 1949, the *Daily Mirror*'s Sunday counterpart, the *Sunday Pictorial*, wrote a piece under the headline 'The truth about British Television':

> Are the programmes bad?
> Yes. Transmission most days is only an hour in the afternoon and about two hours in the evening … Afternoon programmes are mainly old American films. They are terrible … Major sports promoters are bitterly opposed to television because they know attendances will suffer. Consequently most sportscasts are of amateur events … Variety programmes are poor because the big combines put a television ban on their stars.
>
> Quoted in Kynaston 2007, p. 304

All the Problems of the World

It seems to be the fate of all new media to be blamed for the social ills of the age. Fifty years before the advent of television, the newfangled cinemas were seen as a root cause of juvenile delinquency and, as part of their sentence, young miscreants would be ordered by the courts to stay away from them. Fifty years after the dawn of the television age, computer games are today alleged to be responsible for turning our youths into bedroom-bound sociopathic recluses (albeit with very dexterous thumbs). In the 1950s it was television that was getting it in the neck. From its earliest days, the local press were fearful of its potential impact upon people's habits (no doubt including their reading of local newspapers). They forecast the death-knell for the cinema and social life generally, and called for discipline in the way it was used. They even suggested setting aside a separate room for viewing it (a luxury not available to most households in the years of post-war housing shortage).

From the early days of television broadcasting the BBC hierarchy itself fretted over the potentially intrusive nature of the new medium. In the early 1950s, the Controller of Television (as we have seen, a much less important position than it is today) pleaded with parents not to allow their children to watch too much television, while T. S. Eliot, no less, underlined his concerns, based on his experience of the much more pervasive television coverage in the United States:

> I find only anxiety and apprehension about the social effects of this pastime, and especially its effect on small children.

In Scotland the Controller of Scottish Broadcasting, Melville Dinwiddie, sounded positively apologetic about the impact of Scotland's inclusion in the television network:

> Sound broadcasting as such is upsetting enough when reading and lessons and other school tasks have to be done, but here is a more intensely absorbing demand on our leisure hours, and families in mid-Scotland will have to make a decision both about getting a receiver and about using it. At the start, viewing will take up much time because of its novelty, but discrimination is essential so that not every evening is spent in a darkened room, the chores of the house and other occupations neglected. We can get too much even of a good thing.
>
> *Radio Times*, March 1952

Despite this, more and more people wanted television. *House and Garden* even found it necessary to introduce an article to its Spring 1949 edition entitled 'Make Room for Television'. They suggested that 'for winter viewing, a good place for television is near the fire where chairs are usually gathered'. Lest this appear to be an early piece of stating the blinking obvious feng-shui to rival 'don't put the television behind the settee', we need to bear in mind that televisions had rather more demanding requirements in those days. They were bulky and intrusive objects when they were not operating, (which was for most of the day), and required relative darkness for viewing, while those in the room not watching might need more light for whatever they were doing. Curtains or Venetian blinds to divide up the room were suggested as an option.

But it was once commercial television was getting established, in the late 1950s that television really came to be blamed for every social and physical ill of the period. Among those listed by

Sandford were killing civilised conversation, causing divorces, children's nightmares, juvenile street crime and systematically doping the critical faculties of the electorate. New ailments included TV Neck, TV Crouch and TV Dyspepsia. TV Dyspepsia was rediscovered in 1975, this time known as TV Tummy and caused by prolonged slumping in front of the idiots' lantern. Doctors prescribed getting up and walking about every forty-five minutes.

It began to dominate people's lives in all sorts of other ways; television dinners and special trays from which to eat them appeared on the market, for those poor slaves who were unable to tear their eyes away from the set long enough to eat. Coronation chicken was originally claimed to have been devised as a dish that could be eaten off a tray without missing a moment of the 1953 ceremony. Sociologists studying an overspill housing estate in Essex argued that television exacerbated the problems of isolation, already felt by residents torn from their close-knit community of Bethnal Green. Television, they said, 'complements and reinforces the isolation of the immediate family and the lack of opportunities for community life'.

One thing you could at least say about those early television schedules was that the risk of children being exposed to too much television was relatively remote. At first, broadcasting only began at 3.00 p.m. weekdays and 5.00 p.m. Sundays, and stopped for an hour between 6.00 and 7.00 to enable parents to prise young television addicts from their seats and get them to bed. Adult programming then only continued until 10.30 or (on special occasions) 10.45 p.m. Even during these hours, there would be interludes, during which we would be entertained by features such as the potter's wheel (a film showing a pot being made, to a musical accompaniment).

But gradually the viewing hours grew towards our present wall-to-wall coverage. From an initial maximum of thirty hours a week it gradually rose to fifty a week (or eight in a day) in 1961, until all restrictions were lifted in 1972. It is thought that, among television owners, viewing hours overtook listening to the radio hours as early as 1955. By 1959, a survey found that the average viewer was watching five hours a day in the winter and three and a half hours in the summer. By 1961 they had settled on a standard of viewing hours per person per week, which in that year came out at (a surprising reduction to) thirteen hours a week, rising in subsequent surveys to eighteen in 1981 and to twenty-four in 2001 – that's the equivalent of one full day a week glued to the box. By the 1960s, television-watching was consuming more of the British public's leisure hours than any other activity. A survey conducted between September 1965 and March 1966 found that the adult population of England and Wales spent 23 per cent of their leisure time watching television, compared with (for men) gardening (12 per cent) and physical recreation (11 per cent) and (for women) crafts and hobbies (17 per cent) and social activities (is this social science speak for nattering?) (9 per cent). There is also a class-based dimension to it – ever since the 1960s, surveys have shown that social classes D and E (the less skilled) have watched more television than the As and Bs.

The costs of owning a set fell dramatically over the years. In the immediate post-war years, a television set could cost you 115 guineas, the price of a small, reasonable car, and half the nation's sets were owned by the top 12 per cent of earners. But by 1980 the cost of a black-and-white television had fallen (even allowing for inflation) to £62. By then, colour television had come and in 1970, the cheapest colour set was roughly £50 more than its black-and-white counterpart. But the costs of every type of set continued to fall until, by 1993, owning a television accounted for just 2.2 per cent of a household's expenditure. Colour television rapidly outstripped black-and-white, despite the sets (and their licences) costing more. Just under 100,000 colour sets were licensed in 1969 but, by 1977, there were around 10 million of them, outnumbering black and white for the first time.

The Battle over Commercial Television

Always keep a hold of nurse
For fear of finding something worse.

Hilaire Belloc

Television is at last given the freedom of the air. The event is comparable with the abolition of the law that kept motor cars chugging sedately behind a man carrying a red flag ... Now it's the 'go' signal, the green light for TV, too – with no brake on enterprise and imagination.

TV Times, 22 September 1955

Advertising on the broadcast media was by no means a novelty. The BBC itself had carried 'sponsored broadcasts' until 1927, when it was nationalised and went from being the British Broadcasting Company to the British Broadcasting Corporation. Throughout the 1950s, listeners to Radio Luxembourg would have been used to hearing radio advertisements. There had even been an attempt at television advertising. A company named Teleposters took to selling advertising space in panels surrounding the main television picture, on television screens installed in bars, canteens and other public places.

In the immediate post-war years the BBC was regarded as 'a powerful and definitive expression of national will and character'. It also had resources that were guaranteed in a way that applied to no other medium, and was ranked alongside 'Parliament, Monarchy, Church and the Holy Ghost' in terms of its influence. The Conservatives had a long-standing commitment to open the BBC to private competition and the Corporation's monopoly was safe only as long as the Labour government survived. Almost from the start of post-war broadcasting a battle was fought for the hearts and minds of opinion formers. Lord Reith, never one to engage in over-statement, likened the potential impact of commercial television to 'dog racing, smallpox and bubonic plague'. Winston Churchill's opposition to the BBC was more political. He had had run-ins with them since the 1926 General Strike and had been effectively airbrushed out of history by the Corporation during his wilderness years of the 1930s. He described them as 'tyrannical' and said they were 'honeycombed with Socialists – probably with Communists'.

Not everyone in his party agreed with him. Lord Brand joined *The Times*' correspondence on the subject:

This is the age of the common man, whose influences towards the deterioration of standards of culture are formidable in all spheres. It is discouraging to find that it is in the Conservative party which one would have thought would be by tradition the party pledged to maintain such standards, that many members in their desire to end anything like a monopoly, seem ready to support measures which will inevitably degrade them.

Quoted in Kynaston 2009, p. 106

While Liberal politician Lady Violet Bonham-Carter argued that

broadcasting by the BBC has no other aim but good broadcasting. Broadcasting by sponsoring has no other motive but to sell goods.

Ibid.

J. B. Priestley complained in his *New Statesman* column that after a few more years of mass communication on the level of that which he had recently been watching (television parlour games and *Chu Chin Chow on Ice*) 'the crowd may be permanently half-witted'. If dumbing down was the fear, it is perhaps as well for the supporters of commercial television that the American coverage of the Coronation was not shown in Britain. In this, solemn scenes in Westminster Abbey were intercut with commercial breaks, including some featuring J. Fred Muggs, a chimpanzee whose antics pre-dated the Brooke Bond chimps' appearances in commercials. One can imagine bemused American viewers shaking their heads and saying, 'That Duke of Edinburgh's let himself go a bit.'

Others that we would now call celebrities queued to associate themselves with one side or the other in the argument. The National Television Council campaigned for BBC's continued monopoly. They could call upon the likes of the Archbishop of Canterbury, William Beveridge, E. M. Forster, Harold Nicholson, Bertrand Russell and the Workers' Education Association. In opposition to them was the Popular Television Association, supported by ex-BBC executive Norman Collins, actors Rex Harrison and Valerie Hobson, Somerset Maugham, Charles Stanley of the Pye Company (who manufactured televisions), A. J. P. Taylor and cricketer Alec Bedser. Perhaps more importantly, the popular press were stridently on their side. A poll, published by the *Daily Express* in July 1953 indicated that 45 per cent of the public were in favour of 'sponsored television programmes', compared with 36 per cent who opposed them and 19 per cent 'don't knows'.

But if Churchill was opposed to the BBC monopoly, he was out-Churchilled in rhetorical terms by Lord Hailsham, supporting the Corporation:

> We are fighting for our lives in the present generation, no less than in the period of the war. During the period of the war, when in Europe the men had to suffer the peril of death to hear the truth, there was a voice of freedom to which attention was universally paid. It was the voice of Britain and it was the voice of Britain's public service broadcasts. Are we now to condemn this as a dangerous monopoly, as a weapon which we tremble to use in peace as in war? Are objective truth, objective justice, objective standards of duty and of conduct so utterly unworthy of advertisement that we must hand over to purely commercial interests the greatest instrument for good that has been devised since the printing press?
>
> Quoted in Kynaston 2009, p. 350

Lord Reith naturally wanted to preserve the monopoly. In a parliamentary debate in May 1952, he advanced some insultingly paternalistic reasons for doing so. He argued that hire purchase had

> made it possible for more sets to be used in the homes of people with lower incomes than the homes of the better-off. It was an interesting sociological phenomenon and if television's popularity among these people continued it was surely a grave responsibility on Parliament to prevent television services, which were now of such a high standard, from becoming a by-word for crude and trivial entertainment.

The Effects of Competition

> A charming young lady brushed her teeth, while a charming young gentleman told us of the benefits of the toothpaste with which she was doing it.
>
> Bernard Levin reviews the first ever television
> advertisement for *The Manchester Guardian*

The election of the first post-war Conservative administration led to the launch of the first commercial television broadcasts, on 22 September 1955. The Independent Television Authority was given rather greater powers of regulation than many had expected (somewhat along the lines of the BBC Governors' model) and the appointment of Sir Kenneth Clark as its first chairman lent respectability to the organisation (though he feared that 'he had constructed a handsome building that was being lived in by barbarians'). Sponsorship of programmes, on the American model, was not allowed. Instead, spot advertisements were allowed at intervals in the programmes. The press were fascinated by the advertisements. In *The Manchester Guardian* Bernard Levin reviewed them, rather than the new channel's programmes, awarding top prize to Messrs Cadbury, 'whose advertisement, though inept in the extreme, has for two days had me singing the damnably catchy little tune which accompanied it'.

The values of the would-be new broadcaster were very different to those of the BBC, whose ethos was, as we saw, summed up by Lord Reith as 'give the public slightly better than it thinks it likes'. Although the commercial broadcasters may not have stated it in quite these terms, their mantra might have been 'nobody ever went bust underestimating the taste of the Great British public'. In fact, Roland Gillet, the controller of the commercial station Associated Rediffusion, came pretty close to saying it in those terms, when he said,

> Let's face it for once and for all, the public likes girls, wrestling, bright musicals, quiz shows and real-life dramas. We gave them the Halle Orchestra and … visits to the local fire station. Well, we've learned. From now on, what the public wants, it's going to get.

So, the commercial stations had the most populist programming; they poached around 500 staff from the BBC in a six-month period during 1955/56 and – once they had got over initial cash-flow problems – they had far more to spend on programmes than the BBC (around £60 million in 1960, compared to the BBC's £15 to £16 million). Guess which side won the ratings war? In December 1955, 57 per cent of those surveyed by Gallup preferred ITV, compared to the 17 per cent favouring the BBC. By the end of 1957, ITV had a 72 per cent audience share and, in 1960, 117 of the 120 most popular programmes shown that year were on ITV. But the difference of approach of the two channels brought into sharp relief the class divides in British society. Many middle-class families banned their children from watching mind-rotting commercial television, while in some rougher schools, watching BBC was seen as a sign of being a sissy. An unholy alliance of the Labour Party, leading academics, the *Daily Express*, *The Manchester Guardian* and senior clergy (perhaps not so unholy in their case), united in calls to have commercial television closed down.

This is not to say that quality of output was totally disregarded by the commercial sector. The commercial regulators, mindful of the BBC ethos that you should not try to maximise audiences by pandering to the lowest common denominator of taste, set quality thresholds of their own when awarding franchises. But, once competition was a fact of life, both sides had different reasons for wanting to maximise their share of the viewing public. For the commercial stations, it was a simple question of maximising advertising income. Where quality thresholds obliged them to provide the dreaded 'culture' it generally got pushed into the non-peak hours to minimise loss of advertising revenue.

The BBC's position was different, and more ambiguous. On the one hand, if its ratings got too low, its opponents would argue that it no longer had a function and the licence fee was no longer justified. If, on the other hand, they successfully went for ratings by more populist programming, its opponents would argue that it was no longer sufficiently distinct from the commercial competition, and a separate licence fee was no longer justified. The BBC did not try to compete on populism, at least in the short term. It is estimated that their percentage of serious programming went up, rather than down, between 1955 and 1957 (which may help to explain the ratings figures quoted earlier). Between January 1958 and June 1960 about 33 per cent of the BBC's programming was classed as 'serious' compared with just 10 per cent of ITV's.

But there does appear to be some evidence of 'dumbing down' in later years, as the competition grew hotter. A study carried out by the *Observer* suggested that, between 1980 and 2000, the proportion of broadcasting overall falling into the 'light' category (however that may be defined) roughly doubled, while the proportion of 'serious' programming fell by about a third. One thing the BBC was forced to do was to increase its spending on television; this exceeded the radio budget for the first time in 1958/59, about the same time as the number of combined television and radio licences exceeded those for radio only.

Television under the Spotlight: Pilkington

> Much that is seen on television is regarded as of very little value. There was, we were told, a preoccupation in many programmes with the superficial, the cheaply sensational. Many mass appeal programmes were vapid and puerile, their content often derivative, repetitious and lacking any real substance. There was a vast amount of unworthy material, and to transmit it was to misuse intricate machinery and equipment, skill, ingenuity and time.
>
> The BBC know good broadcasting; by and large, they are providing it. We conclude that dissatisfaction with television can be largely ascribed to the independent television service.
>
> The Pilkington Report

As early as 1950, the *Daily Mirror* was calling for a Royal Commission into television before broadcasting hours were extended. It called television 'the biggest time-waster ever invented' whose real menace was

> its hypnotic effect. People will sit watching for hours – even when they don't care much for the programmes they're viewing ... The human animal is naturally lazy. Its so easy to sink into an armchair and switch on entertainment until bedtime ... the vision of a nation of tiny selfish groups mechanically entertained day after day in semi-darkness is enough to make the H-bomb appear almost innocuous.
>
> *Daily Mirror*, 22 March 1950

It took until July 1960, but their wish was eventually granted. The Macmillan government set up an inquiry into the future of broadcasting. It was chaired by Sir Harry Pilkington, a glass manufacturer who, by his own admission, knew nothing whatsoever about the subject. He was advised by Richard Hoggart, author of a popular book of the day, *The Uses of Literacy*. The main thing Hoggart knew about television was that he hated it – especially the commercial variety. Perhaps predictably, the inquiry's 1962 report gave BBC television a relatively clean bill of health (and, perhaps more importantly, an extra channel – BBC2, Europe's first regular colour-television service), while concluding that ITV was mainly responsible for 'worsening the moral climate of the country'. Its programmes, the inquiry said, were cheaply made, designed to appeal to the widest possible audience and catering for the lowest level of public taste. They recommended that the Independent Television Authority be given a stronger regulatory role.

> Those who say they give the public what it wants begin by underestimating public taste and end by debauching it.
>
> > The Pilkington Report

Equally predictably, the report divided the nation. Populists were outraged: 'Pilkington tells the public to go to hell,' screamed the *Daily Mirror*'s headline, while Woodrow Wyatt in the *Sunday Pictorial* went in for savage parody:

> How dare you prefer watching commercial television to looking at what Aunty BBC so kindly provides for you? ... The ITV programmes are 'naughty' and 'bad' for you. They are produced by ordinary men and women who like the same things as you do ... Pilkington is out to stop all this rot about you being allowed to enjoy yourself ... You trivial people will have to brush up your culture.

Among the casualties of Pilkington were what were officially called 'shoppers' guides' and unofficially 'ad mags'. These were a form of mini-soap opera, in which the characters had stilted conversations, endorsing a string of products. Probably the best-known of these was *Jim's Inn*, set in a pub bar in fictitious Wembleham. Despite having little more artistic merit than reading the Argos catalogue, its peak viewing figures rivalled some of the BBC's most popular broadcasts, and many of the great and good of broadcasting were drawn to appear in ad mags. Pilkington decided that these blurred the distinction between programmes and advertisements, and were a way for the television companies to evade the amount of advertising they were allowed to show. Those few ad mags that were not dropped voluntarily by the television companies following the Report's publication were later made illegal by Parliament.

BBC2 was duly launched in 1964. In the British tradition of trouble-free launches that goes back to the *Titanic*, the studios (and large parts of central London) were blacked out for the opening night by a power cut. A kangaroo named George, inexplicably hired as a mascot for the opening evening, was trapped in a disabled lift at the studio. Perhaps God was an ITV viewer after all?

A whole raft of other reasons for objecting to television emerged. Intellectual elites condemned it for discouraging more worthy activities, and in some circles non-ownership of a set was seen as a mark of intellectual superiority (Melvin Bragg's take on this was that these people distrusted or even envied the hold that the medium had on the public). Another group disliked the American cultural imperialism that the medium promoted. Popular though they undoubtedly were, American programmes were subject to strict quotas (14 per cent of total output until 1993 and 25 per cent thereafter). Some objected to the 'obscene' profits (130 per cent per annum on average) the commercial broadcasters were making by the 1960s. But by the 1990s, over a quarter of all advertising expenditure was on television commercials, and by the year 2000 £4.6 billion was being spent on television advertising. Others saw television undermining the moral fibre of the nation and weakening the work ethic:

> Advertisements that are set in pubs or other convivial milieus may glamorise a hedonistic, insouciant approach to life that is the antithesis of hard work and steady application, and inimical to those values that promote economic growth.
>
> > Williams, p. 60

Trendy 'Yoof' Television

It took a while for television to register the existence of a huge potential audience of young people. Surprisingly, it was the BBC that led the way with *Six-Five Special*, launched in February 1957 and playing all the different musical genres that appealed to the youth market – skiffle, rock and roll, blues, jazz and folk. It was hosted by one Pete Murray who, with his Brylcreem and suits, looked to modern eyes as if he had been born middle-aged. However, he spoke some alarming form of pidgin English that young people apparently understood but for which the older viewer needed (and was initially given, by Murray's co-presenter) subtitles:

> We've got almost a hundred cats jumping here, some real cool characters to give us the gas, so just get with it and have a ball.
>
> Asa Briggs, *The History of Broadcasting in the UK*, Vol. 5, p. 202

This from a Corporation that not long before insisted that its announcers wore dinner suits and spoke with received pronunciation. People thought the BBC management had taken leave of its senses, until they saw that it was getting audiences of 10 million plus and record promoters were ready to kill to get their acts on it. But popularity did not stop the Young Conservatives accusing the BBC of being besotted with the scatter-brained teenagers who watched it. They complained that it gave the impression that modern youth were only interested in rock and roll, wore nothing but jeans and sweaters and spent their leisure beating time to that dreadful pop music.

ITV responded in June 1958 with *Oh Boy!*, which gave the world Cliff Richard and Marty Wilde, and the BBC came back with *Dig This!*, *Drumbeat* and *Juke Box Jury*. Compères like Pete Murray and David Jacobs may not quite have been symbols of teenage rebellion, but the first steps towards a distinctive 'Yoof TV' had been taken.

New Broom

What *Six-Five Special* started at the BBC, changes in senior management completed. As the 1960s dawned, the BBC got a new Director General. Hugh Carlton-Greene was a scion of the Greene King brewing empire and brother of novelist Graham. The following extracts from two of his speeches will show you how far the BBC had come from the days of John Reith:

> I believe that broadcasters have a duty to take into account, to be ahead of public opinion, rather than always wait upon it ... great broadcasting organisations, with their immense powers of patronage for writers and artists, should not neglect to cultivate young writers who may, by many, be considered 'too advanced' or 'shocking' ... Relevance is the key – relevance to the audience, and to the tide of opinion in society. Outrage is wrong. Shock may be good. Provocation can be healthy and indeed socially imperative.
>
> Quoted in Williams, p. 137

> I don't care whether what is reflected in the mirror is bigotry, injustice and intolerance, or accomplishment and inspiring achievement. I only want the mirror to be honest, without any curves, and held with as steady a hand as may be.
>
> Quoted in Briggs, p. 325

It will come as no surprise to learn that these views brought him somewhat into conflict with the likes of Mary Whitehouse, who did not find provocation the least bit healthy and socially imperative. Some of their clashes are discussed in the chapter on censorship. The Clean Up Television campaign, precursor to her National Viewers' and Listeners' Association, reported that the BBC employ those

> whose ideas and advice pander to the lowest in human nature and accompany this with a stream of suggestive and erotic plays which present promiscuity, infidelity and drinking as normal and inevitable.
>
> Ibid., p. 146

Aunty BBC had well and truly cast off her corsets and Lord Reith was still around to denounce it:

> The dignity of the BBC has utterly departed … Hugh and I [are] fundamentally in complete opposition of outlook and attitude. I lead, he follows the crowd in all the disgusting manifestations of the age … Without any reservation he gives the public what it wants; I would not, did not and said I wouldn't.
>
> Quoted in Sandbrook, p. 371

Are We Having Fun Yet?

Here at least Great Britain can perhaps award itself some marks for having increased the gaiety of the nation over these years. How dire might our television have been if the BBC had retained its monopoly and not had its Reithian values challenged by its brash commercial competition? We can all bemoan some of the witless programming and the fact that slumping in front of the box distracts us from more creative activities (like reading my books). But it cannot be denied that the range and quality of output available to us has increased out of all proportion since the early post-war years.

Populism and quality do not need to be mutually exclusive. Carlton-Greene's reign at the BBC gave us cultural excellence (*Civilisation*, the series by Sir Kenneth Clark that received reviews to rival those of the original Renaissance. This was screened in 1969, shortly after David Attenborough had taken over as Director General, but was conceived and made during Greene's tenure); politically significant programming (*Cathy Come Home* (1966), which Leader of the Opposition Edward Heath thought important enough to arrange a private showing, and which led to the establishment of the housing charity Shelter); and controversial productions that led to a radical change in the repertoire of drama. *Up the Junction* (1965) initially attracted hundreds of complaints, but Sidney Newman, head of BBC drama, was able to say of it,

> I am proud that I played some part in the recognition that the working man was a fit subject for drama, and not just a comic foil in a play on middle class manners.
>
> Quoted in Briggs, p. 341

Even so, in March 1969, the month of Greene's retirement, the BBC was able to announce a 51 per cent share of the television audience. Serious fun was being had.

5

Fun on Wheels: Motoring

What Englishman will give his mind to politics as long as he can afford to keep a motor car?

George Bernard Shaw

Post-War Austerity

One of the key characteristics of post-war leisure was the dramatic increase in car ownership. Mrs Thatcher used to call us 'the great car economy'. Motoring became not just a means of access to new leisure opportunities, but also a leisure activity in its own right. The Sunday morning ritual of washing the car would be followed by going out for a (more or less aimless and extremely slow) drive in the afternoon. The curse of the Sunday afternoon motorist was born. People devoted not just a substantial part of their disposable income, but also a good deal of their leisure time, to their cars. But were they having fun yet?

At the end of the war, motoring was in a sorry state in Britain. There had been virtually no civilian car manufacture for years and most of the cars surviving from the 1930s and before had been either laid up, or little used, and often neglected, for the duration of hostilities. Even after the war, some car owners who struggled with the costs of ownership would still lay them up for the winter, rather than incur a full year's running costs.

The prices of even the most modest second-hand cars were at a premium, since new cars were virtually unobtainable. Those we could manufacture were nearly all committed to export, to prop up our ailing economy. A car manufacturer's supply of steel depended upon the proportion of their output they exported, which had to be at least 66 per cent and in some cases was over 90 per cent. Any customer lucky enough to be allocated a new car had to wait between twelve and thirty months for it and had to sign a covenant not to sell it on within two years without government consent, to prevent them profiteering from the inflated price any car could obtain. The importing of foreign cars was completely banned until the early 1950s. Another feature of the worldwide shortage of new cars was that you could sell virtually anything you produced, however unsuitable for its market – hence British cars, many of them at that time untroubled by the added complication of a heater, found a ready market in rather chilly places like Finland.

In this context, it was perhaps unkind to torment the British motoring public by staging the first post-war Motor Show at Earls Court in October 1948. Thirty-two British manufacturers showed off over fifty models, virtually none of which were available to the domestic buyer (in that year, the total number of British cars allocated to the home market was just 60,000). The *Daily Express* called it 'the biggest "please do not touch" exhibition of all time' but, even so, 562,954 people attended the show over the ten days – almost double the previous record. Many of the cars that form part of the nation's collective motoring memories first saw the light of day at the show – the Morris Minor and Morris Oxford, the Hillman Minx, the Vauxhall Velox and the Wolseley 6/80.

As restrictions gradually eased, the numbers of vehicles on the road increased, from just under 2 million in 1948 to around 3 million by 1952. But the real boost to car ownership came in 1958, when hire purchase restrictions were lifted and you could buy a Ford Popular for a down-payment of £4 8s 5d and a period of what were sometimes misleadingly called easy payments. We will look at some of the British products on offer in the post-war years shortly, but first we need to look at what they were driving on.

Roads to Ruin

> Throughout its length it will have two carriageways. The motor road will be carried over or under all existing roads and at important junctions there will be flyovers or underpasses.
>
> The M1, as explained by *The Times*

Even if you had a car, you could not have much fun in it without decent roads, but the roads, too, were in poor shape. In the war years there had not been the investment needed in new capacity to accommodate even a steady growth in traffic, and also precious little maintenance of the network we did have. The roads were certainly not ready to cope with the tenfold increase in car ownership that would be seen between the early 1950s and the late 1960s (by when the proportion of car-owning households had risen to 45 per cent).

We were also decades behind countries like Germany, Italy and the United States in building roads that could cope with the speed and numbers of cars around. This is not to say that the idea of high-speed roads was a new one in this country. As early as 1906, a proposal had been put forward for a new road between London and Brighton, with what they called 'multiple tracks' (dual carriageways to you and me) for overtaking. It was dropped, over fears that the use of the newfangled motor car would be restricted to such roads, and their access to the rest of the road network banned. The idea resurfaced at intervals and, in September 1937, got as far as the Ministry of Transport taking a party of 200 people over to Germany, to look at their new autobahns. This was roughly at the same time that Hitler was (with our agreement) sending delegations of top aviators over to study our airfields and other defence installations. Fair exchange and all that. The Minister of Transport, Hore-Belisha, even approved the building of a north-south high-speed road through Lancashire in 1938. The war may have interfered with the building of it, but it did not stop further such roads being planned. The first plans for a national motorway network were drawn up in 1942 and the snappily named War Cabinet Reconstruction Policy Committee turned its attention in the following year to the development of the post-war road network.

But, come the peace, it dawned on the government that it did not have the legal powers needed to build roads that were not public rights of way to all users. Given that pedestrians, cyclists and herds of cattle did not feature prominently in their plans for the new high-speed network, Parliament had to pass legislation – the Special Roads Act 1949 – to allow the construction of roads that were restricted to motorised traffic only – what we know as motorways. They started with an 8.25 mile stretch of the aforementioned road through Lancashire, largely following the route agreed before the war. Amazingly, given subsequent experience, almost no objections were received to it and such as were made were resolved through negotiation, so there was not even the need for a public inquiry. (As a comparison, the cost of anti-protester security alone during the building of the Newbury bypass in the 1990s came to £30 million, compared with the £4 million it cost to actually build this first stretch of motorway). So it was that, in June 1956, work was started on the Preston bypass – what was to become junctions 29 to 32 of the M6.

Hugh Molson MP from the Ministry of Transport officiated over the ceremony to mark the start of building works. The highlight of this was to be when he pressed a button to activate a green traffic light, on which signal a bulldozer would move in and demolish the first section of hedgerow. However, so riveting was the minister's speech that preceded the button-pressing that the bulldozer driver (a Mr Fred Hackett) fell asleep at the wheel, and had to be prodded awake when the lights changed.

The start of the construction period coincided with the wettest spell of weather in living memory, even by Lancashire standards. Work was delayed for months until the monsoon season abated and, when work finally began, the soil they excavated was found to be too waterlogged for use as embankments. Drier soil from more favoured parts of the country had to be imported. The steep embankments on either side (deliberately built to a gradient of between 1:1 and 1.5:1 to minimise the loss of valuable agricultural land) suffered from landslides, both while the road was being constructed and after it had opened.

The road was finally opened in December 1958, and this time Prime Minister Harold Macmillan was brought in to do the honours. To symbolise that this was the very whitest heat of modern technology, arrangements were made for the Prime Minister to push a button, whereupon the opening ribbon would automatically be cut. In the finest British tradition the technology failed, and the dawn of Britain's motorway age had to be ushered in by hand. Within four hours, a Mr Harold Bradshaw earned the dubious distinction of becoming Britain's first motorway casualty, after he fell off one of the motorway's nineteen bridges.

The road was originally built as a two-lane dual carriageway as a cost-saving measure, but it was provided with a thirty-two-foot-wide central reservation, so that (in the unlikely event that traffic growth ever justified it) a third lane could be added without disturbing the bridges. In this way, it was reckoned to have a 120-year life.

The road was closed after forty-six days. This was not quite the total cock-up that it sounds. Not quite. First, there was a problem with more extreme weather. The waterlogged ground beneath the road first froze, then thawed very quickly, causing instability. Second, the road surface itself was only a temporary one, in line with the standard engineering practice of the day. They used to use the temporary road surface for the road to bed in and then replaced it with a permanent surface, while at the same time fixing any snags that had emerged with the sub-structure. The temporary surface could not cope with the extremes of climate. Thirdly, they realised that no-one had yet worked out how to fix these new roads while keeping them at least partly open – the golden age of the traffic cone had not yet arrived. But Britain had done no real road-building since the 1930s, and nothing as heavily engineered as this had ever been tried before in this country. The likes of grade-separated junctions were completely uncharted territory for British engineers. It had always been recognised that building this stretch of road was to be a learning experience.

Whatever else you may say about the Preston bypass, it certainly was a learning experience. They learned, for example, that the breakdown areas along the sides of the carriageway should be hard shoulders, not soft verges into which the jacks of broken-down cars sank. They learned that a hedge down the central reservation was not an ideal crash barrier and that leaving gaps in the hedgerow encouraged illegal and lethal U-turns by lost motorists. They also learned that providing new roads encourages more traffic. The third lanes, which were thought to be a possible requirement for the far-distant future, had to be installed within seven years of it opening. Virtually all trace of the original motorway has now been removed, after it had to be widened from three to four lanes, and have continuous hard shoulders installed, running underneath the bridges, during the 1990s. (The M1 was to give further graphic evidence of new roads creating their own demand. It was built with a maximum design capacity of 14,000 vehicles a day, and reached that capacity on day one. Today, it carries more like 140,000.)

The Preston bypass nonetheless proved to be the wonder of the age. Coach parties were organised, just to go along it, and motorists flocked to see it. Most drove along it at a sedate 40 to 50 mph – only one motorist was clocked in the early months as exceeding the road's 75 mph design speed (there was no maximum speed limit at first). Such restraint was not to last. Within a year, other motorways – the M1, the M10 and the M45 – were opened and there were soon alarming reports about the number of motorists now thought to be exceeding 80 mph along them (alarming not least because many of their cars were not even reckoned by their manufacturers to be capable of such speeds). The lack of speed limits on motorways came to a head, in part after AC Cars chose the M1 as a test route for their Le Mans entry 4.7-litre Cobras in 1964. Despite being thoroughly responsible manufacturers, who only did their testing at night (in the dark?), at a time when they thought there would be no other traffic (or police?) about, they were pilloried in some parts of the media. This may have had something to do with the fact that their cars were clocked at 181 mph. The purely temporary measure of a 70 mph speed limit on the motorways was introduced in December 1965, and made permanent in 1967. Drivers have been ignoring it ever since.

The early motorways were very dangerous places in other respects. Many of their users had no idea of lane discipline, or awareness of other drivers. Many did not understand the purpose of (or even possess) wing mirrors. The impression was also held in some quarters that U-turns and on-street parking were allowed on these new roads, and that the hard shoulder was the picnic lane. Two motorists died on the M1 during its first week of operation.

Meanwhile, on the rest of the road network, congestion grew steadily worse, as car ownership grew far faster than the capacity of the roads. The 1950s saw the idea of traffic management take root. But the 1950s term meant something different to its modern usage. The approach proposed for Reading town centre was not atypical, involving as it did removal of the pedestrian crossings linking the town centre's main shopping streets (on the grounds that they impeded the free flow of traffic) and erecting railings along the pavements of those same streets, to stop those pesky pedestrians trespassing onto the highway. As the local press put it,

One of the most important matters concerning the highways is to keep the traffic moving ... mobility is vital in this hurrying age ... it is equally obvious that the greater number of crossings, the greater the congestion and delay. This is particularly noticeable in Broad Street, Reading, on a busy morning. Each new advance in quickening the life of the community ... brings with it a parallel restriction of right and privilege. Those who find it necessary to cross the highways of busy towns must bow to the inevitable; spare a little more time to reach safe venues, and avoid hesitancy. It is better not to join the cavalcade who always seem to be fearing that they will be late for their accident.

Reading Chronicle (1951), quoted in Hylton 1997, p. 20

One of the other factors impeding the free flow of traffic was parked cars. There seemed to be a view in the immediate post-war years that cars should be treated rather like the sacred cattle in India, and be free to roam (and park) wherever they wanted in the days of yellow paint-free roads. The problems this caused gradually dawned on people and, in the eyes of at least one local journalist at least, it seemed that America had got the answer:

> Some time ago, attention was called to the fact that in the United States the problem, there even more troublesome, is approached in a different way. A large building is erected and on its many floors cars are parked in such a way that any one vehicle can be decanted in a matter of minutes. Opposite the Reading town hall is the bombed arcade site. Is it possible for the Corporation to take time by the forelock, acquire and utilise this site in the same way as the Americans? This project is far from visionary and might at least be examined. It would pay for itself and would allow the authorities to take a firmer line in regard to those who fail to conform to reasonable parking restrictions.
>
> Ibid.

But never mind about traffic jams! The latest must-have car accessory would at least remove some of the stresses of congestion, as this 1960 newspaper report explains:

> The enjoyment of the motorist on holiday can be assured when he has the world of radio entertainment at his fingertips. Holiday traffic jams can be wearing on the nerves and patience is stretched to the limit when traffic queues travel slowly, but the motorist with a car radio has his otherwise savage breast soothed by music or the test match commentary.

Those who have grown up with current levels of in-car gadgetry may be surprised to know that, even up until the late 1960s, the fact that a car was equipped with so much as a heater was seen as a selling point worthy of mention in used car advertisements.

Buchanan and the Protesters

It was not just the motorists who got fed up with traffic congestion. Tensions grew between the motorist and those who suffered the consequences of the motor car on their towns, villages and countryside. The view that the motor car should be allowed to sweep all before it, and the consensus that characterised the building of the first motorway, was not to last. In 1960, the Minister of Transport – Ernest Marples, a road-builder by profession and the man who gave the railways Dr Beeching – commissioned a report on traffic in towns. Its authorship was entrusted to a civil servant, trained as an engineer and with a background in highway construction. Before the war, he had been one of those who went to admire Hitler's autobahns. By the time his report appeared in 1963, there were 7 million cars on the road and Colin Buchanan struck an apocalyptic note:

> It is impossible to spend any time on the study of the future of traffic in towns without at once being appalled by the magnitude of the emergency that is coming upon us. We are nourishing at immense cost a monster of great potential destructiveness [the motor car] yet we love him dearly. To refuse to accept the challenge it presents would be an act of defeatism …
>
> [The motor car] given its head, would wreck our towns within a decade … The problems of traffic are crowding in upon us with desperate urgency. Unless steps are taken, the motor vehicle will defeat its own utility and bring about a disastrous degradation of the surroundings for living …

Either the utility of vehicles in towns will decline rapidly. Or the pleasantness of surroundings will deteriorate catastrophically – in all probability both will happen.

Traffic in Towns

Buchanan got some things wrong. He overestimated the growth in car ownership – the 27 million cars that he forecast by 1980 was only just surpassed by the turn of the millennium – and some of his solutions, like upper-floor pedestrian walkways linking whole neighbourhoods, did not materialise. But it is a tribute to his vision that his views, which seem so blindingly obvious today, were considered so radical then. The report was as popular as it was controversial. Penguin published an abridged version as a paperback, it was translated into several other languages and the motoring organisations hailed it as 'brilliant' and 'courageous'. But others laid many of the traffic problems of the following decades at his door. Buchanan was also often misunderstood.

His central idea was to draw the bulk of the traffic onto a network of 'primary roads', on which the car would be king. In the 'environmental areas' between these roads the focus would be on restricting the freedom of the private car, so as to promote quality of life. He recognised that areas had a finite capacity for cars before quality of life began to be impaired, and that redevelopment that increased accessibility for traffic involved costs, in terms of environmental degradation and redevelopment pressure. The Buchanan report familiarised us with a host of ideas, including urban clearways, flyovers, yellow lines, pedestrian precincts, one-way streets and other traffic restrictions and the separation of pedestrian and motor car. But it was wrong to suggest that he encouraged, rather than managed, traffic. He simply pointed out the options and the trade-offs that were involved in balancing access with environment. Buchanan was to have important ramifications, in terms of linking transport and land-use planning, the promotion of public transport, evidence-based transport planning and even the organisation of local government. He also later became the President of the Council for the Preservation of Rural England, as if to prove to the sceptics how misunderstood he had been.

Another, much less well-remembered, committee reported at about the same time. The Smeed Committee in 1964 became one of the first to concede the feasibility (if not positively recommending it) of congestion charging. They said that road users should meet all their costs – not just the building and maintenance of roads but also the costs resulting from congestion and social costs, such as risk, noise and fumes. They suggested that the privilege of driving in the centre of London or Cambridge (why Cambridge? Perhaps the chairman was an Oxford man?) should cost the motorist as much as ten shillings an hour – a lot of money in 1964. Charges could be collected by such revolutionary means as wireless identification of cars or meters built into the vehicles themselves. This report scared the life out of the Conservative government of the day and Prime Minister Sir Alec Douglas-Home offered 'to take a vow that, if we are re-elected, we will never again set up a study like this one'. It took almost forty years (2002) before Ken Livingstone's London was prepared to test out the idea.

So it was in the 1970s that that popular British spectator and participant sport, the road protest, emerged. Protesters enjoyed success in getting the widening of London's Archway Road dropped, but only after they had challenged four public inquiries with a combination of technical argument and civil disobedience between the 1970s and the 1990s. The motorway programme offered no end of causes for the protesters. One of the best known was the section of the M3 through Twyford Down in Hampshire. This was part of an Area of Outstanding Natural Beauty, an important chalk grassland habitat with Iron Age trackways, butterfly breeding grounds, a designated Site of Special Scientific Interest and, for some, a site of religious significance because

King Arthur's knights were allegedly buried somewhere on it. But otherwise it had nothing whatsoever to commend it. Protesters called from 1992 for a more environmentally friendly tunnel (rejected on the grounds of £75 million additional costs) or, better still, no road at all. This environmentally unfriendly stretch of motorway opened in 1994.

But in the meantime, the protesters had developed a host of ingenious means of obstructing the works, adding much to the gaiety of that part of the television-viewing nation that was not either passionately pro- or anti-motorway. The whole thing took on the trappings of a small war. When the contractors wanted to erect a temporary bridge across the A33, they gave the exercise the military-sounding name of Operation Market Garden (an unfortunate, if not tasteless, echo of the tragic allied attempt to capture the bridge at Arnhem in 1944). The protesters promptly sought to trump Market Garden with Operation Greenfly, in which they chained various parts of their anatomy to the bridge. Initially, those leading the protest were characterised as 'New Age Travellers' (surely a better name for motorway users than these tent-dwellers?) and were viewed with hostility by locals and certain sections of the press. But opinion gradually changed (aided not a little by the heavy-handed use of force by security guards employed by the contractors) and curious alliances were formed between the likes of Second World War veterans, public schoolboys and the protesters. Ever more eye-catching (if ultimately unsuccessful) ways were found of impeding the construction – tunnels, tree-houses along the road, squatting in front of the machinery. In some small way, a sense of common purpose in the wartime mould came to a diverse group of Britons – not exactly fun, perhaps, but a life-enhancing experience for those who took part.

If the contractors found it hard going to chop down a few trees and plough up a few fields to make a rural stretch of motorway, they found it doubly difficult to progress urban schemes. When they came to build the M11 link road in east London, they needed to demolish the home of ninety-two-year-old Dolly Watson – the house in which she had been born. She (or perhaps more particularly her fellow protesters) became ever more ingenious in their methods of obstruction:

> Whole streets were occupied by protesters, who concreted themselves into barrels, tied themselves to chimneys, built vast scaffolding towers on the roof, strung huge nets from house to house, occupied bulldozers. Two 'Independent Republics' were created – Wanstonia and Leytonstonia – with their own passports and laws, in which the residents claimed to have seceded from the United Kingdom, and refused to recognise the authority of its laws – or its police force.
>
> *www.paulkingsnorth.net/rage.html*

Ever sensitive to this shifting climate of public opinion, the government in 1989 announced the largest road-building programme Britain had seen since Roman times. The White Paper *Roads for Prosperity* promised 500 road schemes, including 150 bypasses, costing a total of £23 billion. Mrs Thatcher waxed lyrical about the 'great car economy' and it was said that her government's view of the public transport alternative could be summarised as 'a man who, beyond the age of twenty-six, finds himself on a bus can count himself a failure'. Many of the schemes ran into widespread opposition and were scrapped by 1996, with a general election looming. An incoming Labour government did for most of the rest, and made it one of its first post-election commitments to reduce the number of cars on the road within five years. This, too, was a promise that was unfulfilled.

We may not all have loved the roads, but we evidently loved the things that went along them. In 1952, only about a quarter (27 per cent) of our personal travel was by car, van or taxi; by 1996, the figure had risen to 87 per cent. At the start of the chapter we saw the sorry state of the vehicles most car owners were driving in the immediate post-war years. But how far and how fast had things improved on that front?

New Roads and Old Bangers

The coming of the motorways threw the inadequacies of the national car fleet into sharp relief. Free for the first time to attempt sustained high speeds, our cars proved horribly unreliable. The RAC estimated that people using the M1 during its first month had a 1 in 400 chance of breaking down and calling them out. The overloaded breakdown services fitted their vehicles with rubber bumpers, to help them push the hordes of stricken motorists out of harm's way.

But even before the motorways highlighted the shortcomings of many of the cars on our roads, there was a lively debate about the need to regulate about some of the lethal old bangers that were at large. The government carried out tests on several thousand vehicles at their centre in Hendon in 1955. They found that

> five out of six cars tested had faults with their headlights, steering, brakes or tyres. For pre-1945 cars, the proportion failing the test was a staggering 97 per cent, and even among cars two years old or less, 77 per cent failed. One car in four had faulty steering. Four out of five had incorrectly aimed headlights. Some cars' brakes failed entirely during the test. Despite this evidence, the tests were opposed by the motoring organisations, on such spurious grounds as 'it is not possible to test the brakes when the car is stationary'.
>
> Hylton 1998, p. 27

Such problems are borne out from personal experience: I spent my formative years travelling in cars in which you could watch the road going past between your feet, and where the passenger door had a tendency to fall off as you went round a corner (rather more of a concern in the days before seatbelts). Despite the objections of the motoring organisations, the compulsory testing of all cars over ten years old was introduced in 1960. It led to the scrapping of a host of old bangers, whose impecunious owners could not afford to maintain them to a safe standard (or the tragic loss of part of our motoring heritage, depending upon who you asked).

Road deaths rose to a record of almost 8,000 by 1966 and, perhaps not by coincidence, 1967 saw a blitz of motoring regulation. The breathalyser was introduced, along with compulsory seatbelts and the compulsory testing of cars was extended to anything over three years old.

The testing of the drivers themselves had only been introduced as recently as 1935, only to be suspended again on the outbreak of war. Possibly as a consequence, by 1941 the number of road deaths had risen by 38 per cent over the immediate pre-war figure, despite there being less than half as many cars on the roads. After the war, anyone who had got a wartime provisional licence was allowed to convert it to a permanent full licence without having to take a test. Testing was suspended again during the petrol shortage caused by the Suez Crisis in 1956, and anyone who had held a provisional licence for one month was allowed to drive unaccompanied during the crisis.

What Were We Driving? The New Bangers

Most of us could not afford race-prepared AC Cobras. In this section we look at a selection of the best-known products of British car manufacturers in which we travelled in the post-war years. I have focussed on British manufacturers, partly because that was what most of us were travelling in at that time, and partly because it tells you a story about British manufacturing over this period. How much fun were we having with their products? Measured against the standards of pre-war cars, reliability, performance and build quality overall may have improved, and for many, the sheer novelty of car ownership no doubt detracted from complaints about the quality of what they owned.

For the most part, however, the story is a pretty depressing one, in which the seeds of the decline of the British motor industry were sown. Many of the home-based models suffered from out-of-date or ill thought-through technology, inertia or a lack of development finance. Others featured genuine advances in styling or mechanics, but suffered from terminal unreliability or basic design faults such as leaking cockpits or galloping rust (resulting again from lack of development or poor build quality). Even on those rare occasions when manufacturers found themselves with a genuine success on their hands, they were all too often sunk by their inability to make enough of them to meet demand, or to make any money from those they did sell.

Most of the cars built in Britain in the immediate post-war years were based more or less on the pre-war models the manufacturers had been producing, some of which were already fifteen years out of date. All too often they had gutless engines, crude suspension and handling, and features such as rod-operated brakes and an opening windscreen, trappings more appropriate to the age of the stagecoach. More fundamentally, the British industry was hopelessly diffused. There were thirty-four British-made (or British-assembled) makes on the market. The worldwide shortage of vehicles in the immediate post-war years may have hidden it temporarily, but the industry was ill-equipped to survive in what was increasingly going to become a global and mass-produced market.

Since 1932, Ford had been building cars for the British market at their works in Dagenham. Pritchard describes them as 'exceptionally cheerful little cars, delightful in their modesty' or as I, as a brief owner of one would put it, with looks and performance that gave them plenty to be modest about. Their immediate basic post-war model was the Anglia EO4A, with such refinements as a 933 cc side-valve engine, three-speed gearbox, mechanical (i.e. negligible) brakes and 6-volt electrics, which meant the headlamps went dim if you put the interior light on. The crude suspension faithfully reproduced the sensation of riding a camel, which made you grateful for the fact that the car would not limp up to more than 55 mph.

But many of the competing makes were no better, or even worse, at the time. The fact that the Ford marque survived and flourished, when many others did not, speaks volumes. One reason for this was price; by 1953, the Anglia's replacement, the Popular, retailed at £390 14s 2d, only marginally dearer than the Reliant three-wheeler, or much above the cost of a motor cycle combination (£270–£300). This was truly an economy model in both price and specification. It had tiny headlights, a single windscreen wiper that gave you only the merest hint of the road ahead in rain, a non-opening fabric roof (which was there purely to save on steel) and no indicators. The crude beam axle arrangement also led many owners to suspect that any form of suspension had been another victim of cost-cutting. But other manufacturers' budget models were scarcely less austere. Sir John Black, the boss of Standard, tastefully described his basic Standard 8 model as 'the Belsen line'.

At about the same time as the Anglia (1948), Alec Issigonis came up with the Morris Minor. At first it too had an extremely lame pre-war 917 cc side-valve engine, giving it a top speed of just 62 mph and a 0–60 time of 55 seconds – at least, that was the speedier two-door model; the additional weight of four doors was felt by some to slow the car to an unacceptable degree. But at least the steering and suspension were state of the (relatively undeveloped) art of the day.

Owners of Minors are prone to go misty-eyed and speak of their character. They were indeed quite modern-looking when introduced. *Autocar* described its 'transatlantic' styling as 'a triumph in good looks' and *Motor* described it as 'the sensation of the 1948 Motor Show' (this being the same show that saw the launch of the Jaguar XK120). But it was not necessarily to everyone's taste; Lord Nuffield, the head of Morris, was said to have likened the Minor to 'a bloody poached egg'. (He did not much care for its designer, Issigonis, either, referring to him as 'that foreign chap'). The model was later upgraded with a decent engine to become the Minor 1000 and lasted until 1971. It also established the company's tradition for neglecting the small matter of making a profit from its products. It has been estimated that at no time during its production did the Minor make much more than £10 a car profit and that, for much of the time, it was being sold at a loss.

Gradually, new models began to emerge to replace the pre-war stop-gaps, their styling influenced by developments in America (whose motor industry had been relatively uninterrupted by the war). The 1947 Austin Devon and Dorset were copied from a 1941 Chevrolet. The American influence grew in the 1950s, with the introduction of the Detroit-styled Ford Zephyr (1950) and Zodiac (1951). These were tough cars, fast for their day (80 mph for the larger Zodiac) and with handling and brakes that gave you at least a sporting chance of remaining on the tarmac at such speeds. A Zephyr won the Monte Carlo Rally in 1953. But the sexiest saloon produced by Ford was surely the Capri (1974–87). Modelled loosely on the American Ford Mustang, it was marketed as 'the car you always promised yourself'. It could initially be had in a wide range of guises, from the anaemic (if affordable) 1.3-litre version to a muscular 3-litre model, capable of 115–20 mph.

The manufacturers' 1956 replacements for their earlier models were even more brashly transatlantic, sprouting tail-fins, two-tone paintwork and whitewall tyres. Ford's principal rivals were Vauxhall, part of General Motors, but their 1957 Victor F was modelled on (or rather 'a dreadful parody' of) a Chevrolet Belair – it was a car which Pritchard describes as 'the warthog of the motoring world … atrocious in looks and little better in performance … one of the worst-styled cars of the 1950s'. On the positive side, they were also so prone to rust that you had to think twice about washing them, so at least you would not have to put up with looking at them for long. *Autocar*'s review of the Detroit-styled Vauxhalls was so bad that the company withdrew advertising from the magazine for six months in protest.

One consequence of the Suez Crisis of 1956 was a fuel shortage, as supplies had to be transported around Africa, rather than through the Canal. Fuel-efficient cars came into their own. This was the age of the bubble car and the minicar, many of which were fuel-efficient but deficient in almost every other respect. They were assisted by the fact that they attracted just half the purchase tax of a conventional car which, considering that the full rate of purchase tax in the mid-1950s was up to 60 per cent of the manufacturer's price, was a major consideration. They also paid only the same road fund tax as a motorcycle.

To take just one example, between 1949 and 1966 over 26,000 people forked out their hard-earned cash for a Bond Minicar. They were advertised under the slogan 'Economy, Comfort, Elegance', on which they scarcely scored 33 per cent. They started life as a two-seater vehicle with a 122 cc (small even for a lawnmower) engine, which produced just 5 bhp and had an eventual top speed of 35 mph. The earliest models lacked even such basic creature comforts as suspension on the rear wheels or electric windscreen wipers (the single windscreen wiper provided had to be hand-operated). The earliest models also had rear-wheel braking only and a positively dangerous steering system operated by wires. Despite having the kind of performance that was only detectable with the aid of scientific instruments, some of the Bonds still had a tendency to fall over at corners. The wheelbase had to be shortened and the rear axle widened to address this shortcoming. The Bond Minicar eventually evolved into a slightly more sophisticated machine, with a more powerful (all things are relative) 250 cc engine and seats in the back for two children (provided they could detach their legs before the journey and take seasickness pills to cope with the ride). But keen-eyed motorists would still spot some differences to even the most basic modern car. Taking the 1955 model as an example:

No reverse gear: It had a 180-degree lock on its steering so you could turn around in twice its own length but, beyond that, to go backwards you had to push it. Some models had the option of a reverse gear that worked by stopping the engine and restarting it backwards. (This meant you could go as fast backwards as you could forwards);

No self-starter: With some models, you had to open the bonnet, climb in and kick-start it, or there was the option of a lawnmower-type starter rope to pull;

No driver's side door: On some models the driver either had to climb over the piece of bodywork where the driver's door should have been, or the passenger had to get out, to enable the driver to leave on the passenger side. This was thrown into sharper relief by the fact that that there was…

No petrol gauge: If you ran out of petrol (which you would, presumably with little advance warning without a petrol gauge) you had to stop, get out of the car (with the complications detailed above), open the bonnet and switch on the reserve tank and restart it. This would have been a difficult and dangerous manoeuvre if you ran out of fuel on the fast lane of a dual carriageway (though what were the chances of a Bond getting into a fast lane anywhere?).

There were advantages; in addition to paying only motorcycle road tax you could drive it unaccompanied on a motor cycle licence, removing the need to pass a driving test. It was also claimed that the aluminium bodywork was rustproof (except that the steel chassis used to rust and sag, causing the bodywork to snap).

But the most original car of the 1950s (though irrevocably associated with the swinging sixties) was the Mini. It was first conceived as long ago as 1953, then shelved, then commissioned in 1957, with the mission of 'driving the bubble cars off English roads for good'. The version introduced in 1959 was only 10 feet long – 2 feet, 4 inches shorter even than the Morris Minor (which was also designed by the Mini's creator, Alec Issigonis). Despite this, the Mini had more interior space than its predecessor. It achieved this by having a transversely mounted front engine with a gearbox in the sump and front-wheel drive.

But at the same time, it was in some respects very primitive. The earliest cars were underpowered by modern standards, with an 848 cc engine producing just 34 bhp, they had sliding windows that used to sprout moss and doors that you opened by pulling a string. They also suffered from other initial design faults. The electrics were very vulnerable to being knocked out by the ingress of water and the cockpit was also seriously prone to being flooded – it was suggested that the best use for the door pockets was for keeping goldfish). It is also thought that the selling price for the Mini (at first starting at £350, or £496 19s 12d with purchase tax) meant that BMC hardly made any money out of the Mini, or even lost money on it. (Ford's engineers studied one in detail and decided they could not have made any money from building them and selling them at the price Austin/Morris charged.) Despite that, they produced over 1.5 million of the little beasts in a production run lasting more than forty years, and earned an enduring place in the affections of the nation.

In the finest traditions of Austin/Morris, having for once arrived at an iconic design with the Mini, they decided they could improve on it. This they did by grafting a new front end copied from the utterly unloved Austin Maxi onto it. This gave us the Mini Clubman (1969–81). Listing the benefits of this in alphabetical order, it gave more space under the bonnet for working on the engine and, well, that's it. On the debit side, it gave a poorly proportioned car, with a squared-off front end and a curvaceous rear. It went out of production long before the car it was supposed to replace (as did the Mini's other supposed replacement, the Metro). They also moved the instruments from the centre of the dashboard to behind the steering wheel, where you could not actually see them.

Rootes Group responded with their own radical idea for a small car – the Hillman Imp, launched in 1963 (though its origins lay, like the Mini, in the fuel crisis of the mid-1950s). The best part about it was the power unit, an all-aluminium 845 cc development of a Coventry Climax motor originally used in fire pumps, but developed for racing cars. The problem was the rest of it. For a start, they put the engine in the rear with the transmission in front of it, which made it seem to a conservative British motoring public somehow foreign and therefore slightly suspect. Even so, it might have been an excellent car, if they had ever finished it. But Rootes Group was in financial difficulty and was forced to launch it before it had been properly developed. This contributed to its reliability problems, and the odd manner of its assembly would also not have helped. The regional employment-creation policies of the government had forced Rootes to locate the factory making Imps near Glasgow, using a largely ex-shipbuilding labour force with no experience of car-making (something that showed in the build quality). Meanwhile, the engines and transmission castings were made in Glasgow, sent over 300 miles to Coventry to be machined and then sent back to Glasgow for assembly.

It was driven down-market to compete, at one stage becoming the cheapest car on the British market – 'a kind of British Skoda', in the days before the renaissance in Skoda's reputation. But, despite its problems, the Imp continued in production until 1976. More than 440,000 were built, though this was well below the target of 150,000 a year.

Gradually the multitude of British manufacturers got whittled down. From 1959 the Standard part of Standard-Triumph was dropped as the new Triumph Herald was launched. Its design influence was not American but Italian, emerging from the studio of Giovanni Michelotti. BMC turned in 1962 to Michelotti's compatriot Pininfarina for the design of their Mark V Morris Oxford (1959–71) and the Morris 1100 (1963–74). The latter was a bigger brother to the Mini, with the same format of front-wheel drive, transverse engine and hydrolastic suspension. The 1100 and its bigger brother the 1300 were for many years Britain's most popular car, outselling even the Ford Cortina – over 2 million of them left the factory between 1962 and 1973. Despite being quite a sophisticated piece of engineering for their day, they failed to win the same place in the popular imagination as the Mini. They were also another loss maker for the manufacturer, making a loss of some £10 for each one they sold, in their efforts to undercut Ford.

In BMC's case, they dealt with the plethora of marques by badge engineering – producing substantially the same car, possibly with minor changes to the specification – under different brand names. The Mini for example could be had in both Austin and Morris forms and in supposedly deluxe versions as a Riley Elf or Wolseley Hornet. These variants sprouted a curious boot, an incongruous radiator grille and more refined interior trim (such as a wooden dashboard and wind-up windows) all of which added to their weight and made them slower than their cheaper counterparts. Issigonis apparently hated these derivatives and they no doubt also had the founders of these once-proud independent marques revolving in their graves. However the ladies loved them. More examples of disastrous badge-engineering appear in the following section.

The Decline and Fall of British Leyland

As you will already have begun to notice, a special place in the chamber of horrors needs to be reserved for the products of British Leyland, in all its manifestations, over this period (Austin/Morris, British Motor Corporation, Rover, etc.) They seemed to have an unerring ability to get their products wrong in one way or another. There was a general tendency towards appalling build quality, leading to unreliability, water penetration, premature rust and bits falling off. Over and above that, their cars were variously incompetently conceived or designed, or the germ of a good idea, let down by poor execution and lack of development.

The Austin Allegro (1972–83) looked to have been designed exclusively for the geriatric market of Eastbourne. One reviewer described it as having a pension book holder on the sun visor and a bi-focal windscreen. In a vain attempt to make it appear sexy, they apparently attempted to film one in a quarry, leaping over obstacles. It snapped. It also included the bizarre distinction of having a square (they called it quartic) steering wheel – it only took the company two years to realise that the latter was a bad idea, after the police placed a bulk order for Allegro Panda cars and replaced all the quartic steering wheels with round ones. Quite the silliest manifestation of this model was the Vanden Plas 1500 (1974–81) in which they tried to present the Allegro as a luxury car, by loading it down with walnut dashboards, Wilton carpets (for the rain to leak onto), a pretentious radiator grille and picnic tables. It also came with all the design and build flaws of its cheaper counterparts.

The sad thing was that the original designs for the Allegro were not at all bad – but it fell victim to the British Leyland approach to design by committee and their cash-strapped need to fit an outdated tall engine under the bonnet (the designer said the engine was 'more suitable for a Leyland truck'). This led to the dumpy vehicle that was known as the 'flying pig', described as looking 'pregnant' and, on account of its build quality, named the 'All Aggro'. (One of its more interesting design features was that the windscreen could sometimes pop out when the car was jacked up.) Despite all this, it sold in large numbers and was, for a time, Britain's most popular car.

In 1970, they found themselves in urgent need of a replacement for the ageing Farina-designed Morris Oxford model, dating from 1959. Where did they turn for inspiration? Of course, to the white-hot technology of 1948. The Morris Minor was the basis for the Morris Marina (1970–81). Journalists at its launch pleaded with the manufacturer to modify the suspension and brakes, since the car at speed showed no inclination to go where you pointed it, or to stop when requested. By 1981, it was seriously (by some estimates, eleven years) overdue for replacement. Where did the company turn for inspiration this time? To the white-hot technology of 1948, of course! They simply re-skinned the Marina and called it the Ital (1981–4), in some people's opinions making it worse than its predecessor – no mean feat.

The company also made some attempts to break into new markets. Their bid for the executive car market in the 1960s was the Austin 3-litre (1967–80), a car so devoid of personality that it is hard to remember what it looks like, even when you are looking at it. In addition, it had an overweight and under-performing 3-litre engine, awful handling and ride and all the usual Austin/Morris faults of poor construction, such as a tendency to rust and fall apart. It is surprising to find that it sold even 10,000 models in its four-year life, and possibly just as well for the company. For, with its proliferation of different marques, if the Austin 3-litre had been any good and sold well, the main sufferers might have been their own Jaguar and Rover ranges.

When Volkswagen introduced the world to the concept of the hot hatchback, the Golf GTI, British Leyland's response was the MG Maestro (1983–92). The Maestro, already nicknamed the 'Popemobile' for its ill-proportioned upright styling, was hardly the right image for a sporting saloon. It was when they belatedly fitted it with an turbo-charged engine that really did go, that they discovered that its real problem was that it couldn't stop.

Sports Cars

If there was one place where you could have had some motoring fun, it should have been in the British sports car. Over the years, they have variously provided the fuel for our youthful fantasies (or at least, some of them) and the antidote to our mid-life crises. However, even their development in the post-war years was something of a mixed bag.

Possibly the first important British sports car of the post-war years, and a truly inspired one, was never really intended to go into full-scale production. The Jaguar company had developed a new six-cylinder engine for their luxury saloons but, come the 1948 Motor Show, the Mark VII saloon was not ready and there was nothing sufficiently exciting to sit the engine in for demonstration purposes. Just weeks before the show, the boss of Jaguar told his team to knock something together. They did so in just three weeks, using a combination of spare parts out of the factory, ideas stolen from the BMW 328 ('to hell with patents, who were the war winners?') and a hand-built aluminium body on an ash frame. No thought whatsoever was given to designing it for mass production. The result of this ad hockery was the beautiful Jaguar XK120, and it took the Motor Show by storm. In its day, it was the fastest production car in the world (120 mph) and, at £998, ultra-competitively priced. To their surprise, Jaguar had customers queuing round the block – far more than could be supplied using the hand-crafted methods of the prototype. It had to be entirely re-engineered with a steel and aluminium body. The company would be equally caught out by the demand for another of its products, decades later.

More typical of the pre-war hangover of the British car industry was one of the first popular sports cars of the immediate post-war period – the MG TC (1945–9). Although it had some engineering improvements over its pre-war predecessors, it looked little different to its 1936 cousin, the TA. An apparently total disregard for aerodynamics limited its top speed to 78 mph. Although around 10,000 were made, the great majority were exported to the United States (the American model featured chrome bumpers and flashing indicators, but was still right-hand drive). They were one of the first of many British sports cars that enjoyed cult status in America – we were making them, but Americans were having most of the fun.

The TD followed in 1950, with some further engineering improvements but still the same quaint old-fashioned looks. By 1952, MG were desperate to develop a more modern product, as newer rivals (some discussed below) came onto the market. However, the Nuffield Group (of which MG was a part) had just merged with Austin to form the British Motor Corporation. In a foretaste of all that was wrong with the post-war British car industry, MG were initially forbidden to develop what was to become the MGA, since it would have clashed with Austin's plans to launch their Austin-Healey 100/4. All MG were allowed was a mildly face-lifted TD, the TF.

One of those rivals to the MGs was the Triumph TR2 (1953). This had its origins in Standard-Triumph's attempts to take over the Morgan Car Company. When this failed, they set out to develop their own sports car. Their first attempt was a bit of a turkey. The 20TS was first shown at the 1952 London Motor Show. It was based on a one-off kit car built by a private enthusiast (and virtually undeveloped from these humble origins). It used an obsolete Standard 9 chassis (for no better reason than that Standard-Triumph had a supply of these lying about in the factory) and the same basic engine that was used to power the Ferguson tractor. To be fair, the engine was also that fitted to the Standard Vanguard saloon and turned out to be quite a good choice. Certainly it produced a good deal more power than the rest of the car could cope with, and the vehicle was variously described as 'a mobile disaster', 'an accident waiting to happen' and 'unfit to be sold'. Belatedly Triumph put the model through some serious development (part of which involved the not very scientific process of driving it around a test track at 100 mph until bits of it broke). What emerged was the TR2, offering a top speed of 103 mph at a knock-down initial price of £787. Early rally success ensured its popularity. Again, the great majority of the 83,000 TR2s and 3s built between 1953 and 1962 were exported.

MG finally responded in 1955 with the MGA, which had its origins in a racing version of one of their old T-series cars, entered in the 1951 Le Mans race. It was better-looking than the TR2 and offered similar performance to it, selling over 100,000 examples. It is perhaps worth noting how modest the performance of many of these cars was, by modern standards. Taking the MGA as an example, its sports car performance figures (95 mph and 0–60 in 13 seconds for the original model) would seem quite slow for even a small modern saloon car. The Wolseley 6/80, the archetypal police car of the 1950s, was even slower. 'Hot pursuit' scarcely applies to a vehicle that can barely wheeze up to 85 mph and took 27 seconds to reach 60. Nor was the MGA's successor (the MGB, introduced in 1962) particularly muscular in its performance, being powered by the same 1800 cc engine that later went into that other sporting icon, the Morris Marina saloon.

Neither the Triumph nor the MG could match the performance of the Austin Healey 3000 (1959–68). This started life as a venture by a small engineering company run by Donald Healey. He negotiated a deal to use Austin mechanical components, but when Len Lord, the Chairman of BMC, saw the car, he negotiated for them to build the whole thing at their Longbridge factory. It proved to be a formidable rally and racing car, with later models having a top speed in their standard form of over 120 mph. Over 73,000 were made.

But in some respects the most fondly remembered Austin Healey was a much more modest performer, one that went on sale a year before the 3000. The Austin Healey Sprite (1958–61) was commissioned by BMC to fill a gap in the market for a small, cheap two-seater sports car. Most of its mechanical components were taken from the Morris Minor 1000 or the Austin A35 and everything possible was done to pare costs to the bone. It had no opening boot (you had to load the luggage from inside the car) and the earliest models had the heater switch inside the bonnet (at least that opened). Its most characteristic feature, the frog-eye headlamps, was also forced on Healey by these economies. He had wanted pop-up headlamps to keep the aerodynamics smooth, but the budget would not run to them. Although the performance from its 948 cc 43 bhp engine was modest (a top speed of just 84 mph) it sold almost 50,000 models in three years, before its more bland Mark II replacement was introduced. This latter was another example of BMC's unnecessary badge-engineering, being made available in near identical Austin Healey Sprite and MG Midget versions.

If the Austin Healey 3000 was commonly described as 'hairy-chested', then the AC Cobra (1962) was positively King Kong. AC (Autocarriers) was a venerable British car maker that started life in 1904 building powered delivery tricycles for tradesmen. By 1961, they were building the AC Ace, an attractive but ageing sports car, when the American racing driver Carroll Shelby proposed buying Ace body/chassis units from them and shipping them out to California, where he would fit them with Ford V8 engines and transmissions. After much re-engineering, the result was the Cobra, and the engines that were shoehorned into them grew steadily in size, from 4.2 litres to 4.7 and ultimately 7 litres. 'Aggressive' hardly does them justice; they appear to run on pure testosterone and understandably became a cult car. After production ceased in 1968, a host of firms sprung up making replicas of varying quality, and Shelby himself bowed to the inevitable and resumed production in the 1990s.

If the AC Cobra was the most muscular of British sports cars, the Jaguar E-type (1961) was the sexiest. It incorporated a lot of aerospace technology and drew upon the Le Mans-winning heritage of the D-type. Once again, Jaguar were surprised that lots of people actually wanted to buy them. When a television company approached Jaguar about using one in their new television series *The Saint* (a piece of product placement for which most manufacturers would have sold their mothers) Jaguar turned them down on the grounds that they could not cope with the extra demand it would generate. That is why Roger Moore ended up driving around in a grotesque set of Swedish wheels. A top speed of 150mph was claimed for the E-type, but in reality even Jaguar had to do a lot of tweaking to get them up to that speed (which was just as well, since the standard tyres fitted to them were not designed to cope with 150 mph). They were nonetheless relatively affordable, remarkably beautiful and able to outperform virtually anything else on the road in their day. Over 72,000 were built between 1961 and 1975.

But even those few British car manufacturers who have prospered since the war have had their darker moments. In the 1960s Morgan, a car company built upon traditional values, yielded briefly to siren voices to modernise (a piece of advice that would have been much more well-founded in the case of the rest of the British car industry). In their case, the result was the Morgan Plus 4 Plus. This featured an unremarkable 1960s-styled glass-fibre body bolted onto the ancient Morgan Plus 4 chassis. It offered unreliability, the traditionally robust handling and ride of a vintage-origin Morgan with none of its character, plus a cramped and uncomfortable cabin – and all this at just double the price of an E-type Jaguar. The surprising thing is that they sold as many as twenty-six of the things (and no, it was twenty-six – I have not missed any zeroes) before it was withdrawn in 1967.

Are We Having Fun Yet?

So were we having fun with our motoring in the 1950s and 60s? The picture is a very mixed one. On the one hand, peoples' eyes tend to go misty when reminded of the empty, unrestricted motorways and the classic sports cars of the era. On the other, journeys off the motorway network (or before the network existed) could be murder, with the only way to pass many towns being to go straight through the middle of them, on poorly maintained and unimproved roads that were totally inadequate for the volume of traffic they were being asked to carry. Nor were the thousands of people who had to live along those same streets having much fun.

Most of us did not own classic sports cars, or have forgotten how temperamental so many of them were. All too often, the rest of us drove around in wrecks, with every journey a cliffhanger as to whether we would even reach our destination. Ask anyone who began their motoring career in those years for their memories of it and it will not be long before they get onto the hideous unreliability of the vehicles they owned. Even the new models of the day were all too often themselves unreliable, with lacklustre performance by modern standards and riddled with design faults. Over-regulated and congested as we might feel, we also travel today in far greater safety than in the days before the seat belt, the MOT test and the breathalyser. Perhaps every generation harbours the myth of the one before them living in a golden age of motoring? Sorry to break it to you, but this may be your motoring golden age – reflect on this, as you sit in your next traffic jam.

1. Absent fun. British sports cars of the 1950s – mostly exported so that other people could enjoy them. The Jaguar XK120;

2. Motoring fun. The Standard 10.

Opposite above: 3. The MGA.

Opposite below: 4. The 3-litre Austin Healey.

Above: 5. And the one some of us could possibly afford – the Austin Healey Sprite.

6. British caravanners seize the opportunity to get away from it all and commune with nature. (West Sussex Past)

7. Bognor Regis enjoys some unseasonably fine holiday weather. The crowds on the beach are temporarily obscured as the waves lap gently around their heads. (West Sussex Past)

8. Some councils went to extreme lengths to prevent topless sun-bathing on their beaches. (West Sussex Past)

9. These ladies manage to enjoy a game of beach cricket, despite having forgotten to bring the ball with them. (West Sussex Past)

Opposite: 10. A moment of pure British holiday-making fun, dating from 1952. The locals still talk about it. (West Sussex Past)

Above: 11. Dinner time at the holiday camp is graced by the presence of youthful Redcoat Des O Connor (right). (Lincolnshire County Council)

Right: 12. These holiday campers do not seem overjoyed at their fifteen minutes of fame as knobbly knees contest winners at Butlins Filey in 1949. (Lincolnshire County Council)

6

Fun is our Business: Teenagers

Adolescence – A stage between infancy and adultery

Ambrose Bierce, 1911

'What are you rebelling against?'
'What've you got?'

Marlon Brando in The Wild One (1953)

If you're not a 'square' (that means a creep who does not know his way around) you're hip to the fact that today's teenager is real cool, a gone cat – and he's here to stay. He's a new kind of biped, jive-talking, rock-and-rolling, fad-crazy, more flamboyant than young people between thirteen and twenty have ever been before.

Good Housekeeping magazine temporarily abandons the
English language as a means of communication in 1957

Teenagers complain there's nothing to do, then stay out all night doing it.

Bob Philips

The latter part of the twentieth century saw the creation of a new class of being, defined largely in terms of its leisure habits – its chosen ways of having fun. Before the Second World War, there was no such thing in England as a teenager (though the term had found some currency in the more affluent United States as early as the 1920s and 30s). For most of the century up until then, the demands of war or economic necessity meant for most people departure from school and an early start in the adult world of work or military service. Such teenage years as they had were spent hanging about in the waiting room for adulthood.

And a pretty dull waiting room it was, too. A 1947 survey of the leisure pursuits of British sixteen- to twenty-year-old boys found that 23 per cent of them listed as their main leisure activity 'doing nothing'. Their moral condition appeared to be no better than their physical torpor. Another 1949 survey of young men in suburban London found that most of them harboured 'unrealistic dreams of becoming champion cyclists, football stars or dance-band leaders'. There were few signs of interest in wider civic or community activities, little evidence of constructive leisure pursuits, weak moral codes in relation to sexual matters and a good deal of emotional disturbance. (Birching and flogging would have been too good for them, had these juvenile punishments not been abolished in 1948.) Or perhaps the authorities had another solution to the problem? This from the letters page of the *Daily Mail* in October 1949:

Teenagers are pampered with high wages, first-class working conditions and excellent facilities in education. Their outlook is centred in trashy books and films. The boys are hoodlums in embryo, while the girls are brazen and unrefined. A rigorous period of military training might make men and women of them, if they had the courage to face it.

Even after the Second World War was over, a major distraction from their state of suspended animation still existed for most British male teenagers, in the form of conscription (or National Service, as it was known after the war). Between 1949 and 1960 around 2.3 million young men were called up for up to two years, to enable the government to fulfil its overextended military commitments throughout the world. Views on its value differed:

half adult boarding school, half lunatic asylum ...

Mel Calman's view of National Service

It is in truth an education in itself – the finest in the world; quite apart from the training and instruction the National Service man will receive, he will meet and live with men drawn from all classes of society, of all trades, of all standards of education, and of various religious and political faiths ... discipline is the foundation of the army ... Discipline starts with the individual and there is nothing debasing about it; quite the reverse.

A Guide for the National Service Man (1953)

Some of the conscripts welcomed the chance to get away from boring homes and boring jobs and see a bit of the world. At the same time, many others looked for ways of falsifying their medicals or otherwise avoiding conscription (pretending to be an idiot or a homosexual were common ploys – there was also the rather more unusual route of standing for Parliament, which some older people took as a means of getting out of military service). Opinions were equally divided as to the effects of conscription on the conscripted. Some thought it created a social melting pot, radicalising many of those who took part; others argued that it reinforced the existing social order, with promotion to officer being largely restricted to those with the right schooling and the right accents.

In terms of leisure, it meant a chance to spend evenings in pubs and dance-halls with a group of fellow eighteen- and nineteen-year-olds, free of parental control. For some, it meant an opportunity to engage in large-scale brawls with gangs of local teddy boys, having been conveniently trained in the arts of combat by one's employer. National Service may have been instrumental in helping to create a separate category of 'youth' in the minds of both the conscripts and the population generally. But how far it helped create the rebellious model of youth is more open to question. As Kynaston put it,

the whole basis on which the army was run was consciously designed to encourage conformity and stamp out independent, critical thinking, especially of a left-wing variety. Instead, it offered a wonderfully self-contained world in which tradition, hierarchy, authority and discipline were privileged above all else.

Kynaston, p. 372

The army was as conservative in sartorial matters as it was in every other respect. Off-duty conscripts were forbidden to wear civilian clothes 'of any unorthodox pattern' (army speak at the time for teddy boy outfits – of which more later). If they had nothing conventional to wear, they had to go out on the town in their uniforms (for anyone below the rank of corporal, wearing plain clothes off-duty was a privilege, not a right). One lieutenant-colonel at the Royal Engineers' barracks at Malvern even went so far as to make his troops parade in their civvies before a night on the town, to weed out any deviant dressers. But if National Service was trying to enforce conformity, other unwholesome influences from across the seas were at work to undermine the fabric of British society. We will come to those shortly.

What Made the Teenager?

A number of factors drove the teenage revolution. One was their sheer numbers. By the early 1960s, the post-war baby-boom generation were working their way through their teens; almost 40 per cent of the population was under twenty-five. Second was their financial muscle. Young people's incomes almost doubled in real terms between 1958 and 1966, no doubt helped by improved educational standards that enabled more of them than before to flourish in the workplace. An average young person was earning around £10 a week in the early 1960s, around 70 per cent of which was typically disposable income. A shrinking working week left them with more time on their hands and, initially, few places to spend their time or money. In some cases, it was entrepreneurs from their own generation that came forward with the fashions and the leisure activities to fill the gap. A further factor may well have been a reaction against the austerity that dominated the immediate post-war years. Rationing was not finally abolished until 1954.

The authorities responsible for dealing with the new teenage phenomenon were not always keenly attuned to their tastes. In 1960, a youth leader in Huddersfield was sacked for allowing the young people in his club to play billiards, table tennis and darts, and to listen to rock and roll. The County Youth Service wanted him to offer instead a crowd-pleasing diet of handicrafts, classical music and drama festivals. Two years later, the London Union of Youth Clubs showed a better appreciation of the interests of youth, but equally dubious judgement. In an exercise designed, we were told, 'to mould the citizens of tomorrow' they sent a hundred teenage girls to spend the night at sea on a ship full of sailors. Sandbrook reports that

> The point of the exercise was never entirely clear, but it takes little imagination to speculate that the evening did not unfold quite as the youth service would have wished.
>
> Sandbrook, p. 421

Before the teenager, the clothes young people wore and the music they listened to differed little from those of their parents. Even the Top 20 show on Radio Luxembourg in the early 1950s was not aimed at teenagers; its main advertising sponsor was Horace Batchelor, a man selling a 'guaranteed' method of winning the football pools – an activity forbidden to the under-21s. Come the transformation and young people made a point of differentiating themselves from the rest of the population (and often from other teenagers) with a bewildering variety of tastes in music and fashion, each one seeming to many of their parents' generation more outrageous than the last, and very probably representing the end of civilisation as they knew it.

Rock and Roll, Skiffle and Pop

Rock and Roll is an economic thing. Today's nine- to fourteen-year-old group is the first generation with enough money given to them by their parents to buy records in sufficient quantities to influence the market. In my youth if I asked my father for forty-five cents to buy a record, he'd have thought seriously about having me committed.

Jo Stafford in *Billboard* magazine, October 13 1958

The hypnotic rhythm and the wild gestures have a maddening effect on a rhythm-loving age group and the result is a relaxing of all self-control.

Letter from the Bishop of Woolwich to *The Times*,
13 September 1956, calling for rock and roll to be banned.

This new race of beings had to have their own music and dancing. The term 'rock and roll' was originally black American slang for sexual intercourse. Its first recorded reference was in a blues song in 1922, but it came to prominence in the 1950s. At that time, it was first brought into popular usage by disc jockey Alan Freed in 1952, but it really took off with the release in this country of the film *Blackboard Jungle* in 1955. This was a film about classroom violence and a lack of respect for authority in an American school. One of the things that marked it out was its title music, a song released without conspicuous success the previous year by a former country and western singer. Its title was 'Rock Around the Clock' and the singer was Bill Haley. The film earned some minor notoriety when the US ambassador to Italy objected to it being shown at the Venice Film Festival.

Someone in Hollywood spotted the potential of the title music and came up with the film of the tune. The film *Rock Around the Clock* had a flimsy plot about rock and roll being discovered in a dance-hall in a backwater and transported to New York, where it took the nation by storm. Its content was deemed inoffensive enough for it to get a U certificate, and its initial showings here went off without incident. But reports began to come in about minor disturbances in some south London cinemas, with the audience getting up and dancing in the aisles, and word began to arrive from America about rock-and-roll riots at showings over there. Like many reports of teenage misbehaviour since, it probably suffered from a good deal of exaggeration in the media, according to whom the trouble soon escalated. Lighted cigarettes were being thrown, fire hoses discharged, seats slashed. Dancing spread out of the cinemas, into the streets and onto the bonnets of parked cars. In Bootle, police with batons had to be called in to deal with a crowd of hysterical dancing teenagers reported to number about a thousand.

The film made a star of Bill Haley and his group, the Comets. They made a visit to England in early 1957, amid scenes as riotous as those that accompanied showings of the film itself. Haley was an unlikely pop idol. He was, by teenage standards, ancient (in his thirties) with a curious kiss curl on his forehead and a taste in loud checked suits that made him look like a cross between an overweight Tintin and Rupert the Bear. One disappointed fan described him as the 'fat, kiss-curled housewife from the middle of America, the uncle you never wanted'. Even so, the musical establishment did not know at first what to make of rock and roll. When *Rock Around the Clock* was first listed in the Decca catalogue, it was classed as a foxtrot, and music critics, struggling to find a vocabulary to describe the new phenomenon, fell back on analogies with classical composers like Carl Orff and Beethoven, 'who built his musical structures on ideas that were striking because they were basic'. Eroica and roll, anyone?

Haley's fame was relatively short-lived; he was replaced in the teenage pantheon by someone more representative of their idealised selves. American television would only allow Elvis Presley to be seen from the waist upward, in case the gyrations of his lower regions made female viewers come over all unnecessary. He did not have the same effect on sections of the British music press. This from the *Melody Maker* reviews of his 1956 hits 'Hound Dog' and 'Heartbreak Hotel':

> I have heard bad records [but] for sheer repulsiveness coupled with the monotony of incoherence Hound Dog hit a new low in my experience. There must be some criteria left, even in popular music. If someone is singing words, surely one has the right to demand that the words are intelligible.
>
> … If you appreciate good singing, I don't suppose you'll be able to hear this disc [Heartbreak Hotel] all through.

Unsurprisingly, the *Daily Mail* was equally unsupportive of rock and roll, condemning it in terms that they would not get away with today:

> It is deplorable. It is tribal. And it is from America. It follows ragtime, blues, Dixie, jazz, hot cha-cha and the boogie-woogie, which surely originated in the jungle. We sometimes wonder whether this is the negro's revenge.
>
> *Daily Mail*, 5 September 1956

For a time, many of the British pop stars that emerged were, to varying degrees, pale imitations of Elvis – people like Terence Nelhams, Ronald Wycherley and Harold Webb. (You might know them better as Adam Faith, Billy Fury and Cliff Richard.) It was in the early 1960s that Britain would find its own popular music voice, though again this was borrowed from several American sources.

One of these borrowed sources was skiffle, a genre that was born almost by accident. The trumpeter in one of the popular British traditional jazz bands of the 1950s had a weak lip that he had to rest part-way through the set. A few of the band members, led by their guitarist, took to filling the gap by playing a few country blues or folk music-related numbers, and it soon became clear that these were more popular than the mainstream jazz of the rest of the set. The guitarist was Lonnie Donegan and the musical style he developed came to be known as skiffle, a name coined by the black residents of New Orleans for the musical parties they used to throw. Skiffle was the last word in do-it-yourself music; many of the instruments, like the washboard and the tea-chest bass, could be made or improvised, and the success of the performance owed as much to energy and enthusiasm as it did to musical skill – which in many cases was just as well.

Thousands of young people up and down the country formed their own skiffle groups, but one of these was to go rather further than the rest. This group's other big influence was the American blues, a type of music that was little known and difficult to obtain in Britain at this time. Things were a little easier in this respect in Liverpool, from where the Cunard liners still plied a regular trade with the United States. Local people working on the boats heard this music while over there and bought the records home with them. This particular skiffle group absorbed these new influences and evolved into a band. They went to Germany to learn their trade, and it was there that they cut their first single, 'My Bonnie'. They had to bring it out under the name of 'Tony Sheridan and the Beat Brothers', since their German record company feared that the name they usually performed under would be confused with a rude German term for a gentleman's tummy banana – 'peedle'. Only later, after being turned down as Billy Fury's backing band and refused a recording contract with Decca, did the Beatles get a chance to record in their own name.

Dressing to Kill: Teds, Mods, Rockers and the Rest

> These chaps wear those clothes because they like them … I think it is a passing phase, and not all of them who wear them are rotters at all.
>
> Croydon Councillor D. Stewart on teddy boys in October 1955

The new music also needed a new uniform, or rather uniforms, since much of the history of the teenager has been of one sub-branch opposing another. It was alleged that fear of the mutually assured destruction of the atomic bomb led to a new application of the wartime ethic of 'live for today' and gave us the 1950s beatnik. They were characterised by duffle coats, sloppy jumpers, a fondness for bad modern jazz and worse modern poetry, marijuana and beards (the latter mainly among the men). Their philosophy of 'disengagement', of opting out of the wage-earning rat-race, was borrowed from the French Existentialists of the 1940s, their language was borrowed from negro slang and their living expenses were borrowed in many cases from their middle-class parents. Eldridge Cleaver described them as 'a bunch of white middle-class kids adopting the lifestyle of "niggers"' and they were the ethical, if not the fashion, prototype for the hippies of the 1960s.

Distinctly more working class were the young gentlemen 'dressed in the Edwardian style', as early newspaper reports quaintly put it – Teddy Boys to you and me (apparently the *Daily Express* coined the abbreviated term in 1953). There was a whole generation of young people leaving school, relatively well educated but facing the prospect of two years' disruption to their lives come the age of eighteen, when National Service beckoned. They dismissed the idea of starting a poorly paid apprenticeship when the army would hopefully teach them a trade, and instead entered relatively well-paid, if dead-end, jobs in the interim.

There seem to be various rival explanations for the origins of the teddy boy fashion. One was that it evolved from the characteristic dress of the wartime spivs. They dressed in hard-to-get latest fashions as a form of conspicuous consumption, a way of advertising their ability to obtain the unobtainable for their customers (at a price). At a time when the wartime authorities were trying to enforce the austerity look to save on material, their long and fancy drape jackets with their wasteful use of material were particularly ostentatious.

Another possible explanation was that, when the first West Indian immigrants arrived in Britain in 1948 on board the *Empire Windrush*, some of them wore zoot suits, from which the teddy boy look evolved. In fact, the zoot suit had appeared in Britain in a limited way a few years earlier in 1946, when an East End tailor called Cecil Gee started selling what he called 'the American look'. The style had its origins in the southern states of the USA during the 1940s. It was said to have been based on one of the Civil War riverboat gambler type of outfits worn by Clark Gable in the 1939 hit film *Gone with the Wind*. It had become popular just at the time when the wartime United States authorities were also stamping down on the extravagant use of material in fashion as an austerity measure, and zoot suits were actually banned in the States. Legitimate tailors stopped manufacturing them and a whole underground industry sprang up to take their place. One option for the customer was to buy a suit four or five sizes too large for himself and then take it to one of the bootleg shops to be re-tailored to fit him, according to the dictates of fashion. It became associated with Mexican immigrant gangs, especially after a zoot-suit gang was charged with a sensational murder in 1942. Large-scale fights between zoot-suit gangs and newly enlisted servicemen became relatively commonplace in America in the war years. But when it came to Britain, it was initially seen as a black ethnic fashion, rather than one associated with violence or criminality.

Yet a third possibility is that it all began in the early 1950s, when Savile Row tried to resurrect the Edwardian look (themselves possibly inspired by the zoot suit). At first, they successfully marketed it as a pleasingly classless fashion for all frequenters of dance-halls. But the style was soon appropriated by a group of young working-class men in south London, who took to the streets in their knee-length drape jackets with velvet collars and cuffs, brocade waistcoats, narrow drainpipe trousers, cowboy-style bootlace ties and crepe-soled shoes (all the better for jiving in). The clothes were not cheap – a single custom-made outfit could cost up to £100, at a time when a typical teddy boy might be earning between £5 and £12 a week. The popularity of the style was fuelled by the positive coverage it initially got in the press:

Pre-Khaki Boys Go for the 'Teddy'
In London the teddy boys have arrived and they are a Teenage cult with a craze for clothes. Their philosophy is: Dress in Edwardian style and be happy … the clothes they wear must follow to a detail the dictates of Edwardian-inspired fashion. The youths will do without most of the things that are important to the normal Teenagers so that they can disport themselves in the dashing, colourful, dignified vogues which held sway at the turn of the century.

Daily Record, December 5 1953

But this was soon to go very sour, and middle-class 'respectable' owners quickly relegated their suits to the wardrobe of history.

For some teds, their fashion accessory of choice was the bicycle chain or the cosh, which they used to beat up rival gangs. Very similar delinquent gangs soon appeared across Europe and as far afield as Japan and Soviet Russia. (The world had been starved, once global war ended, of state-approved outlets for violent psychopathic tendencies.) By 1952, the teddy boy look became even more sinister, when two teenage criminals who dressed in the Edwardian style, Christopher Craig and Derek Bentley, sensationally murdered a policeman in the course of a robbery. The fashion's notoriety grew further when, in 1954 a gang of Teddy Boys were charged with murdering a youth on Clapham Common. The rock-and-roll riots associated with *Rock Around the Clock* did the public image of the teddy boy little good and, in 1958, they showed yet more of their dark side, as leading provocateurs of the Notting Hill race riots. North British Ballrooms campaigned for people dressed as teddy boys to be banned from dance-halls, on the grounds that 'that sort of garb is usually the sign of the troublemaker'; some cinemas and dance-halls did the same and in Liverpool a judge made it a condition of some young men's probation that they should not wear what he described as 'fantastic clothes'. He was not using the term in its complementary sense.

Fights between civilian teddy boys and national servicemen became a regular occurrence, and the army issued War Office regulations, withdrawing walking-out passes to all commands, after finding that 60,000 of their soldiers were in possession of Edwardian clothes, and that some of them had been involved in disturbances. Newspapers now started to campaign for the manufacture of teddy boy outfits to be banned and ridiculed their wearers:

> The exaggerated clothes they wear proclaim their basic self-insufficiency. The shoes often have inch-thick soles and raised heels to flatter stunted height … any relationship between this sartorial travesty and the genuine Edwardian style is purely fanciful … The Teddy suit is, in effect, a prop to sagging personalities and a sop to mentalities starved of worthwhile impulses.
>
> *Liverpool Evening Express*, May 1955

Sections of the general public fretted about the fashion. Why did people wear these clothes? Was it pure exhibitionism? Were they propping up inadequate personalities or displaying conspicuous consumption? The Keeper of Antiquities at Leicester Museum advanced the notion that it may be a reaction to the uniformity in dress imposed on young men by conscription, with them expressing a desire to be individualists. Quite the opposite view was also advanced; that it was a search for uniformity, to match the uniforms offered by National Service in the competition for girls at the dance-halls (though few would have seen what National Service dressed their men in as a fashion statement – more a fashion cry for help).

Among the wilder perspectives, there was also the class-conflict interpretation, that 1950s working-class youths were consciously aping aristocratic fashions from the last point in time when fashion was an expression of the rigid class divide, as a way of disrespecting their social superiors. Were the teddy boys perhaps some obscure offshoot of Marxism? Then Dr J. MacAlister Brew advanced the view in *Family Doctor* magazine that it was all to do with the increasing ratio of males to females in the population, with men consequently having to make greater efforts to seek a mate through personal adornment (though, again, whether the average teddy boy had sufficient grasp of demographics to appreciate the need for this must remain in doubt).

There were even those who praised the style. Hardy Amies, dressmaker to the queen, no less, was perhaps better placed than most to separate the fashion statement from the behaviour of those who occupied it. He said, 'It has a certain swagger, the tight trousers and long jackets are elegant.' Prince Philip may have had a narrow escape.

Teddy boys as a group were not universally violent. Narcissism was more their vice and one of the things that most commonly kicked violence off was insults to their dress sense. For some reason, they seemed to object to being called 'flash c**ts'. But they were by no means the first group of young people to be characterised by their distinctive clothing. For example, inner-city areas of Manchester in the late nineteenth century had gangs called scuttlers, who fought wars with each other over territory, girls and even religion (Irish Catholics against English Protestants). The gangs had their own distinctive hairstyles and dress codes. Some of their fashion statements (clogs and heavy studded belts that could be used to fracture skulls) also doubled as weapons.

But by 1958, the teddy boy look was declining rapidly in popularity, to be replaced by new fashions influenced by Italy and by American cinema, and with a sub-genre (associated with motorcycles and leather) morphing into the rockers. If the Teds were narcissistic about their appearance, the mods of the 1960s were positively obsessive. They wore Italian suits with narrow lapels, winkle-picker shoes and shirts with pointy collars. Their transport was the scooter, preferably fitted with its own weight in chrome accessories, and they wore military-style parkas to keep their other finery clean when they travelled. In the days before hair gel they would spend hours putting sugar water on their hair to get it to obey the dictates of fashion. Some even sat on a sheet of brown paper when travelling on a bus, so as not to get any speck of dirt on their immaculate suits. The more hardcore mods tended to wear more make-up than their female counterparts, going in for eye shadow, eye pencil, lipstick and rouge.

The female mod was to be identified by 'pop-art mini-dresses, PVC "kinky" boots, coloured tights, soft bras and hair cropped in accordance with the dictates of Vidal Sassoon'. One unexpected result of this new wave of fashions was its impact on office furniture design. It was difficult to wear a miniskirt with decorum. Disapproving older women said they left too little to the imagination, while most men found they stimulated their imaginations to a quite remarkable degree. To avoid distraction in the office the modesty board began to be fitted to office desks. For a while they became quite a status symbol and female employees would demand them as part of their conditions of service.

The natural habitats of the mod were the boutique and the discotheque, then both new and fashionable, and they warded off the fatigue of a hectic social life with amphetamines, which were at the time both legal and easily and cheaply available.

A tatty backstreet off London's Regent Street became synonymous with 1960s mod fashions. Carnaby Street was to a substantial extent the creation of one man. John Stephen was the son of a Glaswegian grocer, who came to London in 1956, aged just nineteen. He started out working in a store in Covent Garden, specialising in hiring out military uniforms for fancy dress and theatrical events. He later moved to a store called Vince Man's Shop in Soho, not far from Carnaby Street. Its main clientèle was gay men; George Melly remembered it as 'the only shop where they measure your inside leg each time you buy a tie'. Stephen started out with the idea of manufacturing clothes for others to sell. He only got into retailing by accident, after a fire in his workshop forced him to move into premises with a shop window. He opened the first of his Carnaby Street outlets in 1963, and by 1966 owned twenty-four stores there and was a millionaire.

Despite the association between the mods and Carnaby Street, Stephen showed no particular interest in, or knowledge of, the movement. The mods went to him because he was cheap, for they could not afford the prices charged by the real fashion leaders, along the Kings Road. Later, when Stephen tried to increase his prices on the back of Carnaby Street's commercial success, he fell out of favour with his mod clientèle.

The natural enemy of the mod was the rocker (whose interests I summarised in another book as 'Brylcreem, motorcycles, black leather and alcohol'). Their traditional battlegrounds were the seaside resorts on Bank Holiday weekends. Clacton saw an influx of an estimated 1,000 mods during the Easter weekend of 1964 and there was a replay of the action in Margate over the Whitsun weekend of the same year. According to some of those who took part, overzealous police and an over-imaginative press made the situation appear worse than it actually was, with much of the so-called mayhem taking the form of name-calling and other non-violent posturing. But fifty-one of the Margate combatants were arrested and three actually went to prison. On at least one occasion, one of the less fastidious reporters bribed a couple of rival groups to stage a mock fight on the beach for his cameraman. His competitors got to see the fight for free, as the mock battle descended into the real thing. The 'family doctor' in the *Evening News* had the solution to the problem. They were

> all of unsound mind in the sense that they are all suffering from a form of psychosis. Apart from the birch or the rope, depending on the gravity of their crimes, what they need is rehabilitation in a psychopathic institution.
>
> Quoted in Sandbrook, p. 416

Young people got a pretty bad representation in the media generally; as well as their less than sympathetic news coverage in the papers and on television, there was their treatment in books, plays and films. This was the age of what was characterised as the angry young man – rebellious, hedonistic, unprincipled and opportunistic. For example, Alan Sillitoe's book (and later film) *Saturday Night and Sunday Morning* was set in Nottingham and presented such an unsympathetic picture that local Conservative MP John Cordeaux felt obliged to step in and defend his younger constituents:

> It undoubtedly creates an impression that the young men of our industrial towns are a lot of ill-behaved, immoral, drunken Teddy Boys … The principal character could hardly be less typical of the young men of Nottingham … we produce as good a type as anywhere in the country, who work with the best of their ability from Monday morning to Saturday. Many work through the weekend as well.
>
> *Daily Herald*, 6 February 1961

Hopefully, someone then took him to one side and explained that the book was only pretend.

Skinheads

Skinheads had their origins in a bifurcation of the mod movement in the later 1960s. Part of it – the peacock or smooth mods – went more flowery and ornate, anticipating the arrival of the hippies, while another more working-class part became 'hard' mods, whose style of dress celebrated British proletarian culture (possibly because they could not afford the more expensive fancy gear?). They were the forerunners of the skinheads. The fashion started in Britain but spread across the world, and it seems to have fragmented into a host of different sub-cultures, representing more or less any set of values you care to name. The racist, neo-Nazi element among them tended to attract a disproportionate amount of media attention, but they are far from representative of the whole. Traditional skinheads identify themselves in terms of music, style of dress and pride in working-class culture, but not by attitudes towards race. A left-wing element in the movement, represented by the organisation RASH (Red and Anarchist Skinheads), are militantly pro-working class, anti-fascist and anti-racist. SHARP (Skinheads Against Racial Prejudice) focus on the anti-racist element, without necessarily embracing the other politics of the left-wingers. There are right-wing conservative skinhead groups, strongly patriotic without necessarily being xenophobic, and there is even a gay skinhead sub-culture. Yet other groups – such as Oi! skins and hardcore skins – identify themselves in terms of style and musical choices, rather than political stances. Such fine details as the height of your boots, the closeness of your haircut or the colour of your braces or bootlaces can all be political statements.

The white supremacist part of the skinhead movement is surprising, to the extent that early skinheads were heavily influenced by the music and style of Jamaican rude boys. But it may have been no more than a means of legitimising the anti-social tendencies of those inclined towards violence generally, for skinhead aggression was also channelled into gay-bashing and hippy-bashing, as well as Paki-bashing.

Punks

To start at the end: in 2008, *New Statesman* published a piece mourning the descent of Mr Johnny 'Rotten' Lydon from punk idol as lead singer (using the term 'singer' in its widest possible sense) of the punk band the Sex Pistols to a pantomime figure in a Rupert Bear suit, flogging butter on a television commercial. Fans asked whether this was not contrary to all that punk held most dear, the ultimate sell-out? Mind you, he had shown tendencies towards conformity before, by agreeing to compete in the television programme *I'm a Celebrity… Get Me Out of Here!*, where he only briefly regained his rebellious credentials by walking off the set before taking his turn to be evicted. On the other hand, as the article put it,

> Even if you think it was a musical political movement, should that mean that the figurehead of punk rock has to stay a punk forever? Isn't it just as tragic to stay totally true to the stupid things you think at seventeen, as it is to turnabout and do the opposite?
>
> *New Statesman*, 8 October 2008

Good question. But what is/was punk, before it became an advert for butter? For Shakespeare it was a term meaning 'prostitute'. For more recent readers, it is the musical expression of iconoclasm and nihilism (or, to put it in dictionary terms, 'the desire to smash all that has gone before and kill your idols and the rejection of current moral and established beliefs without offering or seeking solutions to change them'). Or, as one of the websites that purports to speak for punk rather more succinctly put it, 'fuck you'.

Punk seems to have spawned a bewildering number of sub-genres. The band Crass became known as the voice of anarchy in Britain and beyond, combining in their act elements of the revolutionary artistic movement Dada and the Baader-Meinhof terrorist gang (who started life as a street theatre group). They rejected the overtures of major record labels but did rather nicely shifting records by word of mouth, without needing to incur the expense of marketing or getting airplay. They gave large sums of money to causes such as the CND and striking miners, attracting the unwelcome attentions of MI5 in the process. Their reputation came to be something of a prison for them; they became frightened even of going on holiday, for fear of being seen having fun and therefore being accused of selling out. More recently they embraced the cause of NIMBYism, when a housing development threatened their rented commune home and the surrounding countryside. They launched an appeal to raise the money to buy the house (difficult to reconcile with the anarchist maxim about 'all property being theft') and were even threatening to stand for the parish council. If they needed money, why didn't they just get a job in a butter commercial, like proper anarchist ex-punks?

There are many claims for the origins of punk. The oldest, dating from around the time of the First World War, was, as we saw, Dadaism, which relied on shock and disorientation for its impact. From the 1940s, there were the left-wing protest songs of the folk singer Woody Guthrie. Moving forward to the 1960s, the elemental structure and slightly anarchic lyrics of early mod bands like The Who and the Small Faces, not to mention early The Kinks, were acknowledged as influences by some punk bands. Also mentioned in despatches were The Troggs, of 'Wild Thing' fame. But the most immediate impetus seems to have been a reaction to the way pop music was going by the early 1970s. The rebellious element in rock and roll had been well and truly tamed, with mainstream acts like Billy Joel being described as 'rock'. It had also become over-technical and manufactured, as bands who were to varying degrees unqualified to do so attempted to emulate the likes of Jimi Hendrix and Eric Clapton. Most of all, it was thoroughly commercialised.

Punk was an attempt to take rock back to its (very basic) roots. There was a strong ethos of do-it-yourself involved, from forming a band, writing material, recording it, right through to arranging for its distribution outside of the conventional channels. Early punks were taught to distrust commercialised media: 'Stop consuming the culture that is made for you. Make your own culture,' they were told. The punk fanzine *Sideburns* took matters to their absolute basics, publishing pictures of the guitar chords A, E and G with the caption, 'This is a chord. This is another. This is a third. Now form a band.' Punk was skiffle with attitude and the Royal College of Music would not have approved.

Much of the music was basic in the extreme, with individual tracks lasting less than two minutes and some whole sets barely exceeding a quarter of an hour (there are limits to what anyone can do with three chords – unless you are Status Quo). Like much skiffle, they depended upon their driving energy rather than the originality of their melodic invention or their musical skill. But unlike skiffle, the lyrics were generally shouted, rather than sung. 'Loud fast rules' – the title of a single by the Stimulators – sums up the punk approach to music. Dancing to punk was virtually impossible, and led to 'deviant' dance forms – notably the pogo (or, as we used to call it, jumping up and down). Like skinhead fashions and music, punk fragmented into innumerable sub-categories – new wave, hardcore, anarcho-punk, emo, queercore and riot grrrl. Some of these even involved learning to play their instruments!

The fan magazines of punk revelled in their amateurish quality, using typewritten or felt tip text, staples and collage and photocopied reproduction. The fashions it generated were similarly chaotic. If any line of descent is to be identified in their fashions, it is from the 1960s rockers, from whom came the basic uniform of T-shirt, jeans and leather jacket. This was embellished with torn clothes, bondage accessories and safety pins forming prominent motifs, along with tattoos and piercings, whose main aesthetic driving force seemed to be their ability to shock the wider public. For some reason, unlike the more wholesome Beatles, none of the mainstream political parties rushed to embrace punk bands as their supporters.

More than other post-war youth movements, punk embraced a variety of anti-establishment sentiments. The classic (if such a term may be used in this context) album by Britain's most famous exponents of punk, the Sex Pistols, was titled *Anarchy in the UK* and their famous track 'God Save the Queen' was definitely not suitable for a state occasion. Other bands wrote about unemployment or the grim realities of urban living. The bands even developed a distinctly edgy relationship with their audiences, involving can throwing, stage invasions and spitting. 'Bet you don't hate us as much as we hate you!' Sex Pistols lead singer Johnny Rotten would shout at his 'adoring' fans. They were able to extend this hate-hate relationship to a much wider audience when they appeared on the early-evening television show *Thames Today* and were encouraged by an ill-advised interviewer to inject a string of obscenities into a million teatimes. Many of their subsequent tour gigs were cancelled as a result, polite record stores declined to stock their music and radio airplay dried up. A Nottingham shopkeeper who displayed their album *Never Mind the Bollocks, Here's the Sex Pistols* in his shop window found himself prosecuted under the 1889 Indecent Advertisement Act.

Like so many youth movements, punk began to decline (in around 1977) just as the mainstream entertainment industry began to smell money. They sought to embrace it but in doing so strangled its appeal to its original audience.

'Exploitation' Films

> The older people and parents were staying home and watching TV. Who wanted to go to the theatre? The teenagers! The kids wanted to get out of the house, and their parents were delighted to get them out of the house … and to pay for them to get them out of the house.
>
> Samuel Arkoff, quoted in Rausch, p. 149

The impact of television and changing post-war leisure patterns meant that the cinema became an evermore youth-oriented establishment. The young brought with them their own values and a different way of watching films (a post-war survey revealed that 51 per cent of young people had their first date at the cinema, which suggests that their concentration on the film may have been rather more sporadic than, say, their parents'). One example of this new focus to the industry was particularly striking.

Few in Hollywood expected the small independent company, founded in 1954 and that came to be known as American International Pictures, to survive for long. Few independents did, and the company's principals – lawyer Samuel Arkoff and sales manager James Nicholson – had little or no experience of the industry. But the Hollywood insiders reckoned without the cultural earthquake that was taking place at the time – the invention of the teenager. AIP were the first company to recognise the potential of this new market.

The company became extremely efficient at making very cheap movies very quickly. Sets and costumes would be re-used, scenes from one film cut into another and actors 'recycled' to play more than one character in the same film. A typical AIP film would cost just $300,000 to produce and would be shot in seven to ten days. They were called 'exploitation' films, and their subject matter could include whatever was the new teenage fad. Rausch lists

> biker films, westerns, drug culture, juvenile delinquency films, monster movies, women in prison movies, Edgar Allen Poe adaptations, gangster pictures, beach party movies, blaxploitation, espionage movies, kung fu, redneck movies, and science fiction.
>
> Rausch, p. 151

Their method of making a film was quite the opposite of the conventional one. They would start with a title, a poster and an advertising campaign which they would test on their target audience. Only if it was successful would they then think about writing a script and making the film. And their titles were indeed truly memorable. Who could resist

I was a Teenage Werewolf (1957)
Attack of the Puppet People (1958)
War of the Colossal Beast (1958)
Teenage Caveman (1958)
Attack of the Giant Leeches (1959)
The Ghost in the Invisible Bikini (1966)
1,000 Convicts and a Woman! (1971)

Such titles could win an audience out of sheer curiosity, regardless of any critical reception the film got, which was often just as well. *I was a Teenage Werewolf* was described as *Rebel Without a Cause* meets *The Wolfman*, and the plot (insofar as it existed) centred around a troubled (to put it mildly) student literally tearing his fellow classmates to pieces. According to one review 'the suspense is minimal, the production values low and the time-lapsed special effects are hokey'. But at least the title and publicity campaign were great.

In *1,000 Convicts and a Woman* the energetically promiscuous daughter of a prison warden sets out to bed the entire staff and inmates of daddy's gaol. Once again, the publicity material gives an indication of the production's artistic values:

> Black man … White man … Any man!
> To the warden's daughter prison was a giant playpen – a cage full of men – to TAKE … to BREAK … or PLAY WITH ANY WAY SHE WISHED.

Just in case the theme has still escaped you, it was subtitled *Story of a Nympho*. Among those reviewing the film were the United States Conference of Catholic Bishops, who awarded it their 'O' classification (for morally offensive). They concluded that 'the exploitation movie's ridiculous ineptness fails to mitigate the unsubtle titillation'. And they should know.

For all the shortcomings of the films, the roll-call of those who cut their teeth at AIP reads like a list of Hollywood greats, including as it does Martin Scorsese, David Cronenberg, Dennis Hopper, Woody Allen, Francis Ford Coppola, Jack Nicholson, Charles Bronson and Robert de Niro, among many others.

Girl Power

> A Spice Girl may have the thighs and hot pants of a feeble hussy, but she possesses the heart and soul of a Tory country squire.
>
> Simon Sebag Montefiore, *Spectator*, 14–21 December 1996

In February 1994 an advertisement appeared in *The Stage* magazine for applicants to join a girl band that was being manufactured. Four hundred people applied and five were eventually chosen 'for their all-round ability and personality' (which is the equivalent of a fond relative saying of a plain niece 'she's got a nice smile'. It meant in this case that none of them was particularly good at anything). Fortunately lack of talent is no barrier to success in the industry and, in their short eighteen-month existence, the Spice Girls turned out to be the most spectacularly successful pop phenomenon since the Beatles. Eight of their nine singles and both their albums were number one hits and they sold some 17 million records, with number ones in thirty countries.

This time it was *The Sunday Times* who saw fit to describe them as 'role models for their generation'. On the face of it, they at least came with something of a political manifesto for their followers – 'Girl Power'. They published what purported to be an instruction manual on it early in their ascendancy. Some even tried to interpret them as prototype feminists. In practice, there turned out to be much less to their message than met the eye. The principles of girl power turned out to be variously platitudinous, incomprehensible or internally inconsistent ('the future is female', 'girls should follow their destiny', 'it's like feminism – but you don't have to burn your bra', and so on). In fact, girl power really started life as a marketing ploy, designed to wean a young female audience away from their devotion to the boy bands who, at this time, were spread all over the pop charts like a bad case of acne.

More so even than their predecessors, the Spice Girls were as much a brand as a musical group – a vehicle for marketing a bewildering variety of merchandise. Insofar as any political philosophy emerged it was the Conservatism of their leading member, Gerry Halliwell, who described Margaret Thatcher as 'the first Spice Girl' (a thought that is not comfortable to visualise if it involves hot pants). Their influence over the thinking of their fans is virtually undetectable, not least because their principal fan base was pre-teen girls who used to attend the concerts with their parents.

The End of the World as We Know it?

For many years, the middle-aged (actively encouraged by media that never allow the facts to get in the way of a good story) have believed that the younger generation were taking society to hell in a handcart. In the 1920s, girls dressed as flappers and youths wearing Oxford bags were proof positive that the end of the world was nigh. Since the war, there have been those ready to argue that every new development in youth fashion or music – teddy boys, rock and roll, mods and rockers, the Beatles and Rolling Stones, skinheads, punks – was irreversibly subverting the morals of the nation's young.

For a variety of reasons, nothing could be further from the truth. First, there was not a homogeneous youth culture to which a whole generation subscribed. As we saw, those members of the middle classes who initially adopted the Edwardian style soon abandoned it as it began to attract negative publicity and be associated with the proletariat. The mods started out as a relatively small and localised group of working-class youths and, while some of the superficial trappings of their fashion may have had a wider influence, they existed (for economic reasons) in a separate world to the fashion-setting celebrities in the West End nightclubs. More important, they also set themselves apart from mainstream youth culture, for example in their contempt for the Beatles (who they regarded as 'girly' and excessively melodic). The mods may have had a point about where the Beatles' main appeal lay; the Secretary of the Beatles Fan Club in 1964 described the typical club member as 'thirteen to seventeen, a girl, middle-class, white, Christian, a B-student'. It may also be worth reminding ourselves that the term 'Beatlemania' was originally coined, not as a description of a youth movement, but to describe the reactions of the largely middle-aged and definitely establishment audience at the Royal Variety Show at which the group appeared.

Student culture also existed as a separate sub-caste of youth. In America, where about 50 per cent of eighteen-year-olds went to university, there was a much stronger alignment between 'student' and 'youth' culture. In the 1960s, American youth also had the unifying prospect of call-up for Vietnam. In Britain, by contrast, less than 6 per cent of eighteen-year-olds attended university at any time in the 1960s.

Second, youth movements tended not to be out of the control of capitalism for long. As soon as they rose spontaneously and began to demonstrate a wider appeal they were hijacked by commercialism (at which point, they often began to lose their appeal to their original devotees). Even where events involving young people were meant to shock the more traditional audience (such as the musical *Hair*, with its nude scenes) the establishment could still defuse them by taking them, metaphorically, to its bosom. As soon as Princess Anne was seen dancing in the aisles at a performance of *Hair*, the show had made its transition into the mainstream. Politicians soon came to recognise the electoral benefits of being associated with popular music cult figures. Long before Tony Blair's discovery of 'Cool Britannia' and his love affair with Oasis, both of the main political parties assiduously courted the Beatles in the run-up to the 1964 election. All Conservative candidates were instructed to mention the Beatles in their election campaigns. Last but not least, all but the most hardcore youth idols ran the risk of being absorbed into the entertainment mainstream and becoming family entertainers (as happened with the Beatles, appearing in America on the *Ed Sullivan Show*, on *Morecambe and Wise* over here, and even in pantomime – oh yes they did!).

Nor were the leaders of British popular music fashion the architects of revolution. Rock and roll was seen by many in the 1950s as subversive, with its sexual innuendo and untamed dancing. As we saw, early American television broadcasts of Elvis Presley were censored. And who was Britain's main contribution to this sinister cult? Cliff Richard.

In the 1960s, members of the leading bands were also singled out as role models for the young. This from *The Times* about Mick Jagger:

> He is the symbol of the young generation and the epitome of part of it ... he is the vanguard of a movement of young people that transcends class barriers.
>
> *The Times*, 1 August 1967

Not so. Jagger was the product of a middle-class background (grammar school and the London School of Economics – one of those 6 per cent of university students). Interviews and surveys showed that he identified strongly with the middle classes and they with him. When he and Keith Richard were (briefly) imprisoned for drugs offences, it was the establishment press that lobbied furiously against the severity of the sentences. A survey of working-class voters in the 21–34 age group showed that a majority (56 per cent) thought the sentences were not severe enough. In subsequent interviews, Jagger refused to advocate the use of drugs, denied that he was any kind of spokesman for youth and generally came across as articulate, well-spoken and firmly conservative. This despite the fact that he and Richard wrote what appear to be some anti-establishment songs ('Street Fighting Man' related to a 1968 anti-Vietnam demonstration and 'You Can't Always Get What You Want' was about student protests).

In similar vein, three of the four Beatles had been products of grammar schools and John Lennon had moved on to Art College. As we have seen, their followers tended to be quite youthful but, if the following thoroughly unpleasant piece of journalism is to be believed, they were hardly the stuff of which revolutionary movements were made:

What a bottomless chasm of vacuity they (the fans) reveal! The huge faces, bloated with cheap confectionery and smeared with chain-store make-up, the open sagging mouths and glazed eyes, the hands mindlessly drumming in time to the music, the broken stiletto heels, the shoddy, stereotyped, 'with it' clothes.

Paul Johnson, The New Statesman, quoted in Fowler, p. 171

The argument here seems to be that the Beatles are not engaged in winning over hearts and minds, so much as purses. They are promoting mindless fan worship and passive consumerism – the Beatles and their fellow pop idols were capitalists, not revolutionaries.

What's in a Cult?

The earlier youth movements were recognisably differentiated from the rest of society. Once you were wearing the uniform, there was no failing to recognise that you were a teddy boy or a rocker. But more recent movements have become so disaggregated and diverse that one is left wondering whether the label that binds them together actually means anything? Take this attempt to define another sub-group, the Goths, which seems to throw its hands up in defeat:

Goth in its simplest form, is a subculture. A group of people who feel comfortable within each others' company. There is no specific thing that defines what you need to do or be to fit into the Goth scene (except of course the implied black clothing). People in the Goth scene all have different musical tastes, follow different religions, have different occupations, hobbies and fashion sense … the Goth scene is just as widely varied as society in general … Most Goths become Goths because they have been spurned by normal society … Goths are free-thinkers, people who do not accept the moral rules of society because they're told, 'This is just how it is'…

www.goth.net

Even then, the author felt obliged to add a footnoted disclaimer:

Please note that the above is the opinion of the author, and that there is no definitive answer to the question 'What is Goth?' so opinions and answers will vary.

Are We Having Fun Yet?

Have all the years of branding this age group, of differentiating them from other parts of the life cycle, had any beneficial effects? It would seem not, to judge from the industry that has grown up around teenage depression and dysfunction. Even the car maintenance manual people, Haynes, have got into the act, publishing a teenager manual for anyone wishing to strip a teenager down to their component parts and reassemble them – assuming you have the right spanners (admittedly, I have not studied the contents in detail). It appears that, in any one year, about one in twenty-five teenagers gets sufficiently depressed to require medical treatment; the rest just get moody. According to one of these self-help sites,

everything seems in a state of flux – their moods, their bodies and their relationships with families and friends. They are painfully conscious of their maturing bodies. They feel socially inept. They swing wildly between being shy and embarrassed to brash and rebellious in a bid to disguise their insecurities and confusion.

indiaparenting.com

The problem may be deeply rooted in our anatomies. According to scientists, humans are unusual in the animal kingdom in the way they develop. Most species, including apes and man's predecessors, passed rapidly from infancy to adulthood. Humans have a puzzling four-year age gap between sexual maturity and prime reproductive age. This is variously thought to allow time for our more sophisticated brains to develop or to learn complex social behaviour (such as downloading pornography using the parental credit card and speaking teenage languages that are totally incomprehensible to their elders).

But to draw us back to our central question, are today's teenagers having more fun than their counterparts in the immediate post-war period, or are these years simply a better-funded and hedonistic source of angst? I refer you back to the survey with which we started this chapter, which found that the adolescents of sixty years ago were characterised by physical torpor, unrealistic dreams of celebrity, weak moral codes and a good deal of emotional instability. Sound familiar today? I rest my case.

7
Fun with your Hands:
Doing it Yourself

Do-it-Yourself

Lord Finchley tried to mend electric light
Himself. It struck him dead; and serve him right!
It is the business of the wealthy man
To give employment to the artisan

Hilaire Belloc (1870–1953)

Give your doors that new look with hardboard panels. The out-of-date panelled door tends to provide a series of dust-collecting ledges that are a nuisance to the busy housewife.

Do it Yourself magazine, April 1957

'Home' is what the English have instead of a fatherland.

Jeremy Paxman

Do-it-yourself was not entirely a post-war phenomenon. One of its origins can be found in a series of *How to…* books and pamphlets published in the 1890s, and the *Daily Mail*'s Ideal Home Exhibition had been giving British males (and, perhaps more importantly, their wives) ideas since 1908. However, a number of factors combined to make the post-war years the golden age of do-it-yourself. There was the revolution in new building materials, tools and techniques that bought a wide range of tasks within the scope of the amateur handyman, or at least left him better able to disguise the incompetent job he had made of them. In parallel to this there was the more home-centred focus to people's leisure time, epitomised by the shift from cinema to television as the entertainment medium of choice.

The Festival of Britain promoted an interest in domestic design. Its Homes and Gardens Pavilion would have been seen by most of the Festival's 8 million visitors. There was the boom in home ownership and the associated pride in ownership, promoted in particular by Conservative governments of the 1950s. As early as 1950, 60 per cent of homes were already owner-occupied, although 40 per cent of these were products of the Victorian building boom, over sixty-five years old and – as we will see – often in need of major renovation. Then there was the increased cost (or near impossibility) of hiring a tradesman in a booming labour market. Into that gap in the market leapt the cowboy builder, who tarnished the image of the building industry generally. If a job was going to be botched, better to botch it yourself and save the labour cost.

People also had the spare time in which to do it themselves; as the average working week fell, a Gallup survey found that one in four people had more spare time than they knew what to do with (always a dangerous situation that would lead some weak souls into bad habits, like DIY). There were grants; the government, mindful of the need to improve the housing stock, gave generous home improvement grants under the Housing Act 1949 and the Rent Act 1954. Many households took advantage of these to install hot water systems and bathrooms, with the result that the proportion of households living without a proper bathroom fell from 40 per cent to just 2 per cent between 1951 and 1984. There was also the fact that so many people were living in awful housing conditions, with little chance of having the wherewithal to move into something better.

On the supply side, the end of the war left a large number of small metal-bashing firms without a government contract and looking for new products to sell; many of them spotted the potential of the burgeoning DIY market. Last and quite possibly least, there was the bizarre fact that the distribution of wartime air raid shelters for home self-assembly gave thousands of householders an introduction to the idea of flat-pack furniture. And there was hardboard and Formica. But more of them later.

The housing stock was in a truly appalling state after the war. Bombing eradicated almost 2 million properties, but many of those left standing were nevertheless in a terrible condition. As late as 1956, some 14 per cent of all households had no electricity supply at all and, for many of those who did, the supply was unreliable or downright dangerous. Some had electric light only and, even for those who enjoyed the luxury of electric sockets, many had far too few sockets for the demands of modern living.

Small wonder, then, that the 1956 Ideal Homes Exhibition attracted 1 million visitors to Olympia, to feast their eyes on such wonders of the age as 'the breakfast bar'. These exhibitions opened people's eyes to the potential for home improvements. Starting with the 'Britain can make it' exhibition in 1946/47, there was an annual Handicrafts and Do-it-Yourself exhibition at Olympia from 1953, a DIY theatre at the Ideal Homes Exhibition from 1955 and free-standing DIY exhibitions at Earls Court from 1958. The publishing industry did not get in on the act until October 1955, when the first edition of *The Practical Householder* magazine appeared. From the start it showed no lack of ambition; issue one carried the first in a series entitled 'Build your own bungalow', offering a '£2,000 architect-designed bungalow which may be built for under £1,000 by any handyman'. Within eighteen months, it was Britain's biggest-selling technical journal, with a circulation of over a million. In March 1957 a rival in the form of *Do it Yourself* magazine was launched and, within three years, it was doing even better, selling 3.75 million copies. DIY became huge business. By 1987, it was turning over £9 billion a year – twice the income generated by the UK tourist industry – and this grew to £23 billion by 2001.

Television advertising of DIY products first appeared in about 1960. Television had already cottoned on to the potential of this activity, and television viewers of a certain age will remember the broadcasts of Barry Bucknell, of whom more shortly. But if his was the daddy of all the home improvement programmes, there was a (now little remembered) grand-daddy, W. P. Matthew (he seems not to have been sufficiently intimate with listeners and viewers to reveal his first names). He began his career before the war doing radio DIY programmes. As a topic suitable for radio this cannot come far above juggling and mime. Somebody at the BBC apparently recognised this, and W. P. got the good news that his first television broadcast had been scheduled. The bad news was that it was scheduled for 3 September 1939, and the normal programmes got rather interrupted that day. But from 1946 to 1955, he broadcast regular do-it-yourself programmes for BBC television.

As soon as ITV came on stream, they signed up W. P. Commercial television loved do-it-yourself programmes. Under the rules within which commercial stations operated at the time, DIY was classified as adult education, and therefore did not count towards the maximum number of hours the commercial stations were allowed to broadcast each day. But they did count towards the amount of advertising space they could sell. An extra seven- or fifteen-second advertising spot paid for the cost of each fifteen-minute programme and a tidy bit besides. Unfortunately for him, W. P. did not benefit from the new arrangements for long, since he died in March 1956.

Out from his shadow came Barry Bucknell (1912–2003). Bucknell had an interesting background; he was a qualified mechanical engineer, who had been apprenticed to Daimler before working in, and eventually running, his father's building and electrical firm. He had been a Labour councillor and chairman of the St Pancras Housing Committee. During the Second World War he was a conscientious objector and worked for the London Fire Brigade during the Blitz. His first exposure to the media was a radio programme on which he spoke about the experience of being a father. An afternoon television programme for housewives – *About the Home* – then called upon him to dispense handyman tips (no doubt, in the spirit of the times, in terms so easy that even a woman could understand them).

From this, he got his own show: *Barry Bucknell's Do-It-Yourself*. The first show, broadcast in the run-up to Christmas, showed how to make a Christmas tree stand and, from that point, there was no holding him back. He was soon the most popular man on television, pulling in some 7 million viewers to his programmes and attracting over 35,000 letters a week. At least some of these viewers may have been watching his shows for their comedy potential, because they were broadcast live. Despite Bucknell's best attempts to manage the process – rehearsing every project with his wife timing him with a stop-watch – nails still got bent over and legs fell off tables. On one famous occasion, he was speaking to camera when the piece of wallpaper he had just stuck to the ceiling fell off and draped itself fetchingly around his head. 'And this,' he continued without pause, 'is not how to do it.' The audiences loved him, and his collar and tie, his Brylcreem and his cardigans.

In 1962 he began one of his most ambitious projects, *Bucknell's House*. The BBC lashed out no less than £2,250 of licence-payers' money on a property in Ealing. They did so against the strong advice of a structural surveyor, who warned that it was riddled with wet rot, dry rot and woodworm. But, over the course of thirty-nine weeks, Barry and his team renovated it, sometimes working through the night to meet broadcasting deadlines. Again, the project was not without its disasters. On one occasion, they filmed the demolition of an internal wall, but so much dust was created that the camera saw nothing of what was going on and, having demolished the wall on live television, a retake was not exactly an option. In addition to renovating the fabric of the house, Bucknell also built the furniture that went into it. Once again, he was rewarded by viewing figures of over 7 million and, at its last valuation, the property that they were told was not worth buying at £2,250 was now worth in excess of £800,000.

Bucknell was a keen sailor and his DIY projects did not stop at the front door. One of his greatest contributions to the fun of the British nation was the Mirror dinghy, which democratised sailing and got some 89,000 households afloat. It started from his youngest son demanding a boat in which to learn to sail, and ended with an 11-foot dinghy, made from thin sheets of plywood, literally sewn together and sealed with glass-fibre. To test whether absolutely anyone really could build one, they erected a polythene igloo in Bucknell's back garden and brought in a student with absolutely no experience of building anything to construct it, during the worst winter in living memory.

The dinghy worked, but it nearly did not get launched at the Boat Show. This was being sponsored by the *Daily Express* and they did not want to allow a rival (the *Daily Mirror* were sponsoring the dinghy) to steal their thunder. A compromise was reached, in which the word 'Daily' was hidden and it became the 'Mirror Dinghy'. But they kept the red sails, to match the red top of the sponsoring newspaper.

In the post-war years, what people wanted was the streamlined, minimalist modern look. Away with all the fussy ornamentation of the Victorians! Panelled doors had to be made smooth and featureless, ornate fireplaces ripped out. However, the making good after the ripping out required a certain amount of skill (though not as much as it took thirty years later to put the original features back in). Fortunately, two products were available to make the 1950s do-it-yourselfer's life a lot easier.

A form of hardboard had been invented in England in 1898, by pressing hot waste paper; a superior product was later developed by compressing wet wood pulp at a high temperature. It gave a material that was relatively dense, totally uniform and easily workable. It was also versatile in the ways it could be finished. You could paint it, wallpaper it, stain it or veneer it. And there was another thing you could stick on top of it…

> Lucky mother whose table is Formica-topped. No need to scrub – one wipe with a cloth and its clean.
>
> Advertisement in *My Home*, September 1951

That other thing had been invented by two Americans, Daniel O'Conor and Herbert Faber, in 1912. They were working for the electrical company Westinghouse and were trying to develop a cheaper substitute for mica (get it?), a mineral which was used in electrical insulators. What they came up with was layers of paper, originally impregnated with the wonder material of the age, Bakelite, and then compressed. It was not until the 1920s that its uses extended from electrical components to making sheet laminates, which could then be finished with a decorative and hard-wearing top layer of melamine. Formica did not find its way to Britain until 1947, and proved itself to be ideal for the shiny, sleek, wipe-down modern look people were after. Do-it-yourselfers used it everywhere, and it became an essential part of the décor in any catering establishment with pretensions to trendiness. Only in the 1980s did its image slip, coming to be regarded as somewhat synthetic and tacky, but today it has acquired something of a retro-chic reputation. Other do-it-yourself products gradually became easier to use – wallpaper no longer needed its edges laboriously trimmed, water-based emulsion paints replaced the more messy oil-based distemper, cellulose wallpaper pastes replaced the difficult-to-mix and slow-to-dry flour and water variety, and from about 1954 power tools took the hard work out of sawing, sanding and screwing things together.

Not just homes, but gardens enjoyed a post-war makeover. The functional vegetable and chicken-raising gardens of the war years were replaced by lawns and flower beds; the most popular rose varieties were subject to a two-year waiting list. *Gardeners' Question Time* made its first appearance on the radio in 1947 and from 1956 Percy Thrower became to the herbaceous border what Barry Bucknell was to the bedside cabinet. When Percy opened his own gardens to the public, 9,000 people queued to see them. From the early 1960s, garden centres became our one-stop shop for everything horticultural and containerised plants held out the promise of instant transformation of your plot.

Do-it-yourself became hugely popular. One local paper ran a contest for the best item of do-it-yourself, with cash prizes for the best efforts by men, women, children and pensioners. Pensioner Mr P. M. Woods was highly commended for his formica-topped coffee table, the top of which was made from an old bedstead and the legs from selected firewood. But the first prize for ingenuity must go to fourteen-year-old Clive Johnson, 'with his remarkable examples of taxidermy, with which he received no practical assistance whatsoever'. I am guessing that these were some kind of junior Frankenstein's monsters, for the ghoulish youth and his products were notably absent from the photographs of the winners. All of which brings us on to the fact that there was also a thriving do-it-yourself culture among a whole generation of youngsters.

Make, Do: DIY for the Young

In the days before the computer games console wove its insidious mind-rotting spell on the nation's youth, young people used to do things. They collected things (82,000 members of the train-spotters' club in 1952), spied on things (the 1950s I Spy Tribe boasted half a million members), joined organisations (there were over two million Scouts, Guides and the like at their peak); and they made things. As evidence for the latter, I draw your attention to a 1959 volume, snappily entitled *A Third Book of Hundreds of Things a Boy Can Make*. As the title implies, there were first and second books in the same series, not to mention three companion volumes of things for girls to make. If, despite these sterling efforts, a boy ran out of things to make, there were also *A Book of Things a Boy Can Do*, *One Hundred Harmless Scientific and Chemical Experiments for Boys* (though my recollection is that the word 'harmless' would instantly remove any interest they had for small boys) and the intriguingly titled *Fun for Boys and Girls* (about whose contents I could not possibly begin to speculate). In fact, the *Things…* series, which had its origins as far back as the 1920s, also offered companion volumes for 'little folk' (as distinct from boys and girls? Did they mean midgets?), housewives, handymen and people at war.

The first thing to strike you about this book is that it is refreshingly free from the icy grip of the health and safety brigade. Possibilities for death or injury jump out from every page. Taking the opportunities for a more lingering death first, there are instructions for making a range of smoking materials, from various kinds of ashtrays and a pipe-rack to a pipe itself (the latter requiring nothing more than a cherry tree that is surplus to requirements).

For the means to cause more immediate damage, any budding psychopath would be gratified by the range of weapons on offer in the book. In relation to his design for a catapult, the author tells us 'it is every boy's ambition to possess a sling and to practice with this until he has reached such a state of prowess that he is able to hit any target with his missile' – including, presumably one's small playground enemies? More terrifying still is the bow-and-arrow set, complete with murderous-looking steel-tipped arrows. The author's guidance on the use of these consists of just the three words 'and good hunting'. Scariest of all is the razor-blade knife – literally made by bolting a razor blade to some bits of plywood. In those days, making such things may have earned you marks towards your school certificate in woodwork. Today they are more likely to get you an ASBO.

But why put individual lives at risk when there are opportunities for wholesale loss of life? These come in the form of the river raft, what looked to my untutored eyes like a seriously rickety structure of five-gallon oil-drums, old planks and rope. Just in case the river current will not carry you over the weir quickly enough, the author encourages you to expedite the process by erecting mast and sails. He does at least advise the builder to make sure first that the oil-drums do not leak but, as for training in seamanship (or should that be pondsmanship?) his instructions are brief to the point of non-existence, not to say downright mysterious. He tells his reader, 'It only remains for you to run up a mast, hoist your petard and sail off.' According to my recollection, a petard is an explosive device of the kind used for blowing down the doors of besieged medieval castles. From this we get the expression 'hoist with his own petard', when the operator of such a device gets blown up, along with the castle door. What kind of demented vessel of war is the author creating, and did I miss the instructions for making a petard in volumes one and two?

After diligent searching, I did finally find one concession to health and safety. In the instructions for making a mains electric table lamp, the small boy is at least advised not to try making the bulb-holder himself.

Along with health and safety, another modern feature that is absent from this volume is political correctness. Nowhere is this more evident than in its choice of home-made fancy-dress outfits. According to our author, the golliwog outfit

> is a costume that comes under the heading of the humorous and the grotesque. It is made by blacking your face with burnt cork or using grease paint, leaving a broad rim of flesh around the mouth and the eyes. Cover the hair by sewing twelve-inch pieces of black wool on a tightly fitting beret or the crown of an old felt hat. Let the wool stick up all over and the effect will be most realistic.

Humorous? No. Grotesque? Most certainly. But I think the word that was missing, were you to wear such an outfit on the city streets today, is 'suicidal'.

One other thing that strikes you on reading this book is the low threshold of amusement that the boy of 1959 must have had. Today, if a child does not have access to the latest specification games console, it is virtually grounds for reporting the parents to the Cruelty Man. In 1959, the author thought the following worth mentioning under the heading 'tricks with paper': 'Another curious trick is to roll a sheet of notepaper into a circle and fasten it with a rubber band. You will then be able to place several books on top and they will be supported without any trouble, as illustrated.'

Then there is the trick caricature face. For this, you take a postcard and draw the rear part of a caricature head on it. Instead of drawing the front part, you attach a fine chain through strategically placed holes, roughly where the forehead and Adam's apple should be. The author explains, 'Now hold the card face upwards and gently jerk this in a horizontal position and the black chain will fall into the most realistic and lifelike attitudes. Every time you jerk the card, you will see a different caricature of the features. You will be able to have so much fun with this card and it will amuse your friends for many hours.' Many hours of fun? This is a definition of fun we have not come across before. I almost lost the will to live just writing it down.

Finally, we have evidence of how little the teenage popular music culture had apparently filtered down to the boys of 1959 (or possibly how out of touch with them our author was). Whereas modern youth would want nothing less than an exact replica of the guitar used by his favourite hit band, this earlier generation were being encouraged to make a cigar-box ukulele. 'All you need is a cigar-box, some wood, strings and pegs and a lot of patience.' Being tone deaf would also help when it came to listening to the results.

Looking further into the literature, some of them had more ambitious projects. *The Adventure Book for Boys* (1959) contained detailed instructions for mounting a manned expedition to Mars, though the need for a rocket the height of a twenty-four-storey building might have put something of a strain on the resources available in dad's shed. *The Scout Annual* (1960), alongside plans for building a canoe and tips on camping in winter, contained a rather alarming cookery section. This told you how to kill a horse and extract nutrition (the use of the word 'food' would be stretching the definition a little far) from just about every part except the tail. After butchering the more obviously edible parts, 'his skin, after having the hair scalded off, was boiled with his head and feet for many hours, chopped up small, and with the addition of a little saltpetre was served up as brawn'. The bones were first used to make soup and then ground up to adulterate flour. The horse would by then of course have no further need for its oats. The best part of these can then be used to make biscuits, but even the husks from the oatmeal could be soaked in water for many hours to form 'a paste akin to that used by bill-stickers. This was called sowens, a sour kind of mess, but very healthy and filling.'

These recipes had apparently been tested by none other than Colonel Baden-Powell himself, at the Boer War Siege of Mafeking, but they seem rather radical measures to teach a young post-war Scout, particularly given that rationing had been phased out by then. And just think how little sister would miss her pony; the brawn would be small consolation.

The Ultimate for DIY Youth: Meccano

> Puzzlingly, the British Library keeps its old Meccano handbooks in the notorious Cupboard, where pornography is stored. The only justification for this must be that Meccano undoubtedly inflamed the imagination of youth and set it coursing in fanciful channels.
>
> E. S. Turner, *An ABC of Nostalgia*

In days of yore, the enterprising young do-it-yourselfer, requiring (as one sometimes did) a dockyard crane, tank or suspension bridge, did not mess around with childish things like plastic interlocking bricks. He used proper engineering materials – girders, steel plates, nuts and bolts, flat trunnions (number 8) – the materials that made Britain great. He used Meccano. This construction kit boasted its ability 'to duplicate any and every movement known to mechanism', and there can scarcely be a mechanical object that has not been replicated in Meccano (plus a good many others that only ever existed in the fevered imaginations of their young inventors).

It was devised (in the finest British tradition) by a man with no formal background in engineering. Frank Hornby was a Liverpool shipping clerk, who apparently spent his formative years in his garden shed, searching for the secret of perpetual motion. He invented what he originally called *Mechanics Made Easy* in 1901, as a game to amuse his children, but by 1907 had patented the name Meccano and opened his first factory. It took off rapidly and, by 1920, there were factories in France and Germany also producing it. Devotees formed Meccano clubs throughout the world, which were united under the auspices of the Meccano Guild. This existed 'to foster clean-mindedness, truthfulness, ambition and initiative', for clearly it would not do to produce a scale model of a 0-6-0 tank locomotive while harbouring impure thoughts. The guild would organise events – including things not obviously related to Meccano, like cross-country runs and motto competitions (attracting entries along the lines of 'Live long, speak true, right wrongs and honour the king').

Meccano soon also built up an enthusiastic following among adults and was found to have practical applications in the real world. In the 1930s, Manchester University used Meccano to help build their differential analyser, a form of mechanical computer that was important to code breakers in the Second World War and which contributed to the university's pioneering post-war work on its electronic counterpart. During the war, officer selection boards for the Royal Electrical and Mechanical Engineers would confront candidates with a pile of Meccano and tell them to replicate a pre-built model. In post-war years, Meccano has been used in prototyping all sorts of projects, from the Austin Mini car to the London Eye and whatever devilish activities they get up to in the Atomic Weapons Research Establishment.

Like so many other talismanic parts of Britain, Meccano is no longer British-owned and made. Since 1959, the main manufacturing base has been in France and in 2000 it was bought out by a Japanese consortium.

Are We Having Fun Yet?

What is the attraction of DIY? An academic explains,

> Ambiguously positioned between work and leisure, it was associated with a cult of suburban family life that presented the home not just as an essentially feminine space, but also as a space protected from the alienating drudgery of corporate life, where men could engage in the construction of domesticity through suitably gendered practices. DIY, therefore, posited the home as a space of empowering self-regulated male work, creative freedom and constructive leisure.
>
> Viviana Narotzky, *Dream Homes and Do-it-Yourself*

I'm glad we cleared that up. While the aspiration of having an ideal home may bring you pleasure, how much fun is there to be had in the actual process of DIY or the contemplation of its results? I can only go on my own experience. You sit there at day's end, your hammer-blackened thumbs still throbbing and your palms raw from where you accidentally glued them to the coffee table. A gentle swishing noise causes you to look up and you watch the books gently sliding down the shelves that you erected at a jauntily asymmetrical angle on the wall. Your wife tries to hide the wreckage from the neighbours' derisive gaze by drawing the curtains, but the curtain track falls from the window, bringing both the curtains and the surrounding wallpaper down with it. Do-it-yourself may be driven by economic necessity, but fun? I don't think so.

8

Fun on the Rates:
Pomp, Pageantry & Official Fun

Received wisdom has it that big state occasions are something that Britain does best. If dressing up in funny uniforms and marching through the streets were an Olympic event, we would be in with every chance of a medal. (Admittedly, the North Koreans are also rather good at organising synchronised activities by its citizens on public occasions, but we would win marks for the more elaborate and comical nature of our dressing-up clothes.)

But what about when the occasion is something more than a state funeral or the opening of Parliament? What about when it is officially designated an occasion for the nation to let its hair down? How good is the state at organising official fun? We have had a number of occasions since the Second World War to find out.

There is one problem we encounter with official fun from the outset. Governments of all persuasions are loath to spend public money on anything as frivolous as fun, so some more serious pretext has to be found for it. It has to be educational, or promoting the national interest in some way. With the 2012 Olympics, the buzz word is 'legacy', the bricks and mortar, green space, new roads or other goodies that are left behind once the original event finishes. Whatever the pretext used to justify official fun, it generally tends to mean a diminution of the 'fun' part into something rather earnest and improving. It wags its finger at the onlooker and says 'see how all this fun is making you a better person' or 'this may look like fun, but there's a serious message behind it all'. At its worst, it can be as embarrassing as someone like Margaret Thatcher trying to insert jokes she does not quite understand into her party conference speeches.

The 1948 Olympic Games

> After all those dark days – the bombing, the killing, the starvation – the revival of the Olympics was as if the sun had come out … Suddenly there were no frontiers, no more barriers, just the people meeting together.
>
> Athlete Emil Zatopek

> The important thing in the Olympic Games is not winning but taking part. The essential thing in life is not conquering but fighting well.
>
> The message displayed on the Olympic scoreboard

It had been twelve years since the last, highly politicised, Olympic Games had taken place in Berlin. Tokyo had been nominated to host them in 1940 and London were asked in June 1939 to host them in 1944, but both venues had had other more pressing engagements to preoccupy them when the time came. The International Olympic Committee met again in 1946 and, at just two years' notice, asked London once again to host the Games in 1948.

Some were rather surprised at the choice, feeling that a bankrupt London could not stage a world sporting event. It was desperately short of housing, and rationing was at its fiercest. Some, like IOC member Avery Brundage (a less than perfect model for the Olympian ideal, who had been expensively bribed to support the 1940 Tokyo bid) had wanted the 1948 Games to go to Los Angeles, which had been able to flourish well away from the front-line. As he put it,

> London, half destroyed by bombs, will have a lot more important things to do than stage an athletics meeting.

But host them we did, and produced a Games that, perhaps more than any other of the post-war period, truly exemplified the Olympic spirit of amateur sportsmanship. It was certainly the most amateur Games. Naturally, there was no purpose-built accommodation for any of the events. Total budget for the entire event was just £650,000, of which nearly £200,000 went on installing a temporary cinder running track inside Wembley Stadium (the cinders were provided courtesy of the fireplaces of Leicester houscholds). Other venues were equally hand-to-mouth; the Olympic pool was a former ice-rink and early rounds of the football were staged at Green Pond Stadium at Walthamstow, home to mighty Walthamstow Avenue F.C. The cycling took place on the Victorian facility of the Herne Hill Velodrome. This had been used as a wartime barrage balloon site and its neglected weed-strewn track was only made usable courtesy of a new – if bumpy – bitumen surface, paid for by a private benefactor. When the cycling events overran one night, cars had to be driven into the stadium to illuminate the track with their headlamps, in the absence of any floodlights. The training base for the British athletics team was one of Mr Butlin's holiday camps (and the joy that the other campers must have had at shouting 'hi-de-hi!' at the pole vaulters can only be imagined).

A record 4,104 athletes from fifty-nine nations attended, though there were some notable absentees. Germany and Japan had not yet been allowed to rejoin the human race (though some left-over German prisoners-of-war had been used to help prepare some of the facilities). Russia and some other Eastern Bloc countries chose not to attend (their own competition – the Cold War – was just getting into full swing and its Blue Riband event, the blockade of Berlin, was nicely under way). One Communist country – Czechoslovakia – chose to come, but then had their gold medal-winning gymnast and President of the International Gymnastics Federation Marie Provaznikova refuse to return home, citing lack of freedom in the Soviet bloc. Some African nations also stayed away from the Imperialist heartland and an Arab boycott was only avoided when it was decided that the fledgling state of Israel was not yet a member of the IOC and therefore could not take part. No events were held on a Sunday, to respect the Christian Sabbath, but no such respect was afforded to Muslim athletes – the Games were even held during Ramadan.

> From what I can remember the opening ceremony was an absolute shambles. We were all late, rushing in, lining up there, higgledy piggledy.
>
>   Ron Cooper, 1948 Olympic boxing competitor

The opening ceremony, if shambolic, was simplicity itself by modern standards. Military bands played, there was a twenty-one-gun salute (apparently we still had twenty-one shells left over from the war), the athletes paraded and the Olympic flame was lit. After a few speeches, 2,500 pigeons were released, lightly pebble-dashing the competitors as they flew back to Trafalgar Square, and King George VI declared the games open. The closing ceremony was equally lavish, featuring as it did a limit of five shillings per head for the catering budget for official guests.

There was no purpose-built competitors' village for the participants at these Games. They were put up in war surplus army and prisoner-of-war camps, schools and colleges, even private houses and tented accommodation in Richmond Park. British athletes who lived anywhere near London were made to live at home. Athletes got a share of a locker, a mirror and a water bottle. They were all asked to bring their own towels (or had to hire them, if they forgot).

The very act of feeding the visiting athletes was pretty well beyond the capacity of the nation. Visitors were asked to bring their own food, and those countries that could afford to do so were asked to make donations towards the cost of feeding poorer ones. The Argentines brought in 100 tons of meat, Holland copious fruit and vegetables and Iceland frozen mutton. The British team had their diet supplemented by food parcels from Canada. British boxers got fit on a diet of custard and jelly, while other British competitors were given the treat of the occasional spoonful of glucose or, if feeling unwell, a shot of sherry and eggs. The British cycling team stayed in a private house, where they were nourished with an athlete's diet of spam fritters and toad-in-the-hole.

For those who relied entirely on British rations for their sustenance, they were at least given the concession of the same higher-calorie 'A-meal' diet allowed to those in the most physical occupations – miners or dock labourers – and free malt drinks to soothe them off to sleep. They also got two pints of liquid milk a day plus half a pound of sweets or chocolate per week. Even so, there were widespread complaints from competitors abut the catering; the Mexican team said the Mexican equivalent of 'to hell with it' and dined out every night. But at least British politicians were able to reassure restive voters at home that the Games had only added 'a totally insignificant' 0.16 of 1 per cent to domestic food consumption.

The female British athletes were expected to make their own uniforms, and the baggy shapeless items in which many of them turned out suggested that, whatever else they excelled at, it was not needlework. Strict instructions were nonetheless given to ensure decency, if not stylishness: 'Shorts should be of black material (sateen or similar) and the inside leg measurement should be at least four inches level across the bottom when worn.' Terry towelling was apparently favoured for the men's shorts in some quarters as 'it didn't slip'. All British competitors were, however, given a free pair of underpants without it affecting their amateur status.

There was not even any purpose-built equipment for the event. The gymnastic apparatus had to be borrowed from Switzerland and even the Union flag for the opening ceremony went missing. The nation's blushes were only spared by athlete Roger Bannister – attending the event as an official – obtaining a spare flag by breaking into a colleague's car boot. Even basic supplies like footballs, boxing gloves or basketballs were only bought on the understanding that they could be sold on later at cost.

There were television pictures of the events for those few (80,000 at one estimate) Britons who had a set. The BBC paid £1,000 for the broadcasting rights, but for most people, it was short-wave radio that carried news of the Games around the world. The games were not entirely technology-free; among the innovations making their debut in 1948 were starting blocks and the photo-finish camera (which was used to separate the gold and silver medals in the closely contested men's 100 metres). For those attending the games in person (including the athletes themselves) transport was in many cases provided by commandeered red London Transport buses or army lorries driven by female volunteers. Some of the buses were later stolen for joyriding by the athletes (no doubt crazed by taking the Horlicks tablets that were the nearest things the competitors of the day had to performance-enhancing drugs).

But drug abuse was much less on the British authorities' minds than preserving amateurism. Denis Watts, the British champion at what used to be called the hop-step-and-jump (the triple jump to you) was banned from competing on no better grounds than that he had applied for a job as a physical education teacher before the games. This attitude, which was not applied with equal strictness by other nations, and the no-doubt debilitating effect of living on British rations for years, may help to account for the fact that Britain's 375 athletes won only three gold medals and the country ended up twelfth in the medals table.

Despite the shambolic, hand-to-mouth nature of what they called the Austerity Games, they were judged to be a great success. They reassured the world that the Olympic ideal, which many feared had perished along with the millions of casualties of the Second World War, was well and truly alive and kicking (not to mention running and jumping). Perhaps most improbable of all, the 1948 Olympics actually made a profit. The final cost of the event was £732,268 and it made a profit of £29,420, on which tax totalling £9,000 was paid. Equally impressive, the greyhound track that had occupied the perimeter of the football pitch at Wembley stadium was back in action within two weeks of the closing ceremony. Now that's what I call legacy!

Has any officially organised piece of fun since then been equally successful?

The 1951 Festival of Britain

> Let us pray that by God's good grace the vast range of modern knowledge which is here shown may be turned from destructive to peaceful ends, so that all people, as the century goes on, may be lifted to greater happiness.
>
> From King George VI's opening speech for the Festival

> The whole design approached you with the fixed grin of the schoolmaster.
>
> One contemporary cynic's view of the Festival of Britain

In 1851, the Victorians held the Great Exhibition – a celebration of the fact that Britain was top nation. All our achievements – technological, industrial, artistic – were put on display in the Crystal Palace for the world to come and admire. Many of the more than 6 million who came to see it were British citizens, for many of whom the sheer novelty of travelling to London on the newfangled steam railway was excitement enough to last a lifetime.

Things were very different a century later. The nation was bankrupted and exhausted by a world war and demoralised by the five years of austerity that had unavoidably followed it. Rationing was, if anything, more severe than it had been during the war years and such consumer goods as we were able to manufacture disappeared tantalisingly overseas to prop up our ailing balance of trade. So the 1951 festival was less about showing off, and more about searching desperately for something to cheer us up – fun! The Foreign Secretary, Herbert Morrison, said it was 'Britain giving itself a pat on the back'. He elaborated on this in a speech at the Mansion House, but in doing so set the festival in a gloomy Cold War context:

The twilight war, the cold war which could go on for another ten or fifteen years [in which] you need something to keep the pride, the self-respect and the national virility of the British people vigorous and successful. If the Festival of Britain had not been thought of before that situation arose then we should have had to invent it.

Quoted in Hylton 1998, p. 12

A cheering thought, then, that the real purpose of the festival was to prepare an exhausted nation for the privations of another fifteen years of war, albeit undeclared. There was another motive – tourism. It was hoped that the festival would give overseas visitors a new excuse to visit a country that was in other respects so shabby and impoverished. A fleet of red double-decker buses was duly despatched to the Continent to drum up trade. But all hopes of getting American visitors to travel anywhere abroad vanished with the start of the Korean War.

The festival was intended to be a national celebration, but the centrepiece – and what most people remember of it today – was the exhibition built on the South Bank of the Thames in London. The area had suffered a lot of bomb damage during the war, though the festival also necessitated the demolition of an imposing early Victorian brewery. In its place was to go 'a gaily coloured scene given over to modern architecture at its most experimental and display technique at its most ingenious'. This task was assigned to a team of thirty or so architects under Hugh Casson, but not everybody was enamoured with the prospect. Speaking at the annual dinner of the Incorporated Association of Architects and Surveyors, Lord Strabolgi roundly condemned the standards of modern architecture in general and those of the festival in particular, and was only able to find consolation in the fact that most of the buildings would be pulled down as soon as the festival was over. Even more sweeping criticism came from the *Daily Express*, who regarded it as worthy, bureaucratic, dull and unaffordable at a time of national austerity, and from Winston Churchill, who saw the whole exercise as a complete waste of time, effort and money. As for the architecture, which those in the know described as International Modernism, Churchill (a man born in Blenheim Palace) thought it was the physical embodiment of Socialism.

The most striking features of the Festival site were

– the Skylon – a 292-foot steel and aluminium cigar pointing vertically into the sky. The joke of the festival was that, like the British economy, it had no visible means of support. In the finest traditions of British scholarship, it was climbed shortly before the opening by Philip Gurdon, a student from Birkbeck College, who wrapped a scarf around the top that some poor workman (whose name was not handed down to posterity) had to climb up and remove;

– a 365-foot diameter dome of discovery, the world's largest domed structure. This featured a series of galleries themed around discovery – including the living world, the sea and outer space.

– the Royal Festival Hall, the first major public building to be erected since the war and the one part of the festival site to survive in the long term. By 1988, it had become a Grade I listed building.

– the Telekinema – a 400-seat cinema showing such novelties as 3D films and large-screen televisions.

The management of the festival was allocated to what were described as 'progressive, public-spirited, high-minded "herbivores"'. Its Director General was Gerald Barry, sometime editor of the left-leaning *News Chronicle*. He had lobbied the then President of the Board of Trade,

Sir Stafford Cripps, to hold such a festival as early as 1945. Cripps was an austere Christian Marxist vegetarian, whose attitude towards fun may be reflected in the nickname given him by his enemies following a BBC announcer's famous spoonerism – Sir Stifford Crapps. Barry was almost as high-minded. He accepted that there was nothing wrong with 'some harmless jollification' but insisted that the festival's main purpose was serious: 'It is intended as an act of national reassessment. It will put on record the fact that we are a nation not only with a great past, but also a great future.' As far as their vision of the nation's great future was concerned, two of the industries featured most strongly in their parade of industrial strengths were coal-mining and shipbuilding.

By some measures, the festival was a success in these entertainment-starved years. 58 per cent of visitors were said to have had a favourable impression of the festival and there were 8.5 million of them in five months. However, numbers had to be boosted by the halving of evening admission prices, after early attendances were disappointing. The much less educational Festival Pleasure Gardens part of the celebrations, in Battersea, managed to attract a similar number of visitors without cutting its prices. It may also be the case that not all visitors were drawn to the festival by the educational exhibits, since it had earned a reputation as an easy place to pick up girls (it would appear that the education they were looking for was not quite the one the organisers had in mind). Due to some inexplicable oversight on the government's part, the festival even made a profit.

While the South Bank site was the main attraction, there were many other exhibitions. In addition to the Pleasure Gardens, there was a science exhibition at the Science Museum; a tented Land Travelling exhibition that went round the nation in a fleet of lorries, and a floating exhibition that toured coastal towns in a redundant aircraft carrier, HMS *Campania*. Glasgow housed the Exhibition of Power and Belfast the Festival of Farming.

Celebrations were staged by local authorities up and down the country, in response to an appeal from H. M. Government. Never let it be said that the British could not make their own entertainment, for who could forget the bonanza of fun laid on by the Knottingley Urban District Council? Their spectacle began with a parade of floats through flag-bedecked streets, led by the Knottingley Silver Prize Band and the fire brigade, to Howard's Field. There, in the presence of no less than three queens (the Festival Queen, the Road Safety Queen and the National Savings Queen) the crowds thrilled to a carnival featuring a tea buffet, fancy dress competition and a sports day that exposed the lack of variety of the aforementioned Olympics by including a sack race, skipping race, slow bicycle race and a three-legged race. But even this paled into insignificance beside the exhibition of local industries in the Town Hall. Here, the community were able to marvel at the variety of local entrepreneurship, ranging as it did from self-locking nuts, through not only ball- but also roller-bearings, glass containers, electric blankets, North Eastern Gas Board gas appliances, to the chemical by-products of tar. (Be still, my beating heart!)

Last and quite possibly least of the attractions in the capital itself was the Live Architecture exhibition, centred on a new public housing estate a free bus ride from the main Festival site. Despite having such unmissable attractions as the Building Research Pavilion and the Town Planning Pavilion, it managed to attract just 86,426 people over the course of the festival.

The Festival Guide Book anticipated its legacy as follows:

It will leave behind not just a record of what we have thought of ourselves in the year 1951 but, in a fair community founded where once there was a slum, in an avenue of trees or in some work of art, a reminder of what we have done to write this single adventurous year into our national and local history.

But they spoke too soon; Labour lost the general election in October 1951 and Churchill as the new Prime Minister was belatedly able to get his revenge on the hated project. There was a good deal of popular support for having the Skylon dismantled and relocated elsewhere. However, the cost of doing so was said to have been £30,000 so Churchill instead had it demolished and turned into ashtrays. Most of the other structures were also torn down.

The Coronation

The Queen's Coronation in June 1953 came with some impressive statistics. A procession almost 2 miles long, with 16,000 participants, took two hours to cover the 4.5-mile route. The number of horse-drawn coaches so far exceeded the number of professional carriage drivers that enthusiastic amateurs (from the right backgrounds, naturally) were pressed into liveried service as temporary Palace servants. Three million people lined the route, including more than 2,000 journalists and 500 photographers from 92 nations. 8,251 guests from 129 nations saw a Coronation lasting almost three hours.

This was ceremony on a grand scale, but was it fun? At the very least, it was a day off work, an excuse for a party and an important, if symbolic, step away from wartime austerity. For many of Her Majesty's subjects, at least part of the fun would have come from the novelty of watching the event on television for the first time – possibly seeing anything on the television for the first time. The BBC outside broadcast ran from 10.00 a.m. to 11.30 p.m., cost the unprecedented sum of £44,000 and used virtually every camera the Corporation possessed. It attracted an audience estimated at anything from 20 to 27 million people at a time when the nation only had about 2 million set owners. A further 11.7 million listened to it on the radio. In some respects the listeners and viewers had the best of it, for those watching from the London streets had to endure some of the worst June weather in living memory. There was rain, an icy wind and a temperature that never rose beyond 12 degrees. Loyal subjects planning to celebrate the event in Northumberland had it even worse, suffering 70 millimetres of rain and flooding. The British weather can usually be relied upon to ensure that no outdoor event suffers from an excess of fun.

One person who may not have been having too much fun under the heat of the television lights in the Abbey may have been the queen herself, given what a sovereign traditionally has to wear in the course of the ceremony. She was swaddled (at various stages) in

– a crimson surcoat;
– the Robe of State of Crimson Velvet – an ermine cape with a long crimson velvet train lined with
   further ermine and gold lace;
– an anointing gown;
– a Colobium sindonis, or shroud tunic;
– a supertunic – an ankle length tunic of gold silk;
– a Robe Royal or pallium regale – a four-square mantle lined in crimson silk;
– a Stole Royal or Armilla – a gold-embroidered and bejewelled scarf;

– a purple surcoat;
– the Imperial Robe of purple velvet.

Winston Churchill and other members of the establishment used the heat of the television lights as an argument against allowing events inside Westminster Abbey to be televised, and it took a determined stand by the young queen to override them all. In the event, the television cameras inside the Abbey were allotted such tiny spaces that the BBC had to select their smallest cameramen to operate them.

Peers and peeresses only ever got to wear their ceremonial robes for Coronations. This gave them an ideal opportunity to have fun by showing off and displaying minute differences in status between themselves and other ranks of the peerage. These are measured in terms of the number of rows of sealskin spots they are allowed to display on their robes, minute differences in the length of their trains and the width of the ermine edging on them, or the number of strawberry leaves or silver balls they have on their coronets. I kid you not; someone had to sit and work all this out.

But the fun was not confined to London. Up and down the country, worthies formed committees to determine how their community would mark the event. Loyal greetings by the van-load flooded into the palace, Coronation Queens were crowned and prizes awarded for the best-decorated street, house, vehicle or child. Decorated floats travelled in procession to recreation grounds. At Treeton, the procession doubled as an entertainment, providing a travelling stage as the Entertainments Committee took their offering to their less mobile citizens (who could not just walk away when they started). In Angmering, the tractor and trailer leading the way took a wrong turning and led the entire procession down a cul-de-sac. Their efforts to turn round in this confined space were later described as being worthy of an episode of *Dad's Army*.

On the nation's sports fields maypoles sprouted like weeds and commemorative trees and benches proliferated like maypoles. There were comedy football and cricket matches and comedy sports days. In Soham they had a ladies' donkey race, in which the comedy element was implied, rather than stated outright. Possibly related to this was the prize of 'a real live donkey', offered for one of the contests forming part of Soham's celebrations.

Teams of Boy Scouts shivered in the rain as they struggled to light their damp commemorative beacons. Children, whether Boy Scouts or not, were presented with Coronation mugs, spoons or free ice creams. In Ridgeway village, items that would be postponed in the event of rain were marked with an X in the programme. That included most of them, and most were indeed abandoned as it poured down all day. Back in Angmering, a series of dances and socials were organised, with separate events for teenagers (an early acknowledgement of their existence as a distinct species) and the over-sixties. It was not yet the era of rock and roll, and the teenagers had to make do with the same band that provided the entertainment at the event for normal human beings – the Accordionaires, a name which does not suggest that they were likely to 'have a maddening effect on a rhythm-loving age group' as the Bishop of Woolwich was later to put it. If it were possible to imagine such a thing, dancing of an even more uninhibited variety than the jive broke out at the Methodist Social Club Concert at Treeton. The Folie-des-ber-jeers, an all-male dance troop, 'proved quite a sensation' with their version of the Coronation Can-Can. Her Majesty surely would not have been amused.

In Reading, the imperial (sorry, Commonwealth) connections came to the fore, as people of all nationalities paraded to celebrate the Coronation. Among the more surprising recruits to the Commonwealth was a party from the Ukraine in full national dress. Given the Cold War, it was not thought that they took part with the blessing of the Russian Embassy.

The Millennium Dome

Even before it was built, the Millennium Dome was mired in controversy. As early as 1996, the dispute was well enough established for the Wonderbra lingerie company to run a campaign for their products with the caption 'not all domes lack public support'. However, no such doubt seemed to stalk the corridors of government in the late 1990s:

> A triumph of confidence over cynicism, boldness over blandness, excellence over mediocrity … Britain need not settle for second best. In the Dome we have a creation that, I believe, will truly be a beacon to the world.
>
> Tony Blair, Prime Minister

> If we can't make this work we are not much of a government.
>
> John Prescott, Deputy Prime Minister

There is an interesting family connection between the Festival of Britain (in which a large dome featured prominently) and the Millennium Dome itself. One of the leading lights behind the 1951 Festival was the Labour government Minister Herbert Morrison. When the Dome project was saved by an injection of public money (after the private sector wisely declined to have much to do with it) Tony Blair put Morrison's grandson, Peter Mandelson, in charge of it.

The design of the Dome was controversial but, as a structure, it was apparently quite something. It was not actually a dome; that would have been self-supporting, whereas this was made of bendy stuff, a bit like posh canvas, held up by poles and strings (all right, Teflon-coated glass fibre, suspended from a series of steel masts by high-strength steel cables – even so, it was still really the Millennium Tent). The basic structure was, we are told, surprisingly cheap (if you regard £43 million as cheap) for something that stood up to fifty metres high and enclosed 100,000 square metres of space. The roof weighed less than the volume of air it enclosed and the novel construction techniques saw it built under budget and within fifteen months.

Or so the architects who designed it tell us. As you can see from the preceding paragraph, they spoke very highly of the Dome. American architects thought different. A poll of them, organised by Forbes magazine, voted it the world's ugliest building (which, given the rich choice of competition fellow architects provide for this prize, is quite something).

Others thought its main shortcoming was not the building, so much as what they put in it. The space was divided into fourteen zones, and you begin to sense the pious, schoolmasterly tone from their list of titles:

Who We Are:
Body
Mind
Faith (apparently added following pressure from the Church of England)
Self-portrait

What We Do:
Work
Learning
Rest (which contained nothing – but very peacefully)
Play
Talk
Money (a highlight of which involved seeing what £1 million in £50 notes looked like – though to one of today's bankers, based in that area, it simply looks like a pay-cut)
Journey

Where We Live:
Shared Ground
Living Island
Home Planet

According to one critic, Iain Martin,

> This is the kind of 'experience' that post-modernist thinkers and designers think should replace old-fashioned museums that aim to impart knowledge. Their cousins in the state education industry have been pursuing a similar approach in schools for several decades with a catastrophic impact on standards and social mobility.

blogs.wsj.com/iainmartin/2010/08/27

Apart from anything else, the organisers did not seem to have thought through the logistics of visiting the dome. In addition to the fourteen main zones, there were two shows, a children's zone and a stage. This gave you about thirty minutes per zone to see everything – and eat – in the nine opening hours initially allocated to it, even assuming you were able to walk through the door the minute it opened. Even with the depleted numbers that turned up, there were queues at the most popular exhibits; had the projected 12 million visitors arrived, the queues would have been unbearable and the crowds very unhappy indeed. In the event, they managed to attract around 6.5 million visitors in twelve months, compared with the 8.5 million who visited the Festival of Britain in the five months when it was open.

In financial terms, the venture was also a dismal failure. According to the *Daily Mail*, the Dome ran out of cash within four weeks of opening, when the first instalment of the twelve million visitors failed to materialise, and went back to the Millennium Commission with the ultimatum, 'give us more Lottery money or we go into liquidation'. Despite the project hoovering up £628 million of lottery money (compared with the £399 million originally planned) it tottered on, semi-insolvent, throughout the year. It had thirty-four County Court judgements against it for non-payment of bills in July alone. These problems did not end with its closure. A government minister later complained that the vacant property was costing over £1 million a month to maintain. (£1 million a month – for a tent?)

The conclusion has to be that official bodies like governments are not much good at fun. Fun is not part of their core business. Governments are mainly there to make us miserable, until we can vote them out in order to allow the next lot to do the same.

So the hard questions have to be asked. Did the government learn nothing from the much more economical way King Ethelred the Unready chose to celebrate the last millennium (by trying to slaughter all the Danes in England)? Will future governments learn from the mistakes made at the turn of the second millennium, or can we expect another debacle in the year 3000? We shall have to wait and see.

The 2002 Queen's Golden Jubilee

The seventy-six-year-old Queen Elizabeth celebrated her Golden Jubilee with a positive whirlwind of activity. She travelled over 40,000 miles and visited fifty countries in thirty-eight days. Even where she was unable to attend, those parts of the world where the monarchy still held sway rejoiced in her absence. (Sorry: that should read: 'rejoiced, comma, in her absence'). It may also be that the countries celebrating – with or without her – were doing so precisely because the monarchy did not hold sway there any more. The first one she visited – Jamaica – was also marking the fortieth anniversary of its independence from Britain. Strangely enough, one of the countries where her reception was the warmest had been one of the first to gain its independence – in 1776. The Empire State Building was lit in royal purple and gold to mark her visit.

She was called upon to do some odd things in the course of her travels. Among her other claims to fame, she became the first monarch to drop the ceremonial first puck in a National Hockey League match, but took no further part in the match.

Even the queen could not be everywhere. Back at home, 40,000 'toolkits' for holding street parties which she could not attend were distributed. She was also absent when the British Antarctic Survey held their celebratory picnic and cricket match on the ice in temperatures of -20 degrees; nor could she light more than one of a chain of 2,006 beacons running not only the length and breadth of the United Kingdom, but also from 300 miles from the North Pole to 1,000 miles from the South Pole, adding to global warming.

Burke's Peerage, well known for its fearless campaigning for republicanism and equality, ensured it would be a People's Occasion by publishing *Her Majesty the Queen's Golden Jubilee: A Celebration*. It was marketed as, and I quote: 'a high-design, top-quality, limited edition, book created specifically for an exclusive hand-picked readership'. I would tell you what was in it, except that I would then have to kill you if you could not prove your direct descent from William the Conqueror. Having said this, I would venture to suggest (at the risk of my future prospects of entering the peerage for my services to literature) that *Burke's Peerage* then sacrificed the last shreds of their exclusivity when they volunteered to create a coat of arms for former President George W. Bush. Many a happy hour could be spent imagining what this might contain.

The Queen's Jubilee tour, while warmly received in some quarters, also acted as a lightning rod for protests around the world. In Jamaica, it was Rastafarians seeking reparations for slavery and their sponsored repatriation to Africa. In New Zealand and Canada, it was republican protests (led by the Prime Minister and deputy Prime Minister respectively of those countries, no less). Sections in Australia held the royal visitors responsible for child-abuse scandals in the Anglican Church.

At home, the occasion prompted the usual rash of street parties and community celebrations, but those of you who have read this far in the chapter will have no need of further description of how they go. If this occasion scores higher on some hypothetical 'funometer' than, say, the

Festival of Britain, it is only because the 'official' part of the agenda had much less detailed control over the agenda. All they provided was the pretext, and if your particular street party provided your idea of a perfect evening's entertainment, in the form of 'tarts and nuns' fancy dress, pork pie-eating contests, followed by wife-swapping, then the palace could claim no credit for it whatsoever.

Are We Having Fun Yet?

More immediately, as I write this, we are in the run-up to the 2012 London Olympics and are licking our wounds after the debacle of our bid to host the 2018 World Cup. We are also in the grip of a recession that, for many of those worst affected, borders on post-war austerity. Given that our greatest triumph of post-war official fun, the 1948 Olympics, emerged from similarly straitened circumstances, does this not suggest a model for the future?

Imagine a future World Cup, played not in expensively built or refurbished stadia. We have perfectly good parks and recreation grounds all over the country and, by this means, could allow even the smallest community to share in the excitement of the tournament. I well remember the rules from my youth; two piles of jumpers (sponsored by Marks and Spencer?) for the goalposts, throw-ins allowed to interrupt the flow of play only if the ball goes into next door's garden (saving on expensive linesmen) and, in the event of an irreconcilable dispute about whether an attempt on goal was in or out, the owner of the ball threatens to call full-time and take his ball home with him. As price of their admission, America could bring the half-time oranges with them from Florida – more savings!

What's not to like? It would be grass-roots and democratic – the People's World Cup; it reflects the British spirit of amateurism and improvisation; even we in our present parlous state could afford it and, best of all, as hosts it would always be our ball that we could threaten to take home, so we might stand a better chance of winning. I'm wasted here; I should be Minister for Official Fun.

9

Fun on the Never-Never: Shopping

Ladies are said, to go a Shoping, when, in the forenoon, sick of themselves, they order the coach, and driving from shop to shop, without the slightest intention of purchasing any thing, they pester the Tradesman, by requiring him to shew them his Goods, at a great expense of time and trouble.

Zackary Zeal, 1764

The awful prevalence of the vice of shopping among women is one of those signs of the times which lead the thoughtful patriot almost to despair of the future of our country. Few people have any idea of the extent to which our women are addicted to this purse-destroying vice.

New York Times, 1881

A vulgar world whose inhabitants have more money than is good for them ... a cockney tellyopia, a low-grade nirvana of subsidised houses, hire purchase extravagance, undisciplined children, gaudy domestic squalor and chips with everything.

The conservative journal *Crossbow* (1962), which clearly disapproved of the working class having fun

In perhaps a millennium or two, humanity will have evolved fully into homo shoppingtrolleyus, a lumbering beast on castors, with four stomachs, one loyalty card and a barcode across its forehead.

Will Self, *New Statesman*, 13 August 2010

Harking back into the past – as books about history tend to do – shopping used to be one of the great trials of everyday life. During the war years it mostly involved forming orderly queues. It did not matter too much what – if anything – was for sale at the front of it. People were known to enter queues without knowing what they were queuing for, secure in the belief that a healthy queue must mean that one or other of the many commodities that were in short supply at the time would lie at the other end. Things got no better in the immediate post-war years, when everything we produced had to go for export. In 1946 the Victoria and Albert Museum hosted a celebration of British craftsmanship under the title 'Britain can make it'. It was supposed to be a morale booster, giving people a foretaste of better things to come, but that cynical lot, the British public, rapidly re-named it the 'Britain can't have it' exhibition.

Our attitude to shopping has changed radically since those early post-war years. It has now allegedly become one of the nation's favourite leisure activities and something else at which we are in danger of leading the world. Figures released by the European Union in 2010 show that, while incomes per head in the United Kingdom are 12 per cent above the EU average, our consumption is 25 per cent higher, second only to Luxembourg (where there is presumably nothing else to do). What this also means is that the UK saves very little of the money it earns, runs high levels of household debt and a chronic balance of payments deficit. New models of retailing have nonetheless emerged over the years to satisfy our apparently limitless desire to consume. We examine a few of these in this chapter, and ask the question 'is shopping until we drop really fun?'

Some of us are allergic to shopping. Given the choice, I would dress like a scarecrow rather than venture into a department store to buy clothes. However if, sufficiently sedated and driven by cattle prods, I am navigated through their doors, my instinct is to try and buy the first item I come upon and get out (and heaven help me if the way to the menswear department is via ladies' underwear). Bear this in mind in the pages that follow; in all other parts of the book I am, of course, the voice of sanity that speaks for the nation. Here, my objectivity may sometimes slip.

As illustrated in the chapter on motoring, our opportunities to consume were heavily restricted in the austerity years that followed the war. We were deluded into thinking that we still had a role to perform (whether we could afford it or not) as world power and peace-keeper. This meant that something else had to give. As the Chancellor of the Exchequer of the day put it: 'we should strive to carry out as much as possible of the necessary sacrifices on current consumption, rather than to burden the future by any serious reduction in investment or the incurring of overseas debt'. What this meant was putting a brake on the creation of a healthy domestic market for consumer goods, such as television sets, radios, refrigerators and the like – in short, as Barnett put it,

> the very products that would constitute the fastest-growing world market of the near future; the market where Germany and Japan would successfully wage their new wars of conquest.
>
> Correlli Barnett, *The Verdict of Peace*

The Conservative government in 1953 eased income tax and purchase tax restrictions but the mantra 'export or die' still applied, and many white goods were either unobtainable or subject to long waiting lists. Others took the opposite view, arguing that a healthy home market would help stimulate home manufacturing and exports but, when they tried encouraging home consumption, it sucked in imports and worsened the balance of trade.

What was undeniable was that a potentially huge domestic market for household goods waited to be tapped. Take domestic laundry for example – fewer than 5 per cent of households had a washing machine in 1950, and a number of those that were on the market were still gas-powered, or had a manual wringer. The option of gas power was just as well for, although the great majority of households had electricity of some description, it was often a grossly inferior system, providing lighting only or just one or two sockets to serve the entire house. It was only in 1950 that regulations were introduced, requiring the fitting of a ring main and a standardised type of socket. For many, from the late 1950s onwards, an alternative to an arduous day devoted to the hand-washing of clothes existed in the form of the launderette. There you could not only get your washing done in a machine, but also catch up on all the neighbourhood gossip.

It is easy to forget how much drudgery was involved in housekeeping, in the days before modern household appliances became commonplace. This, from *101 Things for the Housewife to Do*, published in 1949, illustrates the point:

> The invention of the carpet sweeper followed by the vacuum cleaner has done away with the drudgery of hand sweeping, and the vacuum cleaner especially does the work most satisfactorily

without raising dust. It is now no longer necessary to cover furniture with dust cloths each time the carpet is swept.

Refrigerators were a luxury item, costing almost £100 for a model giving just four cubic feet of storage space. In 1956, just 8 per cent of households had a refrigerator, but the proportion rose to 65 per cent by 1969. Last and quite possibly least, the process had begun of the manufacturers creating new consumer goods we never realised we needed. In 1952, Sony began developing their first transistor radio, which they marketed from 1955 onwards.

The post-war emergence of the teenager also had a strong influence over the shape of the retail high street. Their growing level of disposable income was focussed particularly on specific segments of the retail market. In 1959, teenagers' share of total consumer spending was only around 5 per cent of the total, but they bought 20 per cent of the clothes and shoes, 17 per cent of the drinks and cigarettes, 15 per cent of the snacks, sweets and expenditure in cafés, a third of all cycles and motorcycles and 40 per cent of records and record players.

Fun on the Never-Never

It was under the Conservative governments of the 1950s that the brakes on consumption gradually began to be eased off (and then put on again; and then taken off again; and so on). Increasingly, it no longer seemed to matter if your ambitions were bigger than your wallet. Before the Second World War, buying on hire purchase was considered a very working-class affair; the middle classes could afford to save up for whatever consumer durables they wanted. Things were different after the war, and a large emerging lower-middle class (what *The Times* referred to as 'the artisan and clerical classes') found they had enough of a weekly surplus in their income to commit themselves to regular hire-purchase repayments. By 1953, it was estimated that hire purchase accounted for three quarters of all furniture sales (a market worth around £125 million in 1951), at least half of all television and radio sales, and a quarter of all new motorcycles were also bought on hire purchase. This in turn gave the government of the day a useful means of controlling the consumer part of the economy.

Some called it 'live now, pay later'. Strangely enough, the 'live now' part tended to come to the fore just before the general elections of 1955, 1959 and 1963, with the 'pay later' sting in the tail only emerging after their re-election. For example in February 1952, shortly after the Conservatives' return to power in 1951, a sudden need was discovered to limit to supply of consumer goods for domestic consumption to about two thirds of those made available in 1951. This the government did by increasing the minimum deposit required on goods bought on hire purchase to between 25 per cent and 33 per cent of the total cost, and limiting the repayment periods allowed to between twelve and eighteen months, depending on the goods involved. Come 1954, and the run-up to the general election of May 1955, the government felt a sudden urge to relax the controls again.

Low repayment fun was back, and the list of goods to which the relaxations applied serves as a summary of the popular aspirations of the day: radios, televisions, gramophones, refrigerators, vacuum cleaners, cars, motor cycles and pedal cycles. If any of these were your idea of fun, it became easier than ever to afford them. For a while the new rules were unclear, and there were fears that an unregulated 'no deposit' competition would break out, leading to an unsustainable boom in consumer demand. It did not materialise, but the record level of, for example, hire-purchase funded car sales was enough to force the government to tighten hire-purchase controls again in February 1955, which was shortly before the general election and therefore quite contrary to normal policy.

Once they had safely navigated the general election, the government reverted to type and, by February 1956, you had to be able to put down a full 50 per cent of the price of a car in order to buy the rest of it on hire purchase. Hire purchase companies cunningly got round this crippling requirement by 'lending' their customers the 50 per cent deposit as a separate loan, until the government spotted and outlawed the arrangement. Then world politics, in the form of Colonel Nasser and the Suez Crisis, intervened. The closure of the Suez Canal and the consequent reintroduction of petrol rationing led to a catastrophic drop in car sales, and the government was forced in December 1956 to drop the minimum deposit on a car to 20 per cent of its cost in order to save the motor industry.

Not that concerns about the state of the economy troubled the British consumer. The relaxation of hire purchase controls in August 1954 led to an 8 per cent increase in consumer spending the following year. Spending on consumer durables like televisions and refrigerators leapt by 10 per cent; demand outstripped supply and there were waiting lists of three months for electrical goods, four for furniture and a whole year for cars. In the 1950s as a whole, consumption per head rose by 20 per cent. In just two years, between 1957 and 1959, car ownership rose by 25 per cent, televisions were up 32 per cent, washing machines 54 per cent and refrigerators by 58 per cent. House purchases also hit a record level in 1960, with 326,125 mortgages being taken out.

But the impact of hire purchase paled into insignificance compared with the form of retail credit that was to follow. The credit card had its origins in 1920s America, when the major petrol companies introduced charge accounts for their customers. Railway companies, airlines, hotel chains, department stores and many other services got in on the act, and many a more affluent and mobile American was soon carrying a substantial burden of individual charge cards around with him. From this came the idea of giving trustworthy individuals cards that could be used at a wide range of different outlets. And who were some of the first 'trustworthy' people in Britain to benefit from this arrangement?

In 1966, a northern chain of stores announced a scheme for giving credit cards to young people aged seventeen to twenty-one (twenty-one then being the age of majority). Young people could apply for a credit card allowing them to spend up to £30 in-store and repay it at a rate of one shilling plus interest a week for every pound they owed. If this sounds like high-risk commerce, the card holder had to provide a guarantor (usually a parent) which may explain why the default rate on the pilot scheme compared favourably with their mainstream charge card. However, a director of the store company saw another reason for this. He told *The Times*, 'My experience has been that a youngster getting his first credit account is tremendously proud of it and the status it confers. Because of this, he is quite determined not to let himself down.' His faith in the values of the 1960s teenager (and I speak as one) is truly touching.

But even at that time, there was still doubt about whether the credit card system would ever catch on. The City editor of *The Times* greeted the arrival of the Barclaycard in the following cautious terms:

> The credit card habit has not yet caught on in Britain, but there is evidence that it may do so. It is sensible for British institutions to try to obtain at least part of the market …

The schemes may fail. In the early days of their association hire-purchase business caused some of the banks heavy losses – a total of £10 million has been suggested. Personal loans, too, led to quite a number of bad debts. They may not be able to find enough hotels, shops, and other firms willing to accept the cards. Not enough people may want to use them. But in theory at least credit cards do offer a valuable service to people who otherwise, whether at home or travelling, need to carry an uncomfortably large amount of money about with them.

The Times, 19 January 1966

But the big question remains unanswered – is shopping fun? Let me put it another way:

Shopping: Illness or Crime?

Its like the better moments of sex. Everything else is blocked out of your mind. Its pure selfish pleasure.

Sophie Kinsella, *The Secret Dreamworld of a Shopaholic* (2000)

Shopping is like sex for men, too. They can only manage it for five minutes and then they get tired.

Jeff Green

While some claim that shopping gives them a pleasure that is positively sensual, there can be little doubt that the desire to shop – when it seriously exceeds the available funds – is a major source of crime. Or illness. Or both. Researchers at Stanford University found that almost as many men as women suffered from something called compulsive buying disorder, which led in the worst cases to huge debts, concealing one's purchases from one's partner, bankruptcy, divorce, embezzlement and even suicide. One of the better-known victims of this disorder was Viv Nicholson, who led a modest life as a Yorkshire miner's wife until she won £152,300 on the football pools in 1961. Asked what she was going to do with this very large sum, she famously replied, 'Spend, spend, spend!' Sure enough, she worked her way through the entire sum in short order, during the course of which her husband was killed in a crash in an expensive and powerful car. The *Daily Mail* caught up with her in 2007. Now aged seventy-one, she was applying for jobs from the two-up two-down house around the corner from where she was born, in order to supplement her meagre £87 a week state pension. In addition to the pools win, she had also managed to blow £100,000 worth of royalties from the book, BBC play and stage musical of her life – a story which included five husbands, alcoholism, a spell in a mental institution and suicide attempts. But that's the sort of thing that happens if you let your shopping get out of hand.

As for shopping-related crime, statistics show that shoplifting is yet another dubious area in which Britain is a world leader. We have a shoplifting theft every minute and only the United States and Japan can surpass the £4.8 billion worth of goods stolen in this country to the year to June 2009. The statisticians also found that more women were imprisoned for shoplifting (or 'five finger discounts', as the practice is also known) than for any other offence. A third of all females jailed in 2002 were shoplifters, and not even a spell inside cured most of them – eight out of ten re-offended within two years of their release. So prevalent is it that some boutique owners even use it as a reliable guide to what are going to be the hottest-selling lines. It also tends to be a particularly middle-class crime – in one particularly sad case, Lady Isabel Barnett, a well-known radio and television personality of the 1950s and 60s, was exposed in

1980 as a compulsive shoplifter, and two days later took her own life. Even less in financial need was the film star Winona Ryder, who was a compulsive shoplifter despite being able at one time to command £5 million a film. Much of what she stole she gave away, in a classic sequence of binge and purge that some have likened to bulimia.

So no points for fun, at least so far as these most dedicated of shoppers are concerned.

Self-Service

Self-service is perhaps the single biggest change to have affected British retailing since the war. The very idea of self-service started life as a patent. In 1917, one Clarence Saunders presented himself at the US Patent Office with his idea of a 'self-serving store'. (I say 'his idea' – over in California, the Gerrard brothers were already using it in their Alpha Beta chain of stores.) Nonetheless Saunders secured the rights to it, and then licensed the method to independent grocery stores, which traded under the immortal brand-name of 'Piggly Wiggly'.

The self-service concept introduced many important changes to retailing. Every item in a self-service store originally had to be pre-packaged (admittedly, the first stores only had 605 separate items for sale). Pre-packaging greatly increased the importance of brand recognition and, with a chain of stores that soon went nationwide, that meant nationwide advertising – so in an indirect sense, the self-service concept helped to pay for the floating of commercial television. They also introduced refrigerated displays, uniformed staff (so that customers knew who would be able to direct them to the frozen peas) and the just-in-time method of stock control, which was then adopted by the Toyota car company and subsequently by just about every major manufacturing concern.

But it was not until after the Second World War that the idea took off in Britain. It was estimated that the entire country boasted just ten self-service shops in 1947. There were serious doubts at the time as to whether the idea would catch on at all; in that same year, the trade journal *The Grocer* expressed the view that 'the people of this country have long been accustomed to counter service, and it is doubtful whether they would be content to wander round a store hunting for goods'. Even as late as 1955, the first national conference on self-service methods in the sale of food was being told by many of its delegates that 'self-service shops are becoming so streamlined, so clinically efficient that there is a danger of customers staying away because they miss the social side of shopping'. But they would be proved wrong; in 1950, some fifty self-service stores were trading in Britain. The first full-sized supermarket in the UK opened in Streatham, London in 1951 and the number grew inexorably to 572 by 1961.

Over half of these were owned by three chains – Premier, Victor Value and Fine Fare. But a brash newcomer was close on their tail. Jack Cohen was an East End barrow boy who had launched his own brand of tea under the name of Tesco in 1924. He had gone from barrow to shop by 1929 and in 1956 opened his first self-service supermarket. By the end of the first decade of the new millennium, the company would have over 1,780 more outlets, and would be taking £1 of every £3 the British spent on groceries. In 1964, Resale Price Maintenance (the arrangement by which manufacturers and their distributors could force retailers to sell their goods at a specific price) came to an end, enabling the big chains to use their buying power to cut prices to the public. Even then, there were still those who believed the idea would never catch on. Dorothy Davis wrote in 1966, attempts to copy the discount store in this country met with fierce opposition for many years from the interests favouring resale price maintenance ... And there are other reasons – lack of space, for example – why thorough-going self-service methods will not progress nearly so far or so fast in Britain.

A History of Shopping, p. 296

Her scepticism was not borne out. The supermarket boom gained further impetus, with an estimated 3,400 trading by 1969. In the early years, the concept of self-service shopping still needed to be explained to the bewildered consumer, as this local newspaper report from 1951 shows:

Recent months have seen the changeover of half a dozen of the town's stores to self-service methods and the latest development is the opening of a self-service tea bar. Almost without exception, the new style of shopping has pleased both customers and storekeepers and there has been remarkably little reluctance to accept the experiment.

   The basis of the new method is 'visual appeal' – a sound piece of 'sales psychology' now applied to every phase of advertising and selling. If a woman sees an article she is more likely to buy it than if she has to ask for it. Self-service means that the housewife walks into a spacious shop, takes a basket and wanders past tiers of goods uniformly displayed, with everything clearly marked. She finds the things she originally wanted and is given a reminder of others as her eye is caught. Finally, an assistant checks her purchases and she transfers them to her own basket.

   One local shopkeeper reports a three-fold increase in turnover and felt that the new method would become universal, since salesmanship was a dying art among retail staff.

Quoted in Hylton 1997, p. 17

Five years later, and the same town had the excitement of its very own American-style supermarket:

This gleaming contemporary store, with its huge plate-glass windows, yards of refrigerated display and stacks of brightly coloured groceries, brings new convenience and ease to household buying ... The supermarket is not merely a new kind of grocery. It aims to cut out numbers of trips to separate shops and provide under one roof the widest possible variety of goods. Here is a long counter of fresh vegetables and fruit, the vegetables washed and everything pre-packed in transparent paper with the price and weight already marked ... The shopper will have a wheeled double-decker basket to push around the store. Seven checkouts will cut down waste of time in paying for goods and wrapping them ... In addition, there will be something you will probably be surprised to see – nylons. Yes, nylon stockings and at astonishingly low price and high quality. These always sell very well at American supermarkets.

Ibid., pp. 76–7

Even so, many stores – including multiples like Liptons and Home and Colonial – continued with traditional methods of retailing, hoping (in vain) that personal service over the counter would triumph over the cheaper prices of the supermarket. But although the self-service store was presented as a benefit to the customer – with claims that it did away with having to wait to be served (instead, you had to queue at the checkout) the real driving force behind them was a hard-nosed calculation on the part of the retailer. They rightly judged that the increased likelihood of shoplifting would be more than offset by the savings to be had from employing fewer staff.

These early newspaper accounts of supermarket self-service shopping would have you believe that we had all died and gone to consumer heaven. Since then, though, we have found plenty to complain about in the supermarket model of trading – and complain we do, albeit while continuing to visit their stores in droves. Prepare to engage rant-mode, as we learn from their detractors that supermarkets are responsible for all the ills of our modern society (at least, all those that are not caused by television or fast food – see the chapters on those subjects).

They are to blame for wiping out our local shopping facilities and town centres alike, by driving the independent competition out of business. Far from being creators of jobs, they are claimed to be net destroyers of employment, as their small rivals are forced to shed staff and close down. They are accused of driving farmers to the brink of bankruptcy, by forcing the prices paid to them down to starvation levels. By this means, they have destroyed the British countryside, since only the biggest and most mechanised farms can survive, leading to problems of monoculture and destruction of the landscape, as hedgerows are grubbed up to create single fields comprising entire counties, which can in turn make room for combine harvesters the size of aircraft carriers.

They have limited the choice of fruit and vegetables available to us by abandoning flavoursome, if sometimes less beautiful-looking, varieties for blander ones with a superficially more attractive appearance and a longer shelf-life, in a sort of vegetable Miss World competition. We are told the National Fruit Collection boasts some 2,300 varieties of apple, and are asked how many you will find in your local supermarket? And how many of them will be British? (Come to think of it, who would actually want a supermarket with 2,300 varieties of British apple?) They are also claimed to favour foreign producers over local ones, partly because foreign wages tend to be lower, but also because the foreign competition cuts its costs by reducing standards of animal welfare, so add torturing innocent animals by proxy to the list.

They also add to global warming by flying and trucking in all-year-round strawberries and asparagus from the four corners of the earth. Global warming is further accelerated by their habit of building their hideous giant sheds out-of-town, where only the motorist can access them. And that's another thing – they cause dreadful traffic congestion for us all (as we are trying to drive to the supermarket). Because their business model increases air pollution, it follows that supermarkets are responsible for the growth in childhood asthma and other respiratory diseases. While on the subject of pollution of one kind or another, the self-service business model depends upon large and unnecessary amounts of packaging, much of which we can only burn or landfill, poisoning the air we breathe and our water supply, so put the supermarkets down as being to blame for the eventual death of the planet by pollution while you are at it.

Then there are complaints about all sorts of other evil practices – they are turning us into a nation of alcoholics by constantly plying us with cheap alcohol; getting our kids to pester us to death and themselves into early obesity by artfully stocking low shelves full of must-have consumer goods for tiny tots at the checkouts. There are even claims that supermarkets inflate costs by demanding slotting fees from suppliers – large sums of money charged for the allocation of premium shelf-space to their products. And don't get me started on matters such as mind control and invasion of privacy! The industry invests millions into understanding the psychology of persuasion, so that these dens of iniquity can use their lighting, packaging, product placement and other subtle blandishments to reduce us to their obedient slaves, wandering zombie-like up and down the aisles and filling trolleys the size of a skip with stuff we do not need. For a pittance in rewards, their loyalty cards give them details of our consumption of alcohol and unhealthy foods that many of us would not be prepared to confide to our employers or GPs. Yes, the supermarkets are evil and must be destroyed! (Thank you, nurse, I've taken the medication and I feel much better now.)

You think I exaggerate? See what chef and organic food guru Hugh Fearnley-Whitingstall has to say on the effects of supermarkets:

> This is costing us our landscape, this is costing us our food culture, this is changing the quality of the land we walk on, potentially even the quality of the air that we breathe. I mean, this is big stuff.
>
> *Planning Daily*, 22 December 2010

Small wonder then that the nirvana of self-service shopping, as it was seen in the 1950s, has faded into distant memory. Who could enjoy themselves in a supermarket, burdened with the knowledge of all they are responsible for? Of course, all of this is the fault of the supermarkets. None of this has anything to do with us – the car-driving, wine-swigging, strawberry-chewing, gala apple-guzzling, Tesco share-owning, supermarket-shopping, customer-is-king public. Between 2008 and 2010 the local authorities up and down the country that we elect have been granting planning permissions for new supermarkets at the rate of one per working day.

Since the 1990s the supermarkets have found an entirely new way of tormenting us, again driven by hard-nosed financial considerations. Instead of employing one whole person to staff a single check-out aisle, they can put one employee in charge of several self-service machines, where the customers do the work of the check-out staff. The next logical step in the evolution of self-service must surely be to get us slaughtering and plucking our own chickens.

This is how they work. Each of these self-service machines contains within it a Dalek (I may not be absolutely correct on the technology but you will understand the principle) which, rather than trying to exterminate you with death-rays, attempts to murder you by means of heart attacks bought on by rage and frustration. It starts from the moment you arrive at the check-out and try to be environmentally friendly by putting your own re-usable shopping bag down on it. 'Unexpected item in the bagging area,' it shouts in alarm, causing your fellow customers to look around for whoever is trying to shoplift items. Try and scan that bottle of wine and it bellows 'Approval needed'. Cue for other customers to see if you are now trying to buy Class A drugs or exotic sexual paraphernalia only available from under the pharmacist's counter.

If you are extremely lucky, there will eventually be an assistant on hand to reactivate the machine and you will finally reach the point of settling the bill. 'Insert cash or touch pay with card,' it demands. Before you have had time to find purse or wallet, it is repeating its demand, as if to imply that you are a bad credit risk, and the faster you shovel money into its gaping maw, the more frequent and insistent its demands for money seem to become. If you are lucky, you will simply leave the store feeling incompetent and humiliated. If you are not, you will be arrested by the store detective and taken to the torture chamber at the back of the store that they reserve for shoplifters.

It was forecast that, by 2011, there would be some 15,000 self-service tills in use in Britain, and Tesco has already opened its first entirely self-service store. The shop-workers' union USDAW reports that self-service till rage now accounts for a rising proportion of the 22,000 cases of physical assaults on shop staff each year.

Self-service tills were by no means the first example of technology seeking 'to enhance our shopping pleasure' (as the industry would no doubt have put it). For the past half century new ideas for automating shopping have been coming forward at regular intervals. In May 1961 the Self Service Development Association were telling us that the vending machine was the future of shopping. Their Automatic Vending Exhibition in London had machines that would dispense you anything from six eggs to a bag of sugar; from a 28-pound sack of coal to the distinctly unappetising prospect of a pre-cooked full English breakfast that only required reheating. The shopper of tomorrow, we were told, would be able to meet their every need from these silent sentinels any time of day or night, without even having to enter the store. The Steel Company of Wales took the principle one step further, and tried providing machines dispensing hot snacks in the workers' canteens. The result was a strike by the canteen staff, and serve the company right.

As early as 1969, telecommunications experts (as computer geeks then called themselves) were forecasting a future of home banking and shopping, using computers, but a rather more unusual attempt at automated self-service shopping using computers came even earlier. In 1965 a Wallasey supermarket demonstrated the prototype of a new method of shopping, using the punched card technology of the day. The shopper was to be led into a display of all the goods on offer in the supermarket. Instead of selecting the actual goods themselves, they would take punched cards from a supply kept below the particular display item they wanted. When they had completed their choices, they were to feed their stack of cards through a tabulator, which calculated their bill and took their payment. Meanwhile, their order was relayed electronically to a busy team of elves behind the scenes, who assembled and bagged the shopping and delivered it to a long counter. Many advantages were claimed for the system; it was said to save on time and space; it did away with the laborious business of pricing items individually in the days before bar codes; it ended shoplifting and gave the retailer instant sales information.

But its flaws were rather more fundamental. Shoppers found it a bewildering way of choosing groceries and, perhaps more importantly, small boys found that it was great fun to cause havoc by swapping the punched cards around, so that the can of baked beans that you ordered would be supplied in the form of a 28-pound bag of coal. Aspects of this way of shopping would eventually find their way into the Argos business model but, as a means of revolutionising supermarket shopping, it was doomed.

In 1967, Heals began using a computer to help their customers choose suitable Christmas gifts for that awkward relative. All you had to do was to enter their personal details (under age, for example, you could specify anything from 'less than 4' to 'grandparent'), the amount you wished to spend on them and other relevant details, and the computer would direct you to the perfect gift from their range. In that same year, Tesco went in for a rather more insidious form of technological aid. They spent £300,000 equipping a hundred of their stores with televisions, through which they bombarded their customers with a constant stream of advertisements. The scheme was a guaranteed money-maker for them, in that they more than recouped its cost by selling the advertising space in their stores to the manufacturers of the goods being promoted.

All of which talk of technology brings us naturally enough on to:

E-Commerce

You sit there in your pyjamas, click a few buttons with your wee mouse, and a few days later a wonderful thrilling parcel arrives. There is such a special delight in opening a parcel, tearing through the cardboard, feeling like you've got a fabulous, perfect present from someone who knows you really well, which in fact you have ... Hell being other people, you don't get a mood like that from schlepping up and down Oxford Street on a Saturday afternoon.

India Knight, *The Shops* (2003)

With e-commerce, shopping has come full circle. In the very earliest days of retailing, those who could afford to do so also ordered those goods that they did not grow or make for themselves from the comfort of their own homes. Only instead of doing so via the internet, they sent their domestic servants out to buy them.

Mail order, e-commerce's older brother, dates back to the eighteenth century. Benjamin Franklin launched a company selling scientific and academic books in 1744, promising that 'those persons who live remote, by sending their orders and money to B. Franklin may depend upon the same justice as if present'. The idea had particular appeal in the far-flung corners of the United States; and by the 1880s, some of the big names in mail order, such as Sears and Montgomery Ward, had been established. You could buy a surprisingly wide variety of goods by this means (including fish – not something you would want to get delayed in the post). In immediately post-war Britain, mail order shopping tended to be regarded as something rather working class and, worse still, characteristic of the Midlands and north of England. In 1950, mail order was thought to account for some £50 million of retail sales, a figure which rose to an estimated £150 million by 1958. But in 1967 it was reported that shopping by post had risen by 84 per cent over the period 1961–66, compared with a rise of just 25 per cent in all retail sales over the same period. A significant part of this rise was apparently due to mail order going upmarket, with increased patronage from the southern middle classes, being attracted by more nationally branded goods of higher quality (some of them costing in excess of £100!).

The model for much of this retailing was not pure mail order, but was conducted through a large network of local agents. Many of these were established customers of the company, an army of largely middle-aged ladies who cross-subsidised their purchases by showing their mail order catalogues to friends and neighbours. They collected commission on their sales and went around gathering up the weekly payments from their customers.

The appeal of mail order is easy to understand in the far-flung territories of the Americas, but more puzzling was the fact that the great majority of British mail order customers lived within easy reach of shops selling substantially the same range of goods. More puzzling still was the willingness of so many people to buy things like shoes and corsets by mail order, without first trying them on. Lack of time among working women was one suggestion for it, but another was that they feared the rudeness and condescension of 'superior' shop assistants.

Since the invention of the internet, mail order via e-commerce has become huge business and Britain is Europe's most active market. It is claimed that 21.8 million of us visited the internet daily in 2007 and that we spent the highest average time on it (34.4 hours – that's nearly a day and a half – a month). Small wonder that the internet has now collared around 20 per cent of the UK's total advertising spend – £3.35 billion in 2008.

E-commerce does not necessarily benefit the UK economy. E-companies can be based in countries with more generous VAT regimes, can avoid the cost of providing expensive high street retail outlets (which would provide local employment). They do not even have to print large numbers of mail order catalogues, and can thereby undercut their rivals. But one of its attractions is that it seems as if almost anything can now be bought by this means. When I googled 'mail order', one of the options I was offered was 'mail order brides'. Dimly recalling from my youth that the pre-electronic version of mail order brides – what we quaintly called 'courting' – was something that we used to classify as fun, I decided it would be relevant to follow it up.

I should perhaps start by saying that the companies concerned hotly reject the label of 'mail order brides' – they will tell you that they are reputable agencies, facilitating introductions between people of different nations and adding to the sum of human happiness (and no doubt fostering world peace at the same time). So let us have no sniggering, and accept that their motives are as pure as the descriptions of themselves provided by their clients are accurate.

There are apparently between 100,000 and 150,000 overseas women who advertise themselves on these websites, and ladies from Thailand and Russia seem to predominate. You can forget the traditional jokes about Russian mail order brides ('must have own tractor; send photograph of tractor'). If the pictures in the advertisements are to be believed, most of them are beautiful beyond the specifications of Hollywood. How they can spend time placing such advertisements when it must be a full-time task fighting off the hordes of local admirers with a stick is beyond me. This made it all the more alarming to discover that there is a counterpart market in mail order husbands from the USA and Britain. It was not so much the fact of its existence that was alarming, as what was on offer and the striking asymmetry between the two markets. The websites with pictures of the would-be husbands that I looked at must have been a spoof (please tell me they were a spoof, for they were a parade of grotesques such as any Victorian fairground would have been proud to exhibit). The accompanying texts, with which they hoped to win the hearts of a soul-mate, only made matters worse:

> I'm definitely a classic romantic. I like a candlelight dinner, some quiet background music and a couple hits of ether.
> I'm lonely, how about you? I live in a crappy basement apartment and I'm hoping to go somewhere warm and sunny. If you have money and you aren't in Canada please e-mail me.
> Ever drank paint thinner? Don't! Trust me, it's a bad idea.
> I won't be available for about eighteen months… (but) …I'm up for parole next month.
> I keep in shape by chasing chickens around my backyard. I keep myself clean and take baths weekly.

As a spoof it is brilliant. My only worry is that there might be someone out there who is lonely and desperate enough to take it seriously. All we can conclude from this is that half of those taking part in any such arrangement would not be having much fun.

But dissatisfaction with your mail order spouse may be the least of your online shopping problems. Apparently some three million people fall victim to online scams each year, losing an average of £850 a time. By no means are all of these people who are stupid enough to believe that a former Nigerian general has chosen them at random to be their accomplice in smuggling £10 million out of his country; the scams are many, varied and sometimes quite sophisticated. There are fake lotteries and prize draws, miracle health cures, get-rich-quick investments and forged or simply non-existent tickets for sporting events and entertainments. (Which reminds me: can I interest anyone in some of my valuable shares in 1916 Russian Imperial War Loans? Further details from my website www.oneborneveryminute.com.) Over and above the outright frauds, there are all sorts of other problems with getting satisfaction from a company with whom you have had no physical contact, and who may be located beyond the grasp of British or even European law (always assuming you can even find their postal address). Internet shopping can be anything but fun, if you pick the wrong retailer.

Are We Having Fun Yet?

So what have we learned in our brief journey through the shopping habits of post-war Britain? We found that shopping can cause high levels of debt for the individual household and balance of payments crises for the nation. It can lead to deceit, divorce, alcoholism, embezzlement and suicide. For their part, the big supermarkets have brought about the destruction of the British landscape and the decline of our traditional town centres, the encouragement of lower, foreign standards of animal husbandry, chronic traffic congestion, global warming, poisoning the air, leading to the eventual death of the planet. When I started writing this chapter, I was worried that my personal dislike of shopping might have affected my judgement, but I am pleased to see that I have been able to maintain a balanced perspective on things.

Notwithstanding its dangers, it seems that the internet could be the future of shopping. You may or may not share the views of India Knight, quoted earlier, about the almost erotic pleasure of opening a parcel, compared with the hell of fighting your way along a crowded shopping street. But you are more likely to be interested in the discounts the mail order business model can provide and the almost infinite variety of offers available over the internet – have you ever tried going into Harrods and asking for a Russian bride? So even if some of you are currently having fun shopping, it may not be around long in its high street form for you to enjoy, given the competition the internet offers.

Its salvation may lie in the social dimension of shopping. From the earliest days, shopping was about more than just the exchange of money for goods. The medieval housewife would also exchange news, banter and gossip with the street vendor or market stall-holder. Today, it is said that the charity shops similarly offer a refuge for the impoverished and lonely. When a growing, and increasingly affluent, middle class made the department store a financially viable proposition in the nineteenth century, they deliberately set out to create an ambience that was aspirational – rather brighter and better than their customers' homes. Gordon Selfridge said that his department store was aiming for 'the subdued and disciplined atmosphere of a gentleman's mansion'. He went on, 'This is not a shop – it's a community centre.'

The same principle may hold true for the future, as Elaine Showalter suggests:

> If shopping is going to continue to be a pleasure in the age of the web, it's going to have to offer both men and women a lot more in the way of real comfort and psychological intangibles. It will have to be hooked up to a status and aesthetic aspiration in a way that pleases even those who disapprove of mere consumerism and detest marketing.
>
> The future of shopping, I think, will belong to the places that provide a social service as well as a product ... For women in the twenty-first century, shopping is going to be about belonging to a club.
>
> *Prada Queen* (2000)

For those who like that sort of thing, this may prove to be just the sort of thing that they like. But don't talk to me about shopping fun.

10

Bad Fun. Stop it!: Censorship

Is sex dirty? Only if it's done right.

Woody Allen

Prostitution gives her an opportunity to meet people. It provides fresh air and wholesome exercise, and it keeps her out of trouble.

Joseph Heller

Zeus performed acts with swans and heifers that would debar him from every London club except the Garrick or possibly the Naval and Military.

Stephen Fry

Fun can get out of hand, at which time the question of banning it arises; and if there's one thing that certain sections of the British establishment like, it is banning things. Not that they are particularly good at it; the history of censorship in Britain may be a long one but it has not always been honourable or spectacularly successful. In this chapter we look at the various attempts to control what the various media could say or show. Over the years, this has covered violence, religion, the satirising of politics and the royal family but, most of all, sex in all its rich (and sometimes excessively rich) variety.

It may be worth saying (before I get put on someone's black list) that I am not arguing here for any particular position vis-à-vis what we might neutrally call 'explicit' material. I simply want to show two things. One is the way standards have changed so radically in our lifetimes; before 1961, the selling of *Lady Chatterley's Lover* would have brought the full weight of the law down upon you. By the mid-1980s, the book was to be found on school literature syllabuses, and over the years it has been made into any number of films, television dramas, stage plays and radio programmes. As I observed in my book *Magical History Tour*, all that seems to be missing is the pop-up book. My other theme for this chapter concerns the awful mess the authorities can get themselves into when they try to draw the line between fun and filth. The bad news, reader, is that this involves me dipping my layman's toe into the law relating to obscenity, but the good news is that it is often ludicrous enough to be entertaining. Bear with me.

Censorship in the Theatre

This area of censorship has one of the longest-established track records, so we will start with a short history lesson. A host of officials and others (including the Bishop of London) have at one time or another been responsible for regulating stage productions and from 1581, the duty rested with the delightfully named Master of the Revels. Originally his role was quite a narrow one, of ensuring that any play that the monarch was going to see would be suitable for him or her. This relatively light-touch quality control gradually developed into something wider. The approval of the Master of the Revels told theatre companies and players alike that a production was unlikely to give rise to offence (or litigation). But the spectre of stronger legislation was already waiting in the wings; from the early seventeenth century, the Puritans pushed for legislation banning, for example, the improper use of the 'Holy Name of God'.

Far stricter control was to come with the Licensing Act of 1737, prompted among other things by the conflict between author/political satirist/theatre manager Henry Fielding and the government of Sir Robert Walpole. This act had the effect of closing down unlicensed theatres like Fielding's but, more importantly, it gave a senior court official, the Lord Chamberlain, more or less unlimited power to censor any theatrical production he wished. He fitted this in between his other duties, which included organising state ceremonies, carrying a white staff and wearing a gold or jewelled key, escorting the sovereign to and from his carriage, announcing the names of those approaching the throne, not to mention the arrangement of the sovereign's bedchamber (so a keen appreciation of the arts was clearly an essential prerequisite for the job). Before 1782, he even fitted in being a cabinet minister among his other duties.

The 1737 legislation had the unintended consequence of confusing the statutory powers conferred by the act with the royal prerogative, which the Lord Chamberlain exercised on the king's behalf. This meant that, throughout the nineteenth century, anyone opposing censorship ran the risk of being associated with those dreadful Republican Jacobins in France, who had deposed their monarchy and (as it happened) also abolished theatrical censorship.

This did not stop a long and (sometimes) distinguished line of opponents to censorship speaking up. One of the first was Samuel Johnson, whose savage 'vindication' of the censors expressed 'concern' that 'the task of censorship might place too onerous a burden on government officials already hard-pressed with the work of bribery and corruption'. Johnson's proposal was that the government should abandon half measures and institute a method to prevent the British people from voicing any opinion whatsoever. He suggested that the government should consider simply closing schools and banning the teaching of reading and writing. But the power of the Lord Chamberlain was such that additional layers of self-censorship developed. Pre-censorship involved theatre managers sending scripts for informal clearance before formally submitting them for a licence, and there was even pre-pre-censorship, whereby playwrights would seek guidance on the suitability of certain subject matter before even starting to write.

Although the original motivation of the legislation was the suppression of political satire, its focus soon shifted to obscenity. Edward Piggott, who discharged the responsibilities of the Lord Chamberlain for censorship in 1883, explained its purpose: 'No one acquainted with ancient or modern history of dramatic art will deny that it has always been prone to excesses from which it could only be preserved by an independent and disinterested authority.' He spoke of playwrights who wish to enjoy 'an unrestricted licence in their importation of obscenity', not to mention 'needy and unscrupulous managers' and 'theatrical speculators and parasites who would willingly degrade the one and the other by turning theatres into disorderly houses if not houses of ill-fame'. George Bernard Shaw was to fall foul of this crusade with his play *Mrs Warren's Profession* (1898) – the profession in question being the oldest one – manager of a chain of brothels on the Continent.

Shaw led one of the many attempts to get the legislation changed, in 1909, but the Lord Chamberlain's powers were still intact half a century later. By this time, his views were getting increasingly out of line with the changing climate of public opinion, which the theatre naturally reflected. Some of the decisions emerging from the Lord Chamberlain's office began to look positively bizarre. In one, he banned the stage performance of a sketch in which a commentator describes the outfits being worn by the royal family, as the royal barge sinks beneath the waves. The problem was that the sketch had already been broadcast on the television show *That Was The Week That Was* and seen by millions, with no evidence of any outbreaks of militant republicanism as a result. Spike Milligan's play *The Bed Sitting Room* contained a spoof advertisement for the washing powder Daz 'getting all the dirt off the tail of your shirt'. This was changed by the Lord Chamberlain (for reasons only he could begin to explain) to '... off the *front* of your shirt'.

But even the Lord Chamberlain could not entirely resist the sea-change in public opinion. After the Wolfenden report was published in 1957, the Lord Chamberlain decided to make changes to the way they allowed homosexuality to be depicted on stage (the previous approach had been basically 'not at all' – even something as minor as a reference to Walt Whitman's *Leaves of Grass* in John Osborne's play *Personal Enemy* was red-pencilled as a closet reference to homosexuality). Under his new, more 'liberal' guidance, he wrote to his staff: 'For some time the subject of homosexuality has been so widely debated, written about, that it is no longer justifiable to continue the strict exclusion of this subject from the stage.' However, 'licences will continue to be refused for plays which are exploitations of the subject'. Same-sex embraces continued to be forbidden, as was any play considered to be 'violently' pro-homosexuality (what constituted 'violently' was left unexplained). In terms of language, he decreed that they would allow the word 'pansy' but not the word 'bugger' (an earlier attempt at gritty kitchen sink drama had been somewhat hamstrung by the deletion of every use of the word 'bloody' from the script).

Nowhere was the conflict between the real world and the Lord Chamberlain more apparent than in the case of the Royal Court Theatre. This was founded in 1956 with the aim of bringing forward innovative new work. The founder, George Devine, wanted to discover 'hard-hitting uncompromising writers' who would challenge the artistic, social and political orthodoxy of the day and push at the boundaries. It was a mission that put it in regular conflict with the Lord Chamberlain throughout the 1960s, with three of its proposed plays being banned entirely (*A Patriot for Me* by John Osborne and Edward Bond's *Saved* and *Early Morning*). In the case of *Saved*, this was staged at the Royal Court under the attempted loophole of it trying to pass itself off as a private 'club', leading to them being prosecuted in 1965.

The 1968 repeal of the Lord Chamberlain's powers was achieved despite the opposition of the queen and the then Lord Chamberlain (whose position was the same as that of preceding monarchs and Lord Chamberlains). Aligned with them was Prime Minister Harold Wilson and also commercial theatre operators, who still saw censorship as a useful antidote to vexatious prosecution. The very day after the repeal, the hippy musical *Hair* opened, featuring mass nudity, drug-taking, draft-dodging, opposition to the Vietnam War (then in full swing) and the desecration of the American flag – all things guaranteed to endear it to the traditional theatre-goers of middle England. It nonetheless ran for five years and 1,997 performances, and its audiences included members of the royal family.

Despite the repeal, unofficial attempts at censorship (sometimes through the use of violence) continue to threaten the theatre. A Birmingham-based production of *Behzti* was forced to close in 2004 when the theatre in which it was staged suffered violent attacks, and *Jerry Springer: the Opera* also suffered protests from an evangelical group, Christian Voice.

Obscene? Indecent? Or is it Art?

Back in the mists of time, obscenity was a matter for ecclesiastical law. The first prosecution under the Common Law was not until 1727, when one Edmund Curll was charged with disturbing the king's peace with his publication *Venus in the Cloister or the Nun in Her Smock*. But the prosecution of such misdemeanours proved difficult to mount and in 1857 the first Obscene Publications Act created a statutory offence. This act, known as Lord Campbell's Act after the Lord Chief Justice who promoted it, gave the courts powers to seize and destroy material. It was a very controversial piece of legislation even then, and was only passed on the understanding that it was 'intended to apply exclusively to works written for the single purpose of corrupting the morals of youth and of a nature calculated to shock the common feelings of decency in any well-regulated mind'. That is to say, there was a test applying to the motives of the person who created the material.

The act left the matter of what constituted obscenity to the courts, and it was a case about a decade later that sowed the seeds of a century or so of confusion. *R. v. Hicklin* (1868) concerned the prosecution of one Henry Scott for the publication of an anti-Catholic work called *The Confessional Unmasked* (Benjamin Hicklin was a London magistrate who was mixed up in the case somewhere). Scott was convicted; then the conviction was overturned in a higher court on the grounds that his intention had been innocent, but this decision was in turn overruled in a still higher court, which decided that the intention was immaterial if the publication was in fact obscene.

From this case arose a definition of 'obscene' from Sir Alexander Cockburn, who by this time had succeeded Lord Campbell as Lord Chief Justice. He ruled that the test was 'whether the tendency of the matter charged as obscenity is to deprave and corrupt those whose minds are open to such immoral influences and into whose hands a publication of this sort might fall'. So the test of motive was abandoned and instead there was a judgement to be made, as to whether the kind of people who were likely to read the article concerned were likely to be corrupted and depraved. But who would be the benchmark for reaching such a judgement? Certainly not the wealthy and influential people who helped determine the case, who felt that they were above any possibility of corruption and depravity from such material.

Other shortcomings were to emerge from the Hicklin ruling. A publication could be judged obscene by looking at individual passages from it, rather than at the publication as a whole. A public good defence (arguing that the work had artistic merit) was inadmissible, and material could be destroyed without the author or publisher being given an opportunity to speak in its defence (or even knowing that it was happening).

Over the next century, many works would suffer at the hands of this legislation (perhaps the most famous being James Joyce's *Ulysses* in 1922). By the 1950s, the Society of Authors began to mount a concerted campaign to reform the legislation. They submitted a draft bill to the Home Office in February 1955, but several failed attempts followed until the very liberal (at that point in his career with a small L) Home Secretary, Roy Jenkins encouraged the creation of a viable piece of legislation – a new Obscene Publications Act – which came into force in August 1959.

This gave us a new definition of obscenity. Under the 1959 act an item is obscene if the entire article 'is, if taken as a whole, such as to tend to deprave and corrupt persons who are likely, having regard to all relevant circumstances, to read, see or hear the matter contained or embodied in it'. So there were a number of differences here. First, the work had to be looked at as a whole. You could not just pick out the rude bits and complain about them. Then the new test related to 'persons', not just an individual, who were likely to see it, so a significant number of them needed to be put at risk. The problem once again was, who were the 'persons who were likely … to read, see or hear the matter contained … in it'? Take the case of paedophile material, for example; the most likely audience for it was surely going to be paedophiles, and if they were not already corrupted and depraved before looking at it, then who was? Were they seriously suggesting that large numbers of the general public were going to stumble upon such material and, having viewed it, think 'I might try a bit of that'?

That almost seemed to be the case being made by Lord Wilberforce in the case of *DPP* v. *Whyte* (1972), when he argued that 'the Obscene Publications Act equally protects the less innocent from further corruption, the addict from feeding or increasing his corruption'. So it seemed the fear was that the potential user of this material might wake up one morning and say, 'I'm feeling a bit depraved this morning. I think I'll just go and read some porn and see if it tips me over the edge.'

Other changes to the new law were less ambiguous. It introduced the concept of innocent dissemination. In this, it was a defence if you could prove that you did not anticipate obscenity problems, and did not examine the article in question for such issues. As we shall see, this was to become particularly important in relation to the new media. Slightly more murky, in all sorts of ways, was the defence of 'public good'. This involved proving with the help of expert testimony that the work was 'in the interests of science, literature, art or learning, or of other objects of general concern'. This was to be important in the first major test case for the new act, but it rapidly fell into disuse, at least as far as written material was concerned. By the time it came to the trial for *Inside Linda Lovelace* (1976), a work which to my recollection was never on anyone's shortlist for the Nobel Prize for literature, the judge concluded in his summing up to the jury, 'If this isn't obscene, members of the jury, you may think that nothing is obscene.' The jury still found the defendant not guilty.

Then we have the perennial problem of working out what the words in the law actually mean. What, for example, is meant by 'to corrupt and deprave'? In a judgement in the House of Lords in 1972 (in a case concerning the delightfully named publication *Dingle Dangle No. 3*) Lord Wilberforce complained that the statute did not even explain whether the concern was that the material would cause people to commit wicked acts, or whether the mischief is simply that erotic desires may be aroused. Courts have subsequently held that even erotic desires may be enough to establish obscenity. But, in another judgement, the House of Lords ruled that 'to corrupt' was a very strong word indeed, meaning much more than just leading someone morally astray.

And what counts as 'obscene'? Here, the law has two conflicting definitions. The first, used in the Obscene Publications Act and the Theatres Act of 1968, has its origins in the Hicklin judgement, and relates to some kind of deviation from contemporary community moral standards (which presupposes that common standards exist, or could be agreed). The term is not exclusively reserved for sexual matters (it has been used in relation to drug-taking and violence unrelated to sex), but in its sexual context is almost exclusively reserved for deviant sexual behaviour (involving things like animals, children, violence or extreme humiliation). Certainly, juries almost never convict in cases involving sex between consenting adults. However, this does not stop magistrates using the same law to seize and seek the destruction of material on which they would never secure a conviction from a jury.

But other legislation (like the Post Office Act 1953) has another definition of 'obscene'. This one relies on a dictionary definition, using words like 'shocking', 'lewd' and 'indecent'. So, under this act, material that some hypothetical 'reasonable person' would find shocking and disgusting would be 'obscene'. However, shock and disgust can also be a *defence* against being found obscene in the terms of the Obscene Publications Act. After all, if you find something shocking and disgusting, you are hardly likely to be corrupted and depraved by it, are you?

Then we have the separate category of 'indecency', which appears to be a slightly milder-mannered version of obscenity, covering 'anything which an ordinary decent man or woman would find to be shocking, disgusting or revolting'. All clear so far? If so, can you please explain it to the judges?

Given the confusion about what the law says, it is perhaps no surprise to learn that you don't even need a law in order to prosecute someone for offences against the public morals. Back in 1962 a Mr Shaw published something called *The Ladies' Directory*, a work of reference giving the names, contact details and what one coy legal commentator described as the 'specialised talents' of London prostitutes. He was prosecuted for conspiracy to corrupt the public morals, but appealed his conviction on the not unreasonable grounds that no such offence existed on the statute book. It does not matter, a higher court ruled. According to the judge, Shaw's actions were clearly dangerous to the welfare of society and the courts have a duty to protect public morals. Just because common law has no particular law against such immoral acts, it does not mean that the courts cannot enforce their own decisions.

Lady Chatterley

Perhaps still the most famous (or notorious, depending upon your viewpoint) obscenity trial under the 1959 Act concerned D. H. Lawrence's book *Lady Chatterley's Lover*. This had been banned from sale in Britain ever since its appearance in 1928. It was, however, legal to buy it (and mail order it) from America. I summarised the plot in an earlier book as follows:

> The book concerns the relationship between Lady Chatterley and the family's gamekeeper, Mellors. When Lady Chatterley's husband returns from the First World War, paralysed from the waist down and generally in less than full working order in the marital bliss department, Mellors takes on what the expurgated version might have referred to as 'certain other duties around the estate'. The book is a frank and explicit account of their passionate relationship, with all sorts of allegorical overtones about the class system.
>
> Hylton 2000, pp. 18–19

In August 1961 the paperback publisher Penguin decided to take advantage of the 1959 act to publish an unexpurgated version of the novel in Britain. It was a prime example of the kind of book Roy Jenkins had hoped to see protected by the public interest part of the new act; Lawrence was an established author of serious purpose, and his novel clearly had aspirations well beyond mere titillation. Before it was even published in the normally understood sense of the word, Scotland Yard requested copies, and it was when Penguin supplied them that the book was deemed to have been published, and was immediately prosecuted. (This practice was later deemed to be illegal, on the intriguing grounds that members of the Vice Squad were less prone to being corrupted and depraved, due to their regular exposure to such material.)

Penguin very quickly lined up no less than seventy-one witnesses willing to speak for the literary merit of the book, including many of the literary great and good and, representing God, the Bishop of Woolwich and the Catholic barrister and Member of Parliament Norman St John Stevas. Stevas was also the author of *Obscenity and the Law* (and as such a man who knew a thing or two about mucky books). He urged all Catholics, including priests, to read the book, since its aim was to rid sexual activity of false shame.

For their part, the prosecution could find nobody of note to speak against the book. Their secret weapon was their prosecuting counsel, Mr Mervyn Griffith-Jones QC. He was a Welsh Nonconformist who was to be found prosecuting many of the most famous trials of the 1960s, especially those involving any kind of sex scandal. He it was who earned an eternal place in the halls of ridicule by asking the jury at the trial whether this was a book they would want their wife or servants to read. This illustrated one of the unspoken themes of the trial – the paternalism of the establishment in trying to protect (or prevent) the unwashed masses from being exposed to material that most of the upper classes (though perhaps not Griffith-Jones himself) would have felt perfectly content to read within their own circle. Penguin were planning to publish a paperback book costing 3s 6d and aimed at a mass market. Would the prosecution have taken place had it been a luxury, limited edition, collectors' version of the book?

As the trial proceeded, Griffith-Jones' case seemed to become more and more detached from the law, not to mention reality. He ignored the legal requirement to look at the book as a whole by carrying out micro-analysis of individual passages, to see how many times words like 'bowels' or 'womb' appeared on the page. At one point, he sought to argue that Lawrence's misquotation from the Book of Psalms undermined his integrity as an author. He conducted character assassinations of both Lawrence himself and, more bizarrely, his fictional creation, Lady Chatterley, and he questioned the ability of the mass audience to appreciate the allegorical overtones of the book:

> I submit to you that the tendency of that passage can only be to raise impure and lustful thoughts in the minds of some, indeed many, who will read this book.

The jury may have had views about the murky processes that were going on in Mr Griffith-Jones' own mind during his conduct of the case. Failing that, they may have agreed with him, and simply wished to see impure and lustful thoughts made more freely available to their fellows. In either event, it took them just three hours to return a verdict of 'not guilty'. Not for the last time, the court case gave the publishers the kind of publicity that no amount of money could buy. The first edition of 200,000 copies sold out on the first day and total sales went on to exceed 4 million.

A decade later, another famous obscenity trial took place. This time, the literary merits of the work were most decidedly not at the heart of the case. *Oz* magazine was an underground publication designed to challenge 'the older generation's outdated beliefs and standards of behaviour and morality'. In one edition it said 'the statement of our values is dope, rock 'n' roll and fucking in the streets', which may lead one to wonder how many of the older generation would even have got as far as buying it in order to be challenged by it. In 1971, in response to criticism that they were losing touch with youth, the magazine invited a panel of twenty teenagers to edit the so-called 'schoolkids' edition'. Those who worried about young people living in ignorance of matters sexual should have been heartened by the result, featuring as it did a comprehensive tour of carnal knowledge, taking in homosexuality, lesbianism, sadism and (less conventional and rather scary) a sex scene involving the cartoon character Rupert Bear and 'a gypsy granny' (in case you are wondering what nursery trauma was being relived there, it appears the effect was achieved by a fifteen-year-old pasting the head of Rupert Bear onto an existing X-rated cartoon by the underground artist Robert Crumb).

In a sinister twist to the case, the defendants were not simply charged with publishing an obscene item (the penalty for which was limited to a £100 fine or six months' imprisonment). Instead, the archaic charge of conspiracy to pervert the course of public morals was once again wheeled out, offering the court the scope for unlimited fines and anything up to life imprisonment. This time, the great and the good who were trotted out in support of the defence were more the aristocracy of the counter-culture, including as they did artist and drug activist Caroline Coon, crooner George Melly, disc jockey John Peel and comedian Marty Feldman (who managed to endear himself to the judge by calling him 'a boring old fart'). Nor did the defendants necessarily help their case, by appearing before the court dressed as schoolgirls.

After the longest obscenity trial in history, the defendants were found guilty and sentenced to up to fifteen months' hard labour. But what seemed to cause even greater public outrage than the verdict and sentence was the decision of the prison authorities to shave off their hippy hair, something which the *New Law Journal* called 'a monstrous violation of an individual's personal integrity'. The sentences (if not the haircuts) were later overturned by the Court of Appeal, after they found fourteen errors of law and innumerable errors of fact in the original judge's summing up to the jury. In addition, the head of Scotland Yard's Obscene Publications Squad, who had played a leading role in the prosecution, himself later ended up behind bars, after being found guilty on corruption charges.

Lady Chatterley's Lover escaped censorship in part on its literary merits. But, from 1993, writers could not only be published while writing incompetently about sex, they could win awards for it. It was in that year that Auberon Waugh, then editor of the *Literary Review*, initiated the magazine's 'Bad Sex Awards': their purpose was 'to draw attention to the crude, tasteless, often perfunctory use of redundant passages of sexual description in the modern novel, and to discourage it'. The shortlists in subsequent years have read like great and the good of the literary world, including winners of the Booker and Whitbread prizes and the Prix Goncourt, and those receiving the reward seem to treat it with almost as much reverence as those major prizes. Norman Mailer won the prize posthumously in 2007 and John Updike won a Lifetime's Achievement Award after four consecutive shortlists.

Cinema and Censorship

The first piece of British legislation to affect the industry, the 1909 Cinematograph Act, was mainly aimed at the safety of cinemas, but it also gave local authorities powers to censor films. This power was first used by the London County Council in 1910, unexpectedly to prevent the showing of a boxing match in which a black man, Jack Johnson, so forgot his place that he beat a white man, James J. Jeffries, to win the world heavyweight championship. The industry was appalled at the prospect of 688 local authorities all exercising their own arbitrary and variously demented standards over films and in 1912 founded the British Board of Film Censors (BBFC) as an alternative voluntary body, trying to bring at least uniform regulation to the industry.

They took as their cue the policies employed by the Lord Chancellor's office in vetting stage plays, but they applied the rules much more strictly. The reason for this was that the cinema was considered a more working-class medium and, well, you wouldn't want your servants to be given unsuitable ideas, would you? The board was quite open about this in an early pamphlet, *Censorship in Britain*. They adhered to

> the broad principle that nothing will be passed which is calculated to demoralise the public ... Consideration has to be given to the impression made on the average audience which includes a not inconsiderable proportion of people of immature judgement.

The board's decisions were binding on the industry, and most local authorities also abided by them, but the councils did retain powers to apply their own standards and from time to time have exercised that right. Mostly this was in relation to individual controversial presentations but, in 1932, Beckenham Council opened its own censor's office and began merrily cutting and banning left, right and centre. They were soon forced to abandon this in the face of protesting local cinema owners, who saw their takings plummet, and local cinema-goers, who voted with their feet and went in droves into the neighbouring boroughs to see the more interesting films at their cinemas.

At first, the board had only two classifications – U for Universal and A for Adult (over sixteen), and two absolute prohibitions – no nudity and no depictions of Jesus Christ. This list of prohibitions rapidly grew to forty-three. Most were a minute specification of the board's quaint views on sexual propriety, but quite a number looked like the board trying to ensure that the (working-class) audiences did not come away from the cinema with subversive ideas. There were bans on anything criticising the monarchy, the government, the church, the police, the judiciary and friendly foreign governments. This last was used in 1933 to ban films denouncing the treatment of the Jews in Nazi Germany, which the board described as 'pure anti-Hitler propaganda' (which of course would have been most unsporting). There was also to be no depiction of current controversial issues, such as strikes, pacifism or the rise of fascism in Britain. Even many films tackling social issues from unimpeachably moral standpoints – opposing white slavery or drugs, and informing the public of the effects of abortion or venereal disease, also found themselves banned. In such a climate, it was amazing that any pre-war film-maker would even ask about filming D. H. Lawrence's *Lady Chatterley's Lover*, but someone did (the answer was an emphatic 'no').

Sometimes ingenious film-makers could try to get round these bans by using historical costume dramas as a parable. In the case of the anti-Nazi problem, they did so by telling the story of Jewish persecution by Germans in eighteenth-century Württemberg. But even historical material could be too direct. A 1938 film about the Indian Mutiny, *The Relief of Lucknow*, was banned as being unhelpful at a time when the British government was trying to resolve delicate constitutional matters with the Indians. Likewise a film about 'Hanging' Judge Jeffreys was banned (as if his extreme seventeenth-century attitudes were going to bring the twentieth-century judiciary into disrepute – no, sorry, that's a bad example).

The government has always maintained the fiction that the BBFC was independent of them. In practice, the fact that the Home Office was always closely consulted on the appointment of the President of the Board ensured that the appointee was 'sound'. One such, Edward Shortt, a former Liberal MP, made no secret of his moral mission:

There is in our hands as citizens, an instrument to mould the minds of the young, to mould the minds of the adolescent and create great and good and noble citizens for the future.

1933 Conference speech

In the 1930s, a new phenomenon arrived from America to torment the board – the horror film. The president railed against them in his 1935 Annual Report:

I cannot believe that such films are wholesome, pandering as they do to the love of the morbid and the horrible.

But, morbid and horrible as they were, they were very popular and the board finally compromised by introducing a new classification – H for Horrific. This survived until replaced by the new X certificate in 1951. The U, A and X classifications in turn survived until 1982, when they were replaced by the current U, PG, 15, 18 and (for the naughty private licensed cinemas) R18 classifications.

The advent of the talkies presented yet another new threat to working-class morality – words! From the 1930s, the board operated a voluntary (but strongly recommended) prior vetting of scripts. They were very hot on the toning down of language and repeatedly struck out such words as: (readers of a nervous disposition should skip to the next paragraph now, before I unleash this torrent of filth) 'nuts, bum, lousy, gigolo, belly, bawdy, prostitute, nymphomaniac' and, strangest of all, 'nappy'.

But during the Second World War, the board (who had ceded many of its powers to the government for the duration) daringly allowed even the words 'bloody' and 'bastard' to be used, but only if describing Nazis. Winston Churchill tried to interfere in the censorship of films during the war, most famously in his attempt to ban the wartime classic *The Life and Death of Colonel Blimp* (1943). He failed, and handed the producers the priceless publicity headline 'the film they tried to ban'.

The social dislocation of the war was reflected in the post-war increase in sex, violence and juvenile delinquency in the British cinema. The pace of social change was hotting up, and the board struggled to keep up. The first major post-war storm broke over a British gangster film, *No Orchids for Miss Blandish* (1948) which, despite several enforced rewrites, was felt in many influential quarters to contain too much sex and violence. An important change now was that artistic considerations could be taken into consideration – the quality of the film and the director's intentions finally counted for something, so high-class sex and violence could be all right.

In the 1960s, the barriers fell thick and fast. Discreet female nudity had been allowed in some naturist films since 1951 (often featuring games involving a beach-ball – or so I am told), but the Swedish film *Hugs and Kisses* (1968) was the first to be allowed full-frontal nudity outside the comfortable context of a nudist camp. The display of gentlemen's meat and two veg, expressly forbidden in *This Sporting Life* (1963), was allowed in *Women in Love* (1969). Homosexuality, which was not decriminalised until the second half of the 1960s, was depicted sympathetically in *Victim* (1960) and *A Taste of Honey* (1963). Abortion featured in *Up the Junction* (1967) and drug-taking in *Easy Rider* (1969). The 1970s rolled back the frontiers even further, with Ken Russell's *The Devils* (1970) taking in diabolic possession, *A Clockwork Orange* (1971) promoting sticking the boot in and *Last Tango in Paris* (1973) doing wonders for the sales of butter (or was it margarine? I can't tell the difference). Just in case anyone's exotic tastes were not now being catered for in the public realm, the period also saw the spread of so-called private cinema clubs.

Language was also liberated, with 'bloody' making regular appearances (and not just about Germans) from 1963, 'bugger' following in 1967, and what the *Daily Mail* likes to call the f***-word being admitted from 1970. By now the board had abandoned its traditional role of enforcing its view of public morality, and concentrated instead on stemming any excesses of sex, violence or antisocial behaviour. But concerns remained about what was showing in our cinemas and in 1971 the campaigner Lord Longford set up his own independent commission into film censorship. With a membership that included the journalist Peregrine Worsthorne, novelist Kingsley Amis and, curiously, disc jockey Jimmy Savile, it was perhaps not surprising that they came out in favour of tighter controls. Longford was rather ridiculed in the press (who christened him 'Lord Porn') but his committee did at least come up with a rather better definition of pornography than the one in the statutes: 'That which exploits and dehumanises sex so that human beings are treated as things and women in particular as sex objects.'

The government set up its own commission into obscenity and film censorship. If proof were needed that you can get the result you want from a commission by the careful choice of its membership, this is it. Roy Jenkins appointed Professor Bernard Williams as its chairman; he was a moral philosopher, markedly liberal and one-time husband of Jenkins' political colleague Shirley Williams. Much to nobody's amazement, they recommended that the obscenity laws should concentrate on protecting children, leaving adults free to choose what they watched. The test for what should be banned was the rather limited one of 'proven harm'. According to Williams, Longford got

> the problem of pornography out of proportion with the many other problems that face our society today … given the amount of explicit sexual material in circulation, and the allegations often made about its effects, it is striking that one can find case after case of sex crimes and murder without any hint at all that pornography was present in the background.

Liberal voices even turned the traditional argument about 'corrupt and deprave' on its head, arguing that the removal of the safety valve of pornography could itself be a trigger for sexual crime. Others, further to the left, saw the liberalisation of the pornography laws as part of the class war, seeing them as another way in which the ruling classes exercised control over ordinary people. The question asked by the prosecuting case in the *Chatterley* trial, of whether it was a book you would want your servants to read, echoed down through the years. But by the time the Williams Committee came to report its conclusions, it was to a Conservative government; they declined to act on them.

Censorship by Pulling Rank

> The motion picture theatre is in many ways a local and communial (*sic*) institution and its success is dependent of the standing of its manager and his staff in the local community. Our personnel are loyal, keen and enthusiastic men, who have taken a leading part in the social and economic problems of the communities in which they operate.
>
> Odeon Theatres Annual report, 1951

Sometimes the film-makers themselves prove to be the censors' greatest ally. J. Arthur Rank was a hugely influential figure in British film history, with major interests in the making, distribution and exhibition of films – so much so that his near-monopoly powers came in for close scrutiny and criticism in the 1940s. He was also a devout Methodist, who believed that his films should 'promote family values at home and the British way of life overseas'. From his very first production, *Turn of the Tide* (1934) – a melodrama about sturdy Yorkshire fishing folk – many of his films carried a strong moral message. In 1937 he even set up a separate company, headed by the Revd Benjamin Gregory, the editor of the *Methodist Times*, to make films with an overtly religious theme. Their productions may have gone down well in heaven, but at the earthly box offices they hardly registered.

Rank's values also affected the company's mainstream film-making, as they rejected adult topics like John Osborne's play *Look Back in Anger* and Alan Sillitoe's book *Saturday Night and Sunday Morning*. For reasons which were rather less obvious, Rank also refused to do science fiction and produced almost no musicals (what did God have against music?) Their film *The Kidnappers* (1953) was only allowed to explore its controversial topic on condition that they brought in the name of the Good Lord. He had other bees in his bonnet; he almost rejected major hits like *Genevieve* (1952) (hint of extramarital relations in the plot), *Doctor in the House* (1953) (didn't like films about hospitals and doctors for some reason) and Norman Wisdom's successful first film *Trouble in Store* (1953) (didn't think Norman Wisdom was funny).

No X-rated films were shown in Rank cinemas for many years and the classification had been in existence for a decade before one of Rank's own films, *No Love for Johnnie* (1961) got X-rated. In later years, when Rank's other business interests gave him less time to run the film-making side, he bought in two men of equally conservative tastes, Earl St John and John Davis, to take over the reins. (They managed to combine their conservatism and moralising with rather more colourful private lives – one had a serious drink problem and the other got through six wives – only four of which he owned up to in *Who's Who*.) Their rivals in the cinema industry, who read the change in popular moral codes more accurately (or at least did not choose to ignore it) benefited from the limits Rank imposed on himself. They produced and showed *Carry On* films and the other saucier fare that was more in line with changing tastes.

The British Board of Film Classification (successors to the British Board of Film Censors) nowadays exercise control over who can see what in the cinemas. In theory, the local authorities have the final say but nowadays they almost invariably follow the decisions of the BBFC). Film nowadays is covered by the Obscene Publications Act. This only came about as a result of the 1977 amendment to the 1959 Act. Up until then, the government took the view that the BBFC did a perfectly good job of regulation, but the change was actually introduced at the request of the BBFC. It was done, oddly enough, in an attempt to protect serious films from prosecution. At the time, there had been a number of attempted private prosecutions of films (perhaps the best-known being *Last Tango in Paris*). It seems to have worked, in that no BBFC-approved film has ever been successfully prosecuted under the Obscene Publications Act, and few attempts have been made to do so.

Censorship and the Newspapers

While the battle for our cinema screens was being waged, another one was being fought on the newsagents' shelves. Rupert Murdoch bought *The Sun* newspaper in 1969 and took it rapidly downmarket. From November 1970 the paper featured its so-called 'page 3 girls', semi-naked pin-ups. The example of *The Sun* was followed by the *Daily Mirror* from 1975 and the *Daily Star* from 1978. One of the people this particularly offended was the Labour MP Clare Short, who introduced her Indecent Display (Newspapers) Bill in the Commons in March 1986. The aim of this was to prevent newspapers (but not magazines) from publishing pin-ups. She explained her thinking to the House:

> I agree with the women who think that there is some connection between the rising tide of sexual crime and page 3. Obviously, that is unprovable, but the constant mass circulation of such pictures so that they are widely seen by children must influence sexual attitudes and the climate towards sexuality in our society. These women portray women as objects of lust, to be sniggered over and grabbed at, and do not portray sex as something tender and private.
>
> Hansard, Vol. 93, col. 938, 12 March 1986

Certainly Short's bill was widely sniggered over by her political opponents, who did their best to reduce the parliamentary debate into farce with a series of schoolboy jokes and puns too feeble even for a *Carry On* film. Despite winning quite wide public support, the bill never got government backing and therefore failed to make it to the statute book. A relatively junior Labour MP, one Tony Blair, attempted a new spin on the politicisation of porn debate, by arguing that their opponents' puerile conduct during the debate was typical of the Thatcherites' attitude towards everything – 'Grab what you can, when you can.' He called for the Press Council to be made a statutory body with real teeth. Strangely enough, once Labour had won a general election with the backing of *The Sun*, this item mysteriously fell off the bottom of his 'to do' list.

Censorship and the New Media

As the law gradually came to tolerate what we might call the more esoteric outposts of human sexuality, and new ways of satisfying the demand became available, so new measures were needed to separate the sales of these materials from some of the more impressionable members of society. The Video Recordings Act 1984 gives the Home Secretary the power to classify video recordings, a power which he or she delegates to the British Board of Film Classification. The same act introduced a new R18 classification for films only allowed to be sold from sex shops. These establishments, according to the Indecent Displays Act 1981, were banned from having any of their goods on display in the window, or even visible from any public place. The front door had to carry a warning as to what lurked within, and under-eighteens were banned from even crossing the threshold.

The internet, although covered by the Obscene Publications Act, is notoriously difficult to police. Who do you prosecute and how do you get at them? Publication on the internet means transmitting the item, so first in the queue when blame is being handed out are the Internet Service Providers. But they simply hold their hands up and say 'we are a common carrier, like a telephone company, and can no more be held responsible for an obscene website than can a telephone company for what its customers say down the line'. This is not an entirely convincing argument, in that a website is a rather different kettle of fish to, and much less transient than, a telephone conversation which takes place in real time and is then gone.

They then fall back on the 'innocent publication' justification contained in the 1959 Act. There is no legal requirement on an ISP to monitor the material they carry, only to take it off when its unsuitability is drawn to their attention. In most cases, this gets them off the hook. The ISPs are likely to resist any suggestion that they should exercise any editorial control over what gets sent down their lines since, as soon as that was introduced, the 'innocent publication' line of defence would be lost to them.

Possibly the most famous prosecution involving the internet related to a story which was described as 'a work of erotic, sadistic fantasy set in a world in which women are disposable sex objects that exist solely for the pleasure of men. It contains themes of extreme sadism, misogyny, torture, rape, mutilation, dismemberment, murder, execution and male supremacy over women.' The words are not those of the prosecuting counsel, but of the author himself, a thirty-five-year-old civil servant from South Shields called Darryn Walker. It appeared as a disclaimer (or, no doubt, to those similarly inclined, a piece of promotion) on the overseas website on which he published his short story *Girls Screaming Aloud*. This wholesome little piece of fantasy concerned the kidnap, rape, torture, murder and dismemberment of the pop group Girls Aloud, culminating in the sale of their body parts on eBay (apologies if you had it on your reading list and I've spoiled the ending for you).

It was brought to wider public attention by the Internet Watch Foundation, which takes on the daunting task of policing the internet for indecent material. This led to a prosecution in 2009, thought to be the first of its kind since the 1970s, of written text rather than images. Despite it seeming to be all too easy for young fans of Girls Aloud to stumble across this material while searching the internet for news of the band, defence was able to persuade the court that it could only be accessed by those specifically looking for such material. Those searching for such material might reasonably be held to be in no danger of being corrupted or depraved, since they already were. Mr Walker was found not guilty, but is no longer a civil servant. His defence counsel said of his client's work,

> This type of writing is widely available on the internet in an unregulated and uncensored form. In terms of its alleged obscenity, it is frankly no better or worse than other articles.

The Crimped Crusader

> She who must be dismayed
>
> Nickname for Mary Whitehouse coined by Geoffrey Robinson QC

If there is one person who is forever associated with what different people would describe as holding back the tidal wave of filth, or the imposition of censorship, it was an art teacher from Shropshire. In her youth, she had been a member of the Student Christian Movement and a body which became known as Moral Re-Armament. In the early 1960s her teaching duties at the Madeley Secondary Modern School were extended to include sex education.

During one of these lessons, one of her female pupils fell from her chair in a dead faint, and it emerged that the girl had been witness to some kind of sex-related violence between her parents. The teacher, Mrs Mary Whitehouse, became increasingly of the view that young people were being exposed to a torrent of licentiousness and immorality, and that the media – television in particular – were largely to blame. In her own words 'homosexuality, prostitution and sexual intercourse became the routine accompaniment of the evening meal'. Quite which of the 1960s television channels she was watching to be served with this diet we are not told, nor whether such an evening meal was followed by chronic indigestion.

In May 1964, she and three others decided to do something about it. They had copies of a petition printed and wrote a letter of protest to the *Birmingham Evening Post*. It was the *Post* reporter who persuaded this new pressure group to book Birmingham Town Hall for a rally, failing to point out to her that it seated 2,000 people. Mrs Whitehouse and her fellow petitioners need not have worried. Supporters rallied to the cause by the coach-load (thirty-nine coach-loads in fact, from as far away as Devon and Scotland). The hall was packed and, in a publicity gift that guaranteed the meeting television coverage, a group of 'long-haired students' (her description) rushed the stage and tried to disrupt the meeting. The Clean Up TV Campaign was born and Mary Whitehouse was on the way to becoming a national figure. The following year she created the National Viewers' and Listeners' Association, a body which survives to this day as Mediawatch.

She was soon banging on the doors of television's great and good. Lord Hill, the chairman of the Independent Television Authority, proved reasonably sympathetic to her cause. This was perhaps surprising, given the populist agenda of the commercial station. But her wrath was particularly directed at Hugh Carlton-Greene, the Director-General of the BBC. Greene had set out his stall as a reformer, moving the BBC away from its stuffy Reithian attitudes (a move that Mrs Whitehouse felt inappropriate for a publicly funded institution) and seeking to raise its disastrously low audience ratings in competition with ITV. She regarded him as being 'more than anybody else ... responsible for the moral collapse in this country'. Greene was always unwilling to meet with her, since he reckoned (probably correctly) that the publicity would simply add weight to her campaign. Certainly, Mrs Whitehouse showed an almost ravenous appetite for publicity. In the 1980s, she secured the ear of Prime Minister Margaret Thatcher, giving her opinions even greater coverage (we will return to their impact later).

She certainly found no shortage of material to be outraged about. On television, *Till Death Us Do Part* was condemned for an excess of swearing, along with *Dr Who* ('contains some of the sickest, most horrible material ... teatime brutality for tots'). She also opposed *Tom and Jerry* (violence again) *Jackanory* ('completely irresponsible') and even *Pinky and Perky*. The only conceivable reason I have ever been able to establish for her outrage about this last show was at least implied in the following from Victoria Wood:

> In my day we didn't have sex education; we just picked up what we could from the television, and as far as I was concerned, if Pinky and Perky didn't do it, I didn't want to know about it.
>
> Victoria Wood, *As Seen on TV*

In the theatre, she sought to bring a prosecution under the Sexual Offences Act 1955 against Howard Brenton's 1982 play *The Romans in Britain*. Although this prosecution was not pursued, she managed through it to establish that this piece of legislation – in which a defence of artistic merit could not be mounted – was applicable to the theatre. She also brought a private prosecution in 1977 against *Gay News* for a poem, 'The Love that Dares To Speak Its Name'. Her views on homosexuality were not exactly mainstream and not exactly sympathetic. According to her, homosexuality was caused by abnormal parental sex during pregnancy or just after, and that being gay was a disease, like having acne. She claimed that psychiatric literature proves that 60 per cent of homosexuals who go for treatment get completely 'cured'. She was also one of the driving forces behind the moral crusade the Nationwide Festival of Light (the one launched in 1971 – not to be confused with the Hindu festival of Diwali, or anything of the same name associated with the Blackpool illuminations).

She was a hugely controversial figure. Her supporters (who included national treasures like Cliff Richard and Ann Widdecombe) admired and adored her. Malcolm Muggeridge wrote in his foreword to one of her autobiographies, *Who Does She Think She Is?*,

> As the dreadful tidal wave of filth mounts, but for her the total demolition of all Christian values in this country would have taken place without a word of public protest.

Even some of her detractors had a grudging admiration for her skills. Television impresario Michael Grade described her as

> very witty; she was a great debater, she was very courageous and she had a very sincere view, but it was out of touch entirely with the real world.

Her hardcore opponents lampooned her savagely. A very adult (she would no doubt have said 'pornographic') magazine was named after her, as were a comedy group and a rock band, both of whom decidedly did not reflect her values. On television, a series called *Swizzlewick* featured a thinly disguised Mrs Smallgood and her 'Freedom from Sex' campaign. She echoed the *Catholic Pictorial* in condemning it as 'obscene offerings of adolescent smut'.

Mary Whitehouse was awarded the CBE for services to the community in 1980, retired from active campaigning in 1994 and died in 2001.

How much impact did she have, in terms of stamping out filth (or preventing us having fun, depending upon your point of view)? Probably much less than the amount of press coverage she got would suggest. The arts (and in particular television) were a great deal more liberal when she finished campaigning than when she began; whether that process of liberalisation would have gone further without her constant presence in the wings is impossible to say, and whether that would have been a good or a bad thing a matter of opinion. Her tendency to focus on bad language and sex on television tended to separate her from those who thought television violence was a more pernicious influence. Even such support as she was given by Margaret Thatcher tended to be qualified by the Prime Minister's wider agenda, to deregulate markets, including those for entertainment, rather than impose further layers of bureaucratic control on them.

Sabbatarianism

> Remember the Sabbath day, to keep it holy. Six days shalt thou labour, and do all thy work: but the seventh day is the Sabbath of the Lord, thy God. In it, thou shalt not do any work…
>
> Exodus 21: 8–10

> Today is an English Sunday and by God its gloomy enough for a crossing of the Styx.
>
> Raymond Chandler

I do hate Sundays. I'll be glad when its over. It drives me up the wall, just sitting here, looking at you lot. Every Sunday it's the same, nowhere to go, nothing to do. Just sit here, waiting for the next lot of grub to come up.

Hancock's Half Hour

Many readers of a certain age will identify with Tony Hancock's view of the British Sunday in the immediate post-war years. Everything was closed and there was precious little entertainment to be had by the growing proportion of the population who were not active church-goers. Studies earlier in the twentieth century showed Sunday to be the most common day for committing suicide and there was even a form of mental illness named after it.

Observation of the Sabbath had been maintained with varying degrees of severity for centuries. In nineteenth-century America, virtually every state had a law imposing a no-work rule on Sundays. Earlier, in the seventeenth century, the state of Virginia had punished a third failure to observe the Sabbath with death. Over in Britain, the Lord's Day Observance Society (founded in 1831) was probably the best-known of a number of organisations promoting a work-free Sunday, with not even food preparation or washing up to interrupt a constant round of inactivity, and there could not even be any travel (except between home and church). Over the years it has campaigned against most activities that the Godless could contrive for the Sabbath – the operation of public transport, sporting activities (Prince Philip came in for particular criticism of his sacrilegious polo matches), cycling, the cinema and other public entertainments, television advertising and, of course, the Sunday trading of shops and the sale of alcohol. Nowadays, its focus tends to be more on the last two of these – trying at least to hold back the forces seeking further relaxation of the law, if not actually getting the Sunday trading hours reduced.

One of the movement's strongholds is the Scottish Western Isles. As recently as 1995, they tried unsuccessfully to oppose Sunday ferry sailings to the Islands of Lewis, Harris and Stornaway, their case based as much on respecting the islanders' traditions as on religion. In 2002, they campaigned against flights to the islands and, when this failed, tried the following year to prevent the airport bar being opened, in order that the Godless passengers could not compound their sins with the demon drink. One of the Sabbatarians' dire warnings was that God would judge those who chose to travel on a Sunday harshly. Clear evidence of this had come in the form of the Tay Bridge disaster of 1879, which collapsed with heavy loss of life to travellers on the Sabbath.

Although their days of greatest influence were past by the end of the Second World War, they did secure at least one major post-war victory that shaped our Sundays for many years. An unholy (or, at least, only partially Godly) alliance of the Sabbatarians, the trades unions looking after the interests of shop-workers and small businesses (who feared losing more of their custom to big store competition if Sunday trading came in) led to the Labour government passing the Shops Act 1950. This Act was a minefield of anomalies – you could buy fresh food but not tinned, cycle parts but not a complete cycle, and takeaway food but not fish and chips. You could have your shoes soled and heeled but you could not buy a set of shoelaces if one broke. It was unenforceable in largely Jewish areas, where they observed a different Sabbath, and was hugely unpopular with the general public. Three polls, taken in 1981, 1982 and 1983 showed support for Sunday opening rising from 63 per cent to 73 per cent.

Mrs Thatcher tried to do away with the ban on Sunday trading in 1986 but, in a rare show of defiance, a majority in Parliament rejected her proposal. This time it was a thoroughly unholy alliance of Conservatives, protecting the small traders' day of rest and the disruption of family life generally, and the Labour party, once again batting for shop-workers' rights. It was 1994 before she finally got her own way and the shops could open legally (many had been flouting the law for some time).

The BBC was naturally keen to do its bit to keep Sunday special (that is to say, especially dull). The following is a description of Sunday programming on the radio immediately before the Second World War:

> The BBC Sunday programme began with a morning religious service between the hours of 9.30 to 10.45. There was silence then until 12.30, after which there was various serious music and talks until the evening service at 8.00 in the evening. This was followed by yet more earnest music until the *Epilogue* formally bought the day's observance to a conclusion at 11 o'clock.
>
> Scannel and Cardiff, *A Social History of Broadcasting*
> (Vol. 1), p. 232

Small wonder that large parts of its Sunday audience were lured away to the secular charms of the Continental radio stations. The BBC had religious responsibilities built into its charter from the start – both to educate in the faith and to evangelise. But they were strictly limited to working for the Established Church – there was to be none of that non-conformist religion nonsense. At first, they were entirely limited to broadcasting religious material on a Sunday, and even their hesitant attempts from the 1930s onwards to introduce a modicum of secular material earned them an irate delegation from the Lords' Day Observance Society.

In case you think the Lords' Day Observance Society is a creature of the past, it lives on today, as 'Day One Christian Ministries'. Despite the fact that, by 2007, only 15 per cent of British adults attended church even once a month and, for the growing numbers who were not church-goers but mosque-, temple- or synagogue-goers, Sunday was not even their recognised Sabbath. There was nonetheless still a group in Britain desperate to stamp out fun for at least one day of the week.

Are We Having Fun Yet?

It cannot be denied that, by the turn of the twenty-first century, there was a lot more scope for indulging people's very different ideas of fun than there was in the immediate post-war years. But one man's (or woman's) idea of fun was another's depravity, so where the balance lay between the two was very much in the eye of the beholder. Whether fun or filth, those who sought to contain it have suffered a more or less continuous run of defeats over this period, so this chapter at least must be awarded to the funsters, in all their rich/disgusting (delete as applicable) variety.

Select Bibliography

Akhtar, Miriam and Humphries, Steve, *The Fifties and Sixties – A Lifestyle Revolution* (Boxtree, 2001).

Barrett, Norman, *The Daily Telegraph Football Chronicle* (*Daily Telegraph*, 2004).

Davis, Dorothy, *A History of Shopping* (Routledge & Kegan Paul, 1966).

Fane-Saunders, Kilmeny, *The Radio Times Guide to Films* (BBC, 2004).

Ferry, Kathryn, *Holiday Camps* (Shire, 2010).

Foer, Franklin, *How Football Explains the World* (Harper Collins, 2004).

Foulston, Jill (ed.), *The Virago Book of the Joy of Shopping* (Virago, 2007).

Goldie, G. W., *Facing the Nation: Television and Politics 1936–77* (Bodley Head, 1978).

Good Housekeeping magazine.

Horn, Pamela, *Pleasures and Pastimes in Victorian Britain* (Sutton, 1999).

Hylton, Stuart, *From Rationing to Rock* (Sutton, 1998).

Hylton, Stuart, *Magical History Tour* (Sutton, 2000).

Hylton, Stuart, *Their Darkest Hour* (Sutton, 2001).

Hylton, Stuart, *A History of Manchester* (Phillimore, 2003).

Hylton, Stuart, *The Horseless Carriage* (The History Press, 2009).

Katz, Ephraim, *The Macmillan International Film Encyclopedia* (Macmillan, 1994).

Kynaston, David, *Austerity Britain 1945–1951* (Bloomsbury, 2007).

Lewis, Peter, *The Fifties* (Heinemann, 1978).

Miall, Leonard, *Inside the BBC* (Weidenfeld & Nicholson, 1994).

Murphy, Robert (ed.), *The British Cinema Book* (British Film Institute, 2001).

Pritchard, Anthony, *British Family Cars of the 1950s and 1960s* (Shire, 2009).

Rausch, Andrew J., *Turning Points in Film History* (Citadel, 2004).

Robson, Graham and Ware, Michael, *Illustrated Guide to Classic British Cars* (Abbeydale, 2000).

Street, Peter, *God Save the Queen! Britain in 1952* (Sutton, 2002).

Street, Sarah, *British National Cinema* (Routledge, 1997).

Taylor, A. J. P., *The Oxford History of England: English History 1914–1945* (Oxford University Press, 1975).

Williams, Christopher (ed.), *Cinema: the Beginnings and the Future* (University of Westminster Press, 1996).